European Union Direct Investment in China

China's immersion in the world economy and trading system is a continued source of great interest throughout the globe. This intriguing book focuses on the attempts of European firms to crack this potentially huge market.

The book is divided into three parts, the first being an overview of the Chinese investment environment and the development of foreign direct investment (FDI) over the last twenty years. The second part then goes on to concentrate specifically on the characteristics of European companies involved in FDI into China. The third part looks at different management aspects of EU-invested enterprises within China, using newly acquired data.

This comprehensive overview of European direct investment in China will be of great interest to both students and academics in the fields of Chinese Economics and Business, Organisational Theory and the Theory of the Firm. The concluding business and policy implications of the book will also make it useful to professionals and policy-makers.

Daniel Van Den Bulcke is Professor of International Management and Development at the University of Antwerp, Belgium.

Haiyan Zhang is Research Fellow at the University of Antwerp, Belgium.

Maria do Céu Esteves is the founder and former President of the Institute of European Studies of Macau, China.

Studies in global competition

Edited by *John Cantwell, The University of Reading, UK and David Mowery, University of California, Berkeley, USA*

Japanese Firms in Europe
Edited by Frédérique Sachwald

Technological Innovation, Multinational Corporations and New International Competitiveness
The case of intermediate countries
Edited by José Molero

Global Competition and the Labour Market
Nigel Driffield

The Source of Capital Goods Innovation
The role of user firms in Japan and Korea
Kong-Rae Lee

Climates of Global Competition
Maria Bengtsson

Multinational Enterprises and Technological Spillovers
Tommaso Perez

Governance of International Strategic Alliances
Technology and transaction costs
Joanne E. Oxley

Strategy in Emerging Markets
Telecommunications establishments in Europe
Anders Pehrsson

Going Multinational
The Korean experience of direct investment
Edited by Frédérique Sachwald

Multinational Firms and Impacts on Employment, Trade and Technology
New perspectives for a new century
Edited by Robert E. Lipsey and Jean-Louis Mucchielli

Multinational Firms
The global–local dilemma
Edited by John H. Dunning and Jean-Louis Mucchielli

MIT and the Rise of Entrepreneurial Science
Henry Etzkowitz

Technological Resources and the Logic of Corporate Diversification
Brian Silverman

The Economics of Innovation, New Technologies and Structural Change
Cristiano Antonelli

European Union Direct Investment in China
Characteristics, challenges and perspectives
Daniel Van Den Bulcke, Haiyan Zhang and Maria do Céu Esteves

European Union Direct Investment in China

Characteristics, challenges and
perspectives

**Daniel Van Den Bulcke, Haiyan Zhang
and Maria do Céu Esteves**

Routledge
Taylor & Francis Group

LONDON AND NEW YORK

First published 2003
by Routledge
11 New Fetter Lane, London EC4P 4EE

Simultaneously published in the USA and Canada
by Routledge
29 West 35th Street, New York, NY 10001

Routledge is an imprint of the Taylor & Francis Group

© 2003 Daniel Van Den Bulcke, Haiyan Zhang and Maria do Céu Esteves

Typeset in Goudy by
Newgen Imaging Systems (P) Ltd, Chennai, India
Printed and bound in Great Britain by
Biddles Ltd, Guildford and King's Lynn

British Library Cataloguing in Publication Data
A catalogue record for this book is available from the British Library

Library of Congress Cataloging in Publication Data
Bulcke, D. Van Den.
    European union direct investment in China : characteristics, challenges, and
perspectives / Daniel Van Den Bulcke, Haiyan Zhang, and Maria do Céu Esteves.
        p. cm. – (Studies in global competition)
    Includes bibliographical references and index.
        1. Investments, European – China. 2. Investments, Foreign – China. 3. China – Economic
conditions. I. Zhang, Haiyan, 1956– II. Esteves, Maria do Céu. III. Title. IV. Series.
    HG5782 .B853 2003
    332.67′34051–dc21   2002031815

ISBN 0–415–30377–X

Contents

Figures

Tables

Preface

While this study deals with European Direct Investment in China and consequently the interaction between Europe and China, it is itself the result of a close Sino-European cooperation. This cooperation took many forms. First, while the initiative for the project was taken by the Institute of European Studies of Macau or IEEM (Instituto de Estudos Europeus de Macau), at a time when Macau was still administered by Portugal, it decided on a joint venture with the Centre of International Management and Development – Antwerp (CIMDA), a research centre at the University of Antwerp, Belgium, which had built up expertise in the area of international business activities applied to China.

Second, IEEM and CIMDA agreed that the surveys for the empirical part of the study should be carried out by local Chinese teams. Seven small groups of academics from different universities and institutions were chosen which had previously studied foreign direct investment issues in China. These seven teams from Jinan University in Guangzhou, Fudan University in Shanghai, Shaanxi Economics and Trade Institute in Xian, Nankai University in Tianjin, Sichuan University in Chengdu, China Academy of Social Sciences in Beijing and Wuhan University in Wuhan had already worked together with either IEEM or CIMDA and were brought together in a preparatory meeting in Macau in 1996 and an intermediary seminar in Xian in 1997 during which the first results were presented and exchanged.

Third, the principal researcher Haiyan Zhang coordinated the Chinese teams. Although he was stationed in Antwerp he spent many weeks in Macau to follow-up the project in order to make sure that the different teams followed the same general guidelines for the survey, for example, for the composition of the sample and the integration of the survey results.

Fourth, seminars were organised around the project in which businessmen and government representatives were invited as speakers and participants both in Macau and in Antwerp, Belgium. There was a conference in Macau about 'Major Challenges for European Corporations in the Asian Globalising Economy' in April 1998, which was also attended by the Chinese researchers. The Belgian conference was organised by the China Europe Management Centre (CEMC) in Antwerp in 1998 and consisted of a three-day meeting about 'Belgian and European Direct Investment in China', 'Managing European and Belgian subsidiaries in a growing competitive Chinese environment' and 'A fast changing China in a different Asia'.

Fifth, while the Chinese research teams mainly interviewed the Chinese leading managers of the European subsidiaries located in China's manufacturing sector, several interviews were carried out with managers in the European parent companies who were responsible for the Asian or Chinese operations of their company.

Sixth, preliminary chapters of this study were presented by the authors at academic conferences with European and Asian audiences. The chapter on sourcing (Chapter 8) was presented during the 24th Annual Conference of the European International Business Academy (EIBA) in December 1998 in Jerusalem, Israel and at a seminar organised by the Economic Growth Centre, New Delhi, India. A large section of Chapter 3 was presented as an introductory paper to the aforementioned conference in Macau in April 1998, while a first version of Chapter 7 was accepted for presentation at the International Conference on 'China and Zhuhai in the Globalization of the World Economy' held in Zhuhai, China, in December 1998.

These examples indicate that this study does not give a one-sided view of European direct investment in China, but that on the one hand a close cooperation among the Sino-European research teams and on the other hand an extensive exposure to and communication with government officials, business representatives and academics contributed to a balanced interpretation of the survey results and other evidence about this topic. As the publication of the report had to be postponed for some time, the official data used have been updated until 1999 and 2000.

The authors are grateful to the Macau Trade and Investment Promotion Institute (IPIM) for its financial support that allowed to carry out the project. Also, the contributions of the researchers Chen Xuemei (Jinan University), Dai Bingran and Zhang Jikang (Fudan University), Zhang Jianqi (Shaanxi Economics and Trade Institute), Tong Jiadong (Nankai University), Wang Yamei and Zhao Xizhen (Sichuan Union University), Xue Yanping (China Academy for Social Sciences) and Zhou Maorong and Shen Hao (Wuhan University) are greatly appreciated as their surveys provided essential information for the study. Mention should also be made of Antonio Texeira from the University of Macau and IEEM who performed a number of statistical analyses and helped with the organisation of the workshops. The comments from John Cantwell, editor of this series, were most useful during the period that the publication was being prepared. Last but not least thanks are due to Haiyan Zhang, who as principal author of this study was extremely involved in all the scientific and administrative aspects of the study.

Ceú Maria Esteves   Daniel Van Den Bulcke
Director IEEM   Director CIMDA
Macau   Antwerp

Abbreviations

ADB	Asian Development Bank
BOT	Building, Operating and Transfer
CEE	Central and Eastern Europe
CJV	Contractual joint venture
EJV	Equity joint venture
ETDZ	Economic and technological development zone
EU	European Union
EUDI	European Union direct investment
FDI	Foreign direct investment
FEC	Foreign exchange certificate
FIE	Foreign-invested enterprise
FSA	Firm-specific advantage
FSF	Firm-specific factor
GDP	Gross domestic product
JE	Joint exploration
JV	Joint venture
LSA	Location-specific advantage
LSF	Location-specific factor
MNE	Multinational enterprise
MOFTEC	Ministry of Foreign Trade and Economic Co-operation
NIE	Newly industrialising economy
OECD	Organisation for Economic Co-operation and Development
OIC	Old industrialised country
R&D	Research and development
SEZ	Special economic zone
SIC	Standard industrial classification
SME	Small- and medium-sized enterprise
SOE	State-owned enterprise
TVE	Town and village enterprise
UNCTAD	United Nations Conference on Trade and Development
UNCTC	United Nations Centre on Transnational Corporations
WDS	Western development strategy
WFOE	Wholly foreign owned enterprise
WTO	World Trade Organisation

1 Introduction

During the last two decades China has emerged as one of the fastest growing economies in the world with an average double-digit rate of growth. The remarkable performance of the Chinese economy during the past decades has significantly affected the strategic positioning of global firms in China. For many foreign investors China is no longer a potential market, but one of the most rapidly expanding poles of industrial development and production and export activity in the world. More and more foreign companies have become convinced that they cannot afford to remain absent from such an important market and have consequently decided to become substantially involved in China by way of foreign direct investment (FDI).

While the cumulative inward FDI in China amounted to US$ 349 billion at the end of 2000, the total number of approved FDI projects had reached 364,000 [Ministry of Foreign Trade and Economic Co-operation of China (MOFTEC) 2001]. According to the World Investment Report (UN/UNCTAD 2000), China alone received 4.7 per cent of the world FDI inflows and 19.5 per cent of all FDI that went towards the developing countries in 1999. Yet, these shares decreased significantly during the second part of the 1990s, as they had reached, respectively, 12 and 33 per cent in 1996 (UN/UNCTAD 1997).

FDI and China's economic growth

Multinational enterprises (MNEs) have, gradually, integrated their Chinese operations into their value-adding network in order to strengthen their global, regional and local competitiveness. Since 1992, nearly 400 of the 500 leading global companies listed in *Fortune*, invested in over 2,000 projects in China (UN/UNCTAD 2001). Most of these firms have expanded in size, scope and overall activities within a few years after setting up their first operation in China. Major overseas Chinese and other regional conglomerates have also started to invest in mega-sized infrastructure projects, ranging from superhighways to container ports and power plants in China. Both global and regional MNEs have radically revised their views of the available opportunities in China and have, consequently, adapted their strategic position and organisational structure. The strategic investors of the early 1980s have become 'local players' in China, securing a dominant share of its vast market. They are shaping China's industrial structure and setting new norms with regard to the use of advanced technology. They have established integrated local production lines, achieved 'sustained superior returns' and have become market leaders and long-term partners in the Chinese economy (Shaw and Meier 1994). Most recently, FDI has rapidly expanded into research and development (R&D) activities in China with the establishment of more than hundred R&D centres by leading MNEs (UNCTAD 2001).

Foreign direct investment flows have played a major role in the growth and dynamism of the Chinese economy and in integrating China in the global economy through trade and FDI linkages. In 1999, the so-called 'foreign-invested enterprises' (FIEs) employed more than 20 million people in China, the exports of these enterprises reached US$ 86 billion, while their imports amounted to US$ 89 billion. The relative importance of FDI in China's economy increased rapidly in the early 1990s: the ratio of FDI inflows to the country's gross domestic fixed capital went up from 4.2 to 11.2 per cent between 1991 and 1999 with a record high of 17.1 per cent in 1994, while the output of foreign enterprises increased from 5.3 to 27.8 per cent of the total industrial output of China. During the same period, the share of FIEs in the total tax revenues of China rose from 4.3 to 16 per cent and their shares in China's exports and imports increased, respectively, from 26.5 to 51.8 per cent and from 16.8 to 45.5 per cent (MOFTEC 2000). MNEs as cross-border 'allocators' and 'upgraders' of resources and capabilities (Dunning 1997) have also contributed to China's economic transition process over the past two decades by providing financial resources, technological know-how, technical and managerial skills and marketing expertise. The share of FIEs in the Chinese exports of high-technology products increased from 59 per cent in 1996 to 81 per cent in 2000, as they have become the engine of growth of China's high-technology exports and an essential means of inward technology transfer (UN/UNCTAD 2001). Also, the impact of FDI on the creation of market mechanisms and the establishment of a more competitive environment in the planned Chinese economy has been crucial.

The European Union's direct investment position in China

Although the European Union (EU) constitutes the world's largest home base for FDI, it is relatively underrepresented in the Chinese inward FDI, at least as compared to its overall FDI position in the global economy (discussed later). Apart from a few leading EU MNEs, such as Philips, Siemens, Hoechst, Unilever, Nokia, Volkswagen, Alcatel-Bell, Janssen Pharmaceutica, European firms apparently missed out on the early investment opportunities in China at the end of the 1970s and the beginning of the 1980s when the country gradually opened up to FDI. Between 1979 and 2000 the European Union invested US$ 26 billion in 11,000 enterprises. This total investment amounted to approximately 7.5 per cent of the total Chinese inward FDI. Yet, the fifteen EU countries taken together rank far behind Hong Kong (49 per cent of the total Chinese inward FDI), the United States (8.6 per cent), Japan (8 per cent) and Taiwan (7.5 per cent) as sources of Chinese inward FDI (MOFTEC 2001). As indicated by a report of EU/UNCTAD (1996), the weak FDI position of the European Union in China has directly affected the competitiveness of the European Union in the Asian emerging markets vis-à-vis not only other 'Old Industrialised Countries' (OICs), but also the Asian newly industrialising economies (NIEs).

Although there are encouraging signs that more and more EU enterprises are waking up to the need to be present in China with production activities, many EU managers, especially from small- and medium-sized enterprises (SMEs), still perceive the Chinese investment climate and its bureaucratic and institutional environment as too uncertain and culturally different from their own countries. A better and more complete understanding and anticipation of the changing institutional environment of the Chinese market, more particularly the Chinese FDI investment climate, is absolutely necessary as a precondition to improve the FDI position of the European Union in China. It is crucial, not only that the established EU MNEs adapt their operations even better to the continuously changing Chinese environment, but also that national, regional and supra-national institutions of the European Union more efficiently support their enterprises to participate in the dynamic development of the Chinese economy.

Focus and structure of the report

This study examines the investment patterns of the EU companies in China, more specifically their changing characteristics and perspectives with regard to the Chinese economic and institutional context. The objectives of the study are threefold:

1 To present a complete picture of European Union direct investment (EUDI) in China on the basis of a statistical analysis and surveys and to carry out an accurate assessment of how EU firms operate their subsidiaries in China and which are their experiences and perspectives in its rapidly changing economic and institutional environment.
2 To provide EU institutions and the Chinese government with a better understanding of EU firms' strategic decisions and attitudes about doing business in China and their requests for institutional and administrative support.
3 To find out to what extent EU companies might adapt their strategies for improving their competitive position in China vis-à-vis their global and regional rivals.

The study is divided into three parts. Part I presents an overview of the evolution of the Chinese investment environment and the development path of FDI in China during the period 1979–2000. Two statistical analyses will illustrate the changing patterns of Chinese inward FDI in general and EU investment in particular at both the country and the company level. The patterns and characteristics of EU subsidiaries in China will be compared to those from other countries of origin, especially Western and Asian rivals. Chapter 2 examines the changing context of Chinese FDI policy and the strategic reactions of foreign enterprises with regard to their investment operations in China. The main objective is to capture the dynamic interactions between the firm-specific advantages (FSAs) and strategic options of MNEs on the one hand and the location-specific advantages (LSAs) and FDI policy of the Chinese government on the other hand. Chapter 3 analyses Chinese inward FDI during the last two decades of the previous millennium on the basis of longitudinal FDI data. The changing characteristics of FDI in China are presented against the changing endowments of location factors and China's FDI policy. Chapter 4 focuses on the EUDI in China during the decades of the 1980s and the 1990s. Its main objective is to deal with questions such as: what are the salient characteristics of EU invested enterprises in China; how have these features changed over time and to what extent are the EU enterprises different from firms from North America, Japan and the Asian NIEs?

Part II of the report focuses on the specific characteristics of European companies that are involved in FDI operations in China. The objective of this approach is to identify the FSAs that may have affected the investment decisions of EU companies when they entered the Chinese market. The operating characteristics of EU parent companies, such as their sector distribution, size of operations, degree of internationalisation and investment position in Asia in general and in China in particular, are discussed in order to explain their motivation to invest in the Chinese manufacturing industries and their entry routes and location decisions.

In Part III, different management aspects of EU-invested enterprises in the Chinese manufacturing industries are investigated on the basis of the data from a questionnaire survey. In Chapter 6, the operational characteristics of EU-invested firms in China are studied with a specific focus on their ownership structure, R&D and market orientation. The characteristics of these firms that are analysed in more detail are their geographical location, industrial specialisation, as well as their countries of origin and parent companies. Chapter 7 deals with managerial aspects and competitiveness of EU subsidiaries in China, such as the decision-making process, R&D policy and competitive positioning. The performance of EU subsidiaries in China and the difficulties they encounter in their daily operations are also surveyed. Chapter 9 concentrates on the sourcing strategy of EU subsidiaries in China in order to assess their linkages with the host economy and firms and to illustrate the impact of FSAs and LSAs on this particular dimension of the operations of EU subsidiaries in China. Finally, Chapter 10 concludes by emphasising some business and policy implications of the study. Following up on the recent changes of Chinese FDI regulations, especially with regard to the opening up of the inland regions and new business sectors to foreign investors, this chapter also analyses the location and market factors that could affect the future development of EUDI in China.

Methodology and data sources

The data used in this study were collected from three different sources. The first one consisted of the statistical yearbooks of the MOFTEC in which figures are published on Chinese inward FDI between 1979 and 2000. The second set of data was collected in 1996 and 1997 through contacts with the embassies, consulates and business associations of the EU countries in China. The third set of data resulted from an extensive empirical survey that was undertaken by the authors and their Chinese partners both in a number of European parent companies and in their Chinese subsidiaries in 1997 (year of reference 1996).

Data from MOFTEC

The official statistics on Chinese inward FDI from MOFTEC provide information about the country of origin, location, sectoral distribution and investment forms of FDI flows in terms of the number of projects and contracted and effectively invested capital.[1] These data show the importance and pattern of EUDI as compared to other Western countries and Asian economies. Next to the FDI statistics at the country level, a database of foreign registered enterprises was established on the basis of information from MOFTEC's list of foreign subsidiaries (MOFTEC 1983–1998).[2] This latter data set covers the period 1979–1996 and gives information about the home country of the foreign investor, the total cost of the project, the foreign equity contribution, the geographical location, the ownership structure, the type of business activities and the planned duration of the venture. This database was used on the one hand to emphasise the operational characteristics of EU subsidiaries in China and on the other hand to compare European-invested firms with those from other OICs and Asian NIEs.

Data from EU trade and business associations

The data collected from the trade and business associations of the EU countries in China made it possible to identify 741 European parent companies that established 1,214 manufacturing, trade and service subsidiaries, representative offices/branches and regional headquarters in China. The business and financial information of some 300 European parent companies was collected from annual reports, publications of business associations, business directories such as Who Owns Whom and the CD-ROM AMADEUS.[3] These data are used to analyse the specific characteristics of the European parent companies with FDI operations in China.

Data from questionnaire survey

The survey covers 27 European parent companies and 311 EU subsidiaries in China. The sample of the surveyed companies was selected from the two data sources mentioned above, that is, MOFTEC and diplomatic posts and business associations of EU countries in China. Separate questionnaires were used for the European parent companies and their Chinese subsidiaries.

Taking into account the gradual geographical extension of the FDI policy of the Chinese government and its impact on the location decisions of FDI in China, seven coastal and inland provinces and cities were chosen for the empirical part of this study. Guangdong Province with Guangzhou were included as the first coastal area that benefited from the initial move of the Chinese open door policy, while Tianjin and Shanghai were selected because of the existence of relatively good industrial and trade infrastructure and their historical links with foreign countries. The re-opening of these cities to foreign investors was considered as a new step in the Chinese open door policy. Several provinces of the inland region, for example, Hubei, Sichuan and Shaanxi, were also taken on board to emphasise the impact of the recent changes of the Chinese FDI policy that gives high priority to the inland area on the one hand and encourages foreign companies to participate in the reform of the state owned enterprises (SOEs) on the other hand. Finally, Beijing was added because of its central position in the Chinese political, administrative and economic system. After a pilot study of EU subsidiaries in Xi'an in March 1996, the questionnaire survey was extended to the above-mentioned Chinese coastal and inland provinces and cities.

The principal operating patterns of EU firms in these particular cities/provinces are investigated with regard to entry mode, local-partner selection, sector distribution, market orientation and decision-making. Researchers from seven universities and institutes were involved – each in one particular location – and carried out interviews and prepared survey reports on EUDI in their respective provinces and cities on the basis of a common questionnaire. The main objective of this questionnaire survey was to study the impact of location factors and government policies on the success and failure of EU subsidiaries in China. The comparative analysis of EU subsidiaries located in different Chinese regions is expected to provide a more complete view of the strategic perspectives for corporate management of European MNEs facing different locational factors.

The survey of the European parent companies was mainly conducted through mailing and telephone contacts, while the survey of European subsidiaries in China was in most cases carried out by personal interviews. Chinese academics in the aforementioned seven Chinese cities and provinces gathered information on 311 subsidiaries located in China originating from 13 EU countries. However, only 262 could be included in the final sample, because the rest (i.e. 49 firms) did not really meet the criteria put forward in the study, that is, they were not owned by European firms as such but by individuals (e.g. by Overseas Chinese living in Europe), or they were not operating in the manufacturing sector. Chinese managers answered 95 per cent of the questionnaires, while the remaining 5 per cent of the respondents were expatriates from France, Germany, the United Kingdom and other EU countries. Although the high participation of Chinese managers in the survey might be interpreted as limiting the European perspective of the study, it was precisely one of the objectives of this project to allow Chinese and European managers to evaluate the European controlled enterprises from the Chinese perspective. By contrast, almost all other studies about Western direct investment in China rely very heavily and sometimes exclusively on the views of expatriate managers working in China.

The survey in Europe was designed to emphasise the motivation of EU companies to invest in China and the impact of their Chinese subsidiaries on the group's overall strategic setting and performance. The experience of operating in China and the perception of the Chinese market by EU enterprises in their globalisation process are also commented upon.

Compared to the MOFTEC data, the information gathered in the questionnaire survey has several specific characteristics. First, the survey concentrates on manufacturing firms, while the MOFTEC data have a wider coverage and include the primary and service sectors. Second, the survey targets only firms that were operational, while MOFTEC publishes information about firms regardless of the current situation, for example, cancellation of the project, closure or expansion of the company or investment initiative. Third, the questionnaire survey provides not only quantitative data, but also qualitative information. Of course, both data sets complement each other and allow to get a better grasp of the experiences and challenges of European firms in China.

Part I

Patterns of European direct investment in China

2 Determinants of foreign direct investment and the changing Chinese business environment

This chapter concentrates on the changes in China's FDI policy and the strategic reactions of foreign enterprises with regard to their investment operations in China. The main objective is to capture the dynamic interactions between the FSAs and the strategic reaction of MNEs on the one hand and the LSAs and FDI policy of the Chinese government on the other hand. The chapter consists of five sections. The section on 'Analytical framework' presents a framework to analyse the major locational determinants of FDI in China, especially with regard to the market seeking and the scale/specialisation related efficiency seeking FDI activities by EU MNEs. The section on 'China's specific location advantages and their impact on EUDI' reviews the main changes in the Chinese LSAs, especially with regard to China's industrial policy and the ongoing transition process of the Chinese economy. The impact of LSAs on the changing investment patterns of EU MNEs in China is also focused upon. FDI policy and the relevant regulatory measures of the Chinese government towards MNEs are examined in the section on 'Chinese FDI policy'. Specific attention is given to the gradual liberalisation of the access to the Chinese market, both in terms of the accessibility of different regions and sectors. In the sections on 'Reform of Chinese SOEs and opportunities for European MNEs' and 'Recent developments', the challenges and opportunities that are related to the recent changes of the Chinese business environment in general and FDI policy in particular are studied, especially with regard to the so-called Western Development Strategy and China's entry into the World Trade Organisation (WTO).

Analytical framework

The literature on international production suggests that firms will set up and/or expand value-adding activities abroad for natural resource, market, efficiency and strategic-asset-seeking activities (Dunning 1992a).[1] From a strategic point of view, these investment motives can be regarded as either cost/supply oriented or market oriented (Bartlett and Ghoshal 1989). The cost- or supply-oriented motivations usually correspond to global efficiency seeking strategies, while market-oriented operations are more related to national responsiveness strategies. Figure 2.1 tries to present a framework for analysing different investment strategies and their changes in the emerging markets.

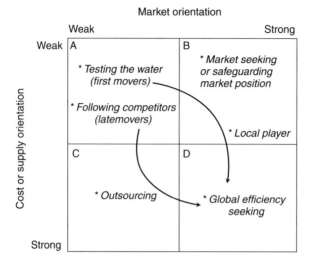

Market orientation

Figure 2.1 Strategy matrix of MNEs in emerging markets.
Source: Van Den Bulcke and Zhang (1997).

From a static point of view, the upper right quadrant (B) in the matrix (Figure 2.1) reflects the market-oriented motivation of companies as a unique or dominant option to penetrate a foreign market and/or to expand, or to protect an existing export market. The most important factors determining the investment decision are related to the expansion into a new market area, the protection of an established market share, the promotion of the parent company's exports and the avoidance of trade barriers. The lower left quadrant (C) shows the case where companies establish new production activities abroad for outsourcing purposes. These firms are motivated by low production costs abroad, the availability of cheap or specific resources and the development of substantial local sourcing capability in the host country. The right lower quadrant (D) refers to the situation where both the host country market and outsourcing abroad are important determinants for the decision to start and/or expand overseas production. Global efficiency is pursued by attempts to create and achieve economies of scale, to diversify markets and products and to build up leading positions in related industries. In the situation presented in the left upper quadrant (A), where the market and supply/sourcing-oriented motivations are relatively unimportant, the creation of a local production facility in an emerging market might be explained by 'strategic' or 'opportunistic' reasons, for example, by 'following competitors' in the case of a defensive move and by 'testing the water' in the case of a reactive and aggressive decision. The investment decision by first-time foreign investors in an unfamiliar market can also be explained by strategic-asset-seeking motivations (Dunning 1992a).

Firms also tend to gradually adjust their strategies over time according to the changes of location-specific factors and their own strategic interests. This means that the supply-oriented option can be switched or extended to market-oriented perspectives when the demand of the local and neighbouring markets become stronger (from A to B or D). A market-oriented production unit could also be used as a first step in building up a supply network for the multinational group's overall efficiency seeking strategy (from B to D). The creation of local sourcing capabilities by market-oriented companies to lower production costs or to follow the local content policy of the host government may also occur.

The widely accepted theories about the determinants of FDI are derived from the OLI-paradigm of Dunning (1981, 1988, 1992a). This approach offers a valuable framework to determine, on the one hand, which are the firm's ownership advantages, and on the other hand, how these advantages can be enhanced within the firm by using, for example, multinational organisational structures and specific locational sites. In other words, the extent and form of the overseas activities of a firm from a particular country depend on three kinds of specific advantages, that is, ownership advantages (O), internalisation advantages (I) and location advantages (L). For a firm to be induced to produce in foreign markets, it must first possess or have access to a set of specific ownership assets, that is, technology, know-how, resources or some other form of tangible or intangible assets that its competitors either do not possess or cannot rely on to in the same way. Second, the firm must be convinced that the internalisation of these ownership assets via a subsidiary abroad is more advantageous than externalisation, for example, via export sales or licensing agreements in the foreign market. Third, natural or created resources must be present in the foreign market, which can be combined with or added to the firm's ownership advantages in order to allow it to produce abroad in a profitable way. The nature and value of these advantages are not assumed to be constant and are likely to change over time (Dunning and Narula 1994). In identifying the forces influencing these advantages, three structural determinants are distinguished, that is, those that are specific to particular countries, those that belong to particular types of industries, and those that are related to particular enterprises. In the following section, the determinants of FDI are analysed from the perspective of both the location- and firm-specific factors.

Location-specific factors

From the perspective of the OLI-paradigm, previous theoretical and empirical studies have shown that the main location factors of the host country affect the patterns and extent of inward FDI. More often, they are related to market characteristics, trade barriers, cost conditions and the institutional and business environment (Dunning 1992b; UN/UNCTC 1992). The significance of these factors could be different according to the strategic orientations of MNEs that are initially determined by the O and I advantages of the firm and the L advantages of the home country. Table 2.1 presents an overview of the main findings of previous studies on the effects of location factors on the FDI patterns of MNEs with different strategic options (UN/UNCTC 1992).[2]

Table 2.1 Effects of location factors on FDI

Location factors	Effects on FDI	
	Cost/supply orientation	Market seeking
Market characteristics		
Size of market	/	+
Market growth	−	+
Proximity to market	−	+
Overseas adaptation	−	+
Regional protectionism	/	−
Pricing control	/	− or +
Resource allocation	/	− or +
Control of distribution channels	/	− or +
Barriers to trade		
Tariff barriers	/	+
Non-tariff barriers	/	+
Local content	/	+
Cost factors		
Transportation	−	+
Wages	−	/
Investment climate		
Tax incentives	+	/
Political stability	+	+
Limitations on ownership	−	−
Foreign exchange control	/	−
Familiarity with a region	+	+

Source: Adapted from UN/UNCTC (1992) and Dunning (1993).

Notes
+ positive; − negative; / not relevant or less significant.

Market characteristics

Market-seeking investors, who are primarily interested in the local market, look at the actual market size and its growth potential, as measured, respectively, by the size of population and production [e.g. gross domestic product (GDP)] and the rate of growth of per capita GDP. The growth of a host country's market is expected to positively affect market-seeking FDI activities. For efficiency seekers, cost and supply conditions are of crucial importance. Because of their globally integrated activities, the local-market factors are less relevant for the export-oriented subsidiaries of these groups. The market growth of the host country as such may even have negative influences on offshore/sourcing-oriented FDI, as a result of the increasing level of wages that are typical in an expanding economy.

As far as the other market-related factors are concerned, the need for proximity to the market as well as for adaptation to local preferences is widely recognised as an influence on FDI decisions for market-seeking options, but evidently not for export-oriented operations. Protectionist measures by individual regions and the state control of pricing, resource allocation and distribution channels have limited the mobility (and consequently increased the cost) of entry for foreign investors, especially in transitional economies such as China (Van Den Bulcke and Zhang 1994a, 1998). Again, these factors are less significant for subsidiaries engaged in offshore activities that are most often located in free trade zones and have fewer linkages with the economy of the host country.

Tariff and non-tariff barriers

Tariff and non-tariff barriers have been among the key location factors leading to overseas production when it is not possible to supply foreign markets via exporting. The degree of effective protection can be a significant determinant of the industry composition of FDI. To attract offshore-oriented foreign investors, countries may set up specific areas, for example, export processing zones, that provide exemptions for import and export duties and grant other incentives.

Performance requirements, such as local content conditions, can also have an impact on foreign-investment decisions, especially for suppliers of intermediate goods. However, the impact of performance conditions, for example, the level of exports and local content requirements on FDI inflows is rather ambiguous, because production costs in the host country may be distorted, or otherwise, lead to a non-optimal performance by the foreign affiliates as such. Therefore, there may be a need for compensatory measures by the host government.

Cost factors

Among the location factors, which may have an effect on the propensity and the direction of FDI, cost factors are very influential. The relative wage rate is strongly relevant for the inflow of FDI for export-processing and cost-based efficiency-seeking operations. Transportation costs might have an important impact on the foreign company's decision for the choice between, either exports to foreign markets or FDI for local market purposes. As far as FDI in export-oriented production is concerned, intra-firm trade has to take transportation costs into account as the normal outcome of the company's integrated cross-border production network.

Investment incentives

Previous research has established that investment incentives of host countries are not often a major factor in accounting for, either realised or potential, entry by foreign market seekers. Nonetheless, there appear to be divergent experiences, especially by small- and medium-sized firms with cost/supply-oriented investment options. Political risk and discriminatory host country policies or regulations are two factors that are ranked as being among the important negative influences on location decisions, however. Also, the control of the ownership structure of foreign subsidiaries and foreign exchange regulations have an important impact on the behaviour of foreign firms, especially those involved in the transfer of technology and local-market-oriented production.

Firm-specific factors

The investment patterns of MNEs are first of all determined by the FSAs and the strategic options of the parent companies. MNEs from countries, which are at various stages of economic development and technological capabilities, occupy different levels on the investment development path (Dunning 1986, 1992a) and the internationalisation process. Next to the initial FSAs of MNEs and the 'country of origin effects', the organisational learning and corporate self-renewal of foreign subsidiaries influence the changing patterns of MNEs (Cantwell 1989; Heldlund 1992; Zander and Sölvell 1992). Both the initial competitive position of the parent company and its previous experience in the host country will, therefore, influence the investment behaviour and specific features of the MNEs' overseas operations and determine the bargaining position vis-à-vis the host government.

China's specific location advantages and their impact on EUDI

As mentioned above, the determinants of FDI for market-seeking investors are mainly related to market attractiveness, trade barriers, investment risks and the host country's attitude to provide foreign investors with positive conditions for business activities.[3] Market-seeking MNEs are attracted by the market potential (size and growth), the costs of market access (entry/participation), the government's control over supply, pricing and distribution, etc. Since European MNEs in China are strongly oriented towards R&D intensive industries (discussed later), intellectual property protection may also have a substantial impact on the entry path and on the type of resources committed by these firms. As trade barriers are often associated with other entry conditions – such as the allowed degree of foreign ownership, the sectoral and geographic location requirements or incentives – they equally influence the investment decisions by MNEs. In the rest of this section, the main changes in China's LSAs and their significance for European MNEs will be emphasised.

Market characteristics

The economic size of the Chinese market has significantly expanded since the end of the 1970s. The total GDP of China reached US$ 961 billion in 1998, which brought GDP at a per capita level at US$ 776 (Table 2.2). The average annual growth rate of China's GDP reached 9.8 per cent between 1977 and 1987

Table 2.2 Size, structure and growth of the Chinese economy (1977, 1987 and 1998)

Indications of size	1977	1987	1998
Population (million)	981	1,200	1,239
GDP (US$ billion)	172	268	961
GDP per capita (US$)	175	223	776
Imports (US$ billion)	8	39	166
Exports (US$ billion)	9	39	208
Structural characteristics (as % of GDP)			
Agriculture	29.4	26.8	18.0
Industry	47.1	43.9	49.2
Manufacturing	31.1	34.4	36.8
Services	23.4	29.3	32.8
Annual growth rate (%)	*1977–1987*	*1988–1998*	*1998*
GDP	9.8	10.3	7.8
GNP	10.0	10.0	7.4
Population	1.5	1.1	1.0
GNP per capita	8.5	8.8	6.5
Gross domestic investment	10.7	11.7	7.6
Industrial production	10.9	14.1	9.2
Manufacturing	11.4	13.4	8.9
Imports of goods and services	19.2	12.5	1.5
Exports of goods and services	18.4	14.4	4.6

Source: The World Bank (1999).

Note
All figures are in current value.

and 10.3 per cent during the period 1988–1998. The existing market size and its expected expansion are undoubtedly among the driving forces of the enormous FDI flows into China during the last decade.

The structure of the Chinese economy has changed tremendously. The proportion of the industrial and service sectors in the GDP increased, respectively, from 47 and 23 per cent in 1977 to 49 and 33 per cent in 1998. The increasing importance of the industrial sector, in particular manufacturing, resulted in the integration of China into the Asian production system and to a certain extent even in the global one. The exports of China increased from US$ 9 billion in 1977 to US$ 208 billion in 1998, an annual growth of 18 per cent during the period 1977–1987 and 14 per cent between 1988 and 1998. This economic performance, especially of manufacturing production and exports, largely explains the boom of China's economy.

However, there is an impressive gap between the coastal and inland regions mainly because of substantial differences in their factor endowments and the speed of the economic transition process. Table 2.3 summarises some salient characteristics of the cities and regions where the surveyed companies of this study are located. Compared to the coastal region, the inland region (e.g.

Table 2.3 Some economic characteristics and location factors of the surveyed Chinese provinces and cities (1996)

	Shaanxi	Sichuan	Beijing	Tianjin	Shanghai	Guangdong	Hubei
Development level							
GDP per capita (CNY)	2,324	2,453	8,665	7,698	13,590	6,174	3,255
Manufacturing in total output value (%)	31	28	32	27	27	24	28
Economic system							
Foreign trade to GDP (ratio)	8	5	137	44	49	98	7
SOEs in total industrial output (%)	61	40	54	33	40	18	38
SOEs in total employment (%)	84	74	76	68	69	60	77
Level of productivity							
Productivity of labour (manufacturing output per employee in CNY)	18,986	26,055	29,222	26,564	46,191	50,909	25,819
Annual wages in SOEs (CNY)	4,639	4,952	8,238	6,963	9,578	8,540	4,991
Annual wages in collective enterprises (CNY)	2,795	3,251	6,516	4,138	6,309	6,395	3,308
Market size							
Population (million)	35	113	13	9	15	69	58
Urban population (%)	48	n.a.	65	57	71	n.a.	n.a.
Total retail value (billion CNY)	63	180	234	86	303	462	134
Total retail value per capita (CNY)	1,801	1,590	18,727	9,120	20,900	6,730	2,326

Source: Calculations based on data from the China Statistical Yearbook (1997).

Shaanxi, Sichuan and Hubei) is characterised by a lower level of development in terms of GDP per capita, a less open economic system (foreign trade to GDP), lower wage rates and lower productivity. Although these inland provinces have a high level of industrialisation, their share in the industrial output and employment is still dominated by the SOEs. While the market potential of the inland region is quite high in terms of population, its actual purchasing power is much lower than in the coastal cities/provinces as measured by total retail value and retail value per capita.

Trade barriers

The existence and the level of trade barriers, such as tariff duties and quotas, customs procedures and specific standards as well as all kinds of technical requirements, have been major determinants for market-seeking investors in China. China often uses prohibitively high tariffs in combination with import restrictions to protect its domestic industry. As import tariffs are much higher for finished goods than for upstream inputs, they result in a high effective rate of protection. Tariffs may range from 3 per cent on promoted imports to over 150 per cent on discouraged imports, such as automobiles. These tariff measures are often associated with a lack of transparency in customs procedures with regard to the necessary documents, registration procedures or licensing system. China's tariff and non-tariff barriers present major obstacles to foreign companies waiting to penetrate the Chinese market by way of exports. These trade barriers consequently encouraged many foreign companies to shift from exporting to local assembly and move on to a local production activity, especially when there are local content requirements. European MNEs producing in the automotive industry have typically followed such a sequence in China (Zhang and Van Den Bulcke 2000).

Over the last 2–3 years, China has gradually reduced its tariffs in order to be admitted to the WTO. To facilitate negotiations for its membership requests, China already in 1996 cut its import duties on some 4,600 items, from an average rate of 35.9 to 23 per cent and scrapped a third of its import quotas (EU 1997). While such reductions of import tariffs increased export opportunities for foreign companies, industries such as automotive and consumer electronics are still highly protected.

A further reduction of import tariffs and the elimination of many non-tariff barriers by the Chinese government, as a result of its newly gained membership of the WTO, will also lower protection in a number of specific industries. As a result, the foreign MNEs that are producing in previously protected industries within China will be facing stronger competition from imported products. For these reasons, many European MNEs that moved into China at an early stage are rationalising their operations within the country by engaging into larger-scale operations and more specialised activities. A number of MNEs are reorganising their links with suppliers, especially by creating local sourcing capabilities and/or bringing with them suppliers from the home country into China.

Business environment

The lack of a well-structured and transparent legal system in China poses serious problems for foreign-owned firms. A clear and strict hierarchical system of norms does not really exist yet. Moreover, there are many diverse regulations issued by different ministries and offices of the central and local/regional governments. Western companies, especially SMEs, are often unable to find out which regulations exactly apply to them. In some cases, unpublished regulations may have precedence over officially published ones. Sometimes, the officially published and unofficially applied rules from the central and local governments are simply contradictory.

However, since the liberalisation of FDI, the Chinese government has made great efforts to build up an appropriate business environment for foreign investors within the context of the transition of the Chinese economy towards a more market-oriented system. With regard to market-seeking foreign investors and their initiatives to expand their scale of operation and their specialisation-based activities, the measures taken by the Chinese government mainly consisted of the introduction of market mechanisms that allow for a better resource allocation and product distribution. First, the foreign exchange restrictions that were the main barrier for foreign enterprises to sell in the domestic market were gradually lifted by the introduction of new regulatory and administrative measures.[4] Also, the unification of the dual exchange rate system in 1994, through the elimination of the so-called Foreign Exchange Certificates (FECs), which existed alongside the local currency Renminbi, was an important step towards the convertibility of the Chinese currency.

Second, the centrally controlled and unified pricing system was converted into a mechanism based on demand factors and production costs. The state plan for the supply of inputs and the distribution of products was gradually eliminated and replaced by market transactions. Market mechanisms such as stock exchanges and labour markets were established and a number of new economic institutions were set up and opened for foreign investors to facilitate transactions of capital, technology, labour and commodities. In 1995, the Chinese government allowed foreign companies to invest through the stock exchange and to set up 'foreign joint stock companies' and 'investment-oriented companies'. The introduction of such flexible investment forms not only improved the investment climate in general, but also allowed foreign companies to achieve a better co-ordination among their different activities in China and thus to operate more efficiently. Additionally, more intensive vertical and horizontal linkages with Chinese domestic enterprises were fostered.

Third, with the increasing use of the market mechanism for business transactions in China, the government introduced a set of regulations to explicitly facilitate market transactions and to stimulate efficiency. Also, the national regulatory framework was brought more into line with international standards, for example, in the areas of contract law, dispute settlement procedures, patent and trade mark protection, accounting systems and copyright protection. Between 1979 and 1994, the Chinese government promulgated more than 500 regulations and laws concerning foreign trade and economic co-operation, of which about seventy concerned FDI. China also signed bilateral and multilateral treaties to protect and promote FDI activities within its territory with no less than sixty-five countries (MOFTEC 1999). Most EU countries signed such bilateral treaties with the Chinese government during the 1980s (Table 2.4).

The most significant change in the Chinese business regulations for foreign-owned firms was the introduction and improvement of intellectual property rights during the 1990s. The introduction of patent law has removed a major obstacle to attract foreign investment in high-tech sectors and has extended the perspectives for the development of industries with high R&D investments and high specialisation. Yet, the full implementation of these regulations is not completed yet.

Table 2.4 Bilateral investment treaties between EU member countries and China

Country	Date	Country	Date
Austria	12.09.1985	Italy	28.01.1985
Belgium/Luxembourg	04.06.1984	Netherlands	07.06.1985
Denmark	29.04.1985	Portugal	03.02.1992
Finland	04.09.1984	Spain	06.02.1992
France	30.05.1984	Sweden	29.03.1982
Germany	07.10.1983	UK/Ireland	15.05.1986
Greece	25.06.1992		

Source: MOFTEC (1983–1997).

Chinese FDI policy

In reviewing the development of the Chinese FDI policy and its impact on the attractiveness of Chinese LSAs for FDI during the last two decades of the twentieth century, three major characteristics can be identified. First, the liberalisation and upgrading process of LSAs by the Chinese government has been closely linked with the geographical extension of FDI incentives on the basis of special tax measures and administrative regulations. Second, China has gradually introduced a set of sectoral and performance requirements for FDI within the context of its economic development strategy that is based on import substitution, export promotion and technological upgrading. Third, the control about ownership/entry forms of FDI has been gradually liberalised with the improvement of the market mechanisms and expansion of the private sector. Figure 2.2 shows the major steps of the liberalisation of the Chinese FDI policy according to these three dimensions.

The specific FDI measures, which were introduced by the Chinese government to support its geographical and sectoral monitoring system, consist of the liberalisation and upgrading of local resources, the introduction of a market system to improve resource allocation and product distribution, the building-up of a legal system geared to market transactions, the decentralisation of macroeconomic management, the diversification of ownership control and the introduction of performance requirements. These measures will be briefly analysed within the geographical and sectoral dimensions of the Chinese FDI policy.

Geographical dimension of Chinese FDI policy

The gradual opening up of specific locations for foreign investors on the basis of preferential tax and tariff measures is quite characteristic of the Chinese 'guided FDI scenario' (Table 2.5). The first major step of the liberalisation process of inward FDI by the Chinese government was the launching of four Special Economic Zones (SEZs) in 1980 in two coastal provinces, that is, Guangdong

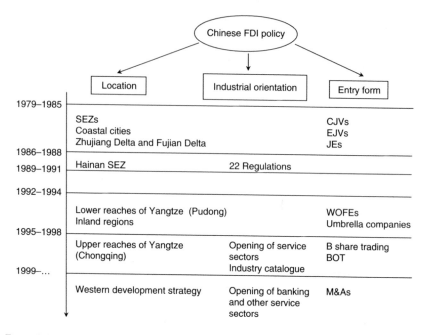

Figure 2.2 Main aspects of Chinese FDI policy and their changes over time.

and Fujian. These areas were chosen to take advantage of their favourable location, that is, their proximity to Hong Kong, good transportation links and close connections to Overseas Chinese business people. Also, the specific administrative and fiscal regulations and the low labour costs were positive elements.

The factors that were mainly related to the geographical location and the specific administrative status of the zones permitted firms from the Asian NIEs to relocate their export processing and assembly operations to China while continuing to rely on the transportation and communication facilities of Hong Kong. Establishing outsourcing bases was by far the most important objective of these companies with investment operations in China. This type of investment commonly involved the relocation – typically carried out in stages – of labour-intensive production processes, such as textile manufacturing and electronics products assembly, in order to benefit from lower production costs in China. For strategic reasons, a number of Western MNEs had also set up an early presence in SEZs. These Western pioneers in China came to the SEZs not to take advantage of the location-bound resources, as was the case for most Asian investors, but for 'testing the water', that is, learning about how to operate in the Chinese market and/or preparing for a long-term involvement.

In 1984, the Chinese government extended the tax and tariff incentives for foreign companies to fourteen coastal cities, including former colonial metropoles

Table 2.5 Chronological overview of China's FDI policies and responses of MNEs (1979–2001)

Period	Government decisions and policies about FDI	Main effects on FDI and responses of MNEs
1979–1982	Abolishment of FDI prohibition by the introduction of Joint Venture Law, Civil Procedure Law, Joint Venture Income Tax Law, etc. Establishment of four SEZs Incentives and regulatory measures of FDI dominated by the bureaucratic control mechanism	Low-cost labour seeking investment with export processing activities Limited integration with domestic market (location mainly in the SEZs) Limited resources and management commitment Preference for contractual JVs and short-term projects 'Testing the water' investment by Western firms (strategic positioning)
1983–1985	Improvement of industrial infrastructure and better access to domestic market by opening up of 14 coastal cities Integration of local-labour-intensive industries into export processing operations by opening up of three River Deltas Introduction of reform measures in urban areas (fiscal, banking, pricing, local economic management, enterprise management) Setting-up of preliminary legal infrastructure for market transactions (contract law and patent law)	Growth of market-seeking investment Introduction of more human-resource-intensive technology More linkages with local market as result of increasing capabilities of local sourcing for export processing manufacture More involvement of local partners for acquiring local market knowledge in establishing EJVs
1986–1988	New regulatory measures (22 regulations) with additional incentives for priority FDI projects (export, import substitution and high-tech) Introduction of performance requirements (export share, product specifics and technological level) 'Marketisation' of resource allocation (foreign exchange-SWAP markets, raw materials, labour) Increasing liberalisation of market resources (supply and distribution network)	Increase of bargaining power of Western MNEs based on relatively high level of technology and new products Increase of large-scale export processing manufacturing industries Decrease of short-term FDI projects (in service sectors)

(Continued)

Table 2.5 (Continued)

Period	Government decisions and policies about FDI	Main effects on FDI and responses of MNEs
1989–1991	Political crisis (aftermath of Tiananmen) and introduction of an 'rectification programme' to control the economic overheating and inflation Neither restrictive nor significant incentive measures for FDI in the updated EJV Law in 1990 Specific administrative arrangements for foreign investors to improve investment climate Increasing support from bureaucracy for local-market-oriented foreign enterprises ('isolated' market)	Reduction of confidence of foreign (especially Western) investors Increase of FDI from Asian MNEs with similar social and cultural background and more risk-taking behaviour Building-up of 'insider' market position by early entered MNEs in a 'isolated' market situation
1992–1994	Opening of inland cities for FDI and introduction of new ownership forms (e.g. umbrella companies and 'B' share trade) Attempts to eliminate unfair competition and improvement of company-level regulations Towards international standards and national treatment of FDI with upgrading of legal infrastructure (taxation, foreign exchange, company law)	Increase of efficiency seeking MNEs by using large-scale production and process technology and/or creation of own marketing and sourcing subsidiaries Diversification into related and unrelated business lines by Asian MNEs as response to booming local market situation Increase of transfer of organisational capabilities by Western MNEs as result of the internationalisation of local business conditions
1995–1998	Opening up of upper reaches of Yangtze River Liberalisation of service sectors to foreign investors Introduction of industrial catalogues Introduction of new FDI forms (BOT, acquisitions of SOEs) Introduction of micro-level control measures for FDI operations (e.g. transfer pricing, evaluation of non-equity contribution for inward FDI)	Increase of FDI in infrastructure and business-related service sectors Expansion into inland region for market potential Take-over of SOEs for insuring market position or entering strategic industries Buy out of Chinese partners or creation of wholly owned subsidiaries for efficiency seeking
1999–...	Opening up of the central and western regions as part of the Western Development Strategy ('Go West') Introduction of incentive measures to attract FDI in local R&D activities Revision of FDI regulations to prepare for WTO membership	Expansion of investment in business services by MNEs into newly opened area, such as inland region Shift by IT MNEs from manufacturing equipment to e-business, software and research and product development Increasing resource commitment by MNEs in local R&D activities

Source: Zhang and Van Den Bulcke (1996), with an update for 1995–2001.

such as Tianjin, Shanghai, Dalian and Guangzhou. The opening up of these coastal cities provided market-seeking MNEs with new opportunities and more extensive markets. They acquired access to a relatively well-developed industrial infrastructure, a larger geographic and densely populated area, a better educated and trained labour force, more reliable transportation and communication systems and improved living conditions. Also, a number of Western MNEs were to some extent already familiar with these cities, as they had established trading and even production activities there during the colonial period (discussed later). These specific location factors allowed foreign MNEs, in particular those from Western countries, to engage into more human-capital-intensive and local-market-oriented activities. The principal motivation for these investments by Western firms during this period was mainly of a 'trade-barrier-circumventing' nature. Local production in China was intended to substitute for the export of goods from the home bases of these firms.

Because China adopted a mixed policy of granting preferences to FDI on the one hand while levying high import tariffs as a means of promoting domestic industries on the other hand, many Western companies switched to local production activities to acquire a foothold in the Chinese market. Yet, a number of large MNEs, especially from Japan and to a lesser extent from the USA, also transferred export processing activities from their home bases or from subsidiaries in other countries to these cities in order to benefit not only from lower cost conditions, but also from the existing trade and transport facilities. For instance, a number of US electronic firms integrated their production facilities in China into their Asian production network. These cross-border ties permitted US-owned firms to exploit the growing technical sophistication and competitive strength of firms that were initially located in Taiwan, Singapore and Korea and had moved recently into the coastal provinces of Mainland China (Borrus 1996). By contrast, EU electronic firms did not follow the same investment path as their US competitors and their operations in China were less integrated into their regional or global production systems (Zysman and Borrus 1994).

In 1985, the regions of the three River Deltas were added to the list of specific FDI areas. The opening up of these additional regions stimulated the integration of the export processing and assembly activities of Asian NIE investors with the small-scale and labour-intensive domestic firms, especially the so-called Town and Village Enterprises (TVEs). The creation of linkages between local industry and foreign processing enterprises provided foreign investors with local sourcing options at lower costs. The pattern of this locally linked cost/supply FDI, and the dynamic changes in the cross-border trade that can be associated with FDI flows, gradually integrated China into the so-called Asian 'flying-geese' pattern of investment. Most of the direct investment carried out by Hong Kong and Taiwanese companies in Mainland China contributed to and accelerated this integrative process. Yet, the impact of such backward integration for Western 'market seekers' was rather limited because of the low level of technology and the poor industrial infrastructure in these newly accessible regions (Table 2.6).

Table 2.6 Types of special economic zones, development areas and other open economic regions in China (1980–2000)

Type of economic areas	Year	Included zones, cities or regions
Special economic zones	1980	Shantou, Shenzhen, Zhuhai and Xiamen
	1988	Hainan
Open coastal areas	1984	Old parts of 14 coastal cities: Fuzhou, Guangzhou, Zhanjiang, Beihai, Qinhuangdao, Lianyungang, Nantong, Dalian, Yantai, Qingdao, Shanghai, Tianjin, Ningbo, Wenzhou
	1985	57 Cities/counties along the Pearl River Delta, Yangtze River Delta and South Fujian Triangle
	1988–1992	Many cities and counties including Bohai Sea Rim, Beijing, Tianjin and parts of Hebei and Liaoning
Economic and technological development zones (ETDZs)	1984	New areas in the open coastal cities: Guangzhou, Zhanjiang, Qinhuangdao, Lianyungang, Nantong, Dalian, Yantai, Qingdao, Tianjin, Ningbo
	1990	Pudong New Area (Shanghai)
	1997	Chongqing
	Since 1985	Many other areas were approved by the State Council (32 at the end of 1994) and provincial and lower levels of governments (586 at the end of 1994)
High Technology industry development zones	Since 1988	52 State Council approved zones and 68 zones approved by provincial and lower levels of governments
Open border cities, Yangtze River cities, Inland provincial capitals	1992	13 Border cities, 18 inland capital cities and 5 Yangtze River cities. Capital cities: Hefei, Lanzhou, Guiyang, Harbin, Zhengzhou, Changsha, Changchun, Huhehaote, Nanchang, Changchun, Yinchuan, Xining, Nanchang, Xian, Taiyuan, Changdu, Urumchi, Kunming Yangtze River cities: Wuhu, Yueyang, Jiujiang, Chongqing
	1997	Chongqing being granted the status of centrally-administered municipality
	1999	Within the context of 'Western Development Strategy', 10 provinces and autonomous regions in the central and western regions are opened to foreign investors and benefit from preferential measures

The setting up of the Pudong economic development zone in Shanghai in 1990 provided foreign market seekers with an even more liberal market access than before. Pudong became one of the most attractive locations for foreign MNEs, as by the end of 1998 more than 5,500 FIEs were already established there with more than US$ 10 billion of foreign capital. In June 1992, the FDI incentives were extended to eighteen inland provincial-capital cities, five cities along the Yangtze River and thirteen border cities in the North East, South West and North West regions. In 1997, Chongqing was granted a set of FDI incentives as had been the case for Pudong, in order to upgrade the investment environment of the upper side of the Yangtze River. A number of Western MNEs have moved into these areas by taking over existing local firms and/or by establishing greenfield production units. The liberalisation and upgrading of the specific locational factor endowments in the inland provinces of China are expected to attract foreign investors, but the investment environment and infrastructure still need to be strongly improved.

In September 1999, the Chinese government announced the Western Development Strategy (WDS). Attracting foreign investment to the Middle and Western regions is among the focal issues of China's new FDI policy. The 'Advice on Further Encouraging Foreign Investment at Present' issued by the General Office of the State Council (Document No. 73, 1999) consisted of six specific measures in order to promote foreign investment in the Central and Western regions, such as relaxing control on a number of manufacturing and service sectors for foreign investment, broadening the scope for these regions to enjoy various preferential policies, developing an export-oriented economy and increasing foreign co-operation. A number of industries and projects with locational advantages in the central and western areas are opened to foreign investment and are enjoying preferential treatment. For instance, FDI in environmental and ecological sectors, such as eco-agriculture and comprehensive use of water resources are strongly supported by these measures to promote sustainable development in these regions.

Foreign invested enterprises in the coastal region are encouraged to relocate in the central and western regions to promote the development of the inland region. All policies that were carried out on a trial basis in the coastal region may also be implemented in the central and western area. Existing development zones in the capital cities in the central and western areas may be upgraded to state development zones after having received the necessary approval.

Foreign invested enterprises in the coastal region are also encouraged to take part in the restructuring and re-organization of the state-owned industrial enterprises in the West. A number of tax incentives are granted to FIEs operating in promoted industries. For instance, during the first three years of having been granted preferential policy, the income tax for these foreign-funded enterprises in the central and western areas can be reduced to 15 per cent as compared to the original rate of 30 per cent. Apart from these preferential policies and measures granted by the central government, local governments are also encouraged to enhance their comparative advantages for attracting FDI.

Sector and performance requirements

Although the Chinese government liberalised FDI for the purpose of import substitution, export promotion and technological upgrading, its FDI policy did not use any incentive nor any regulatory measures to influence the sectoral orientation of foreign enterprises in the early years of the 1980s. As a result of the general uncertainty about the investment environment and the lack of sectoral requirements in particular at that time, FDI was highly concentrated in certain specific service sectors – hotels, restaurants, taxis, etc. – and mainly took the form of short-term and flexible co-operation agreements such as contractual joint ventures (CJVs) or subcontracting arrangements.

In 1986, the State Council issued the 'Provisions for the Encouragement of Foreign Investment', also known as the 'twenty-two regulations'. On the basis of several performance criteria, such as export share targets, technology transfer, sector specificity and production requirements, a set of tax incentives was granted to the foreign direct investors engaging in import substitution, export promotion and advanced technological activities. Also administrative measures were taken to facilitate export and import procedures, to provide foreign companies with additional options to solve their foreign exchange imbalances, to limit external bureaucratic interference in the management of equity joint ventures (EJVs) and to eliminate unfair and costly local bureaucratic interventions.

In 1993, a number of sectors that had until then been closed to FDI were liberalised, especially in services and infrastructure. Since then foreign investors have gradually been allowed to invest in banking, insurance, retail trade, foreign trade, tourism, real estate, legal and consulting services, advertising, maritime shipping and international cargo services. Yet, operations by foreign investors in these subsectors were still limited to certain specific activities and locations. In fact, the access to the service sector is still conditional, restrictive and incomplete.

In June 1995, the Chinese government published foreign investment guidelines, that is, the so-called 'Industry Catalogue'. The object of this regulation was to direct FDI towards the encouraged sectors. The Catalogue divided investment into four categories: encouraged, permitted, restricted and prohibited investment. The list of encouraged FDI consisted of projects that largely involve the transfer of advanced technology and the technical development of leading and basic industries, such as power plants, railways and port infrastructure, machines, microelectronics, steel, non-ferrous metals and chemicals. On the other hand, the service sectors in a second list – such as telecommunications, aviation, rail and sea transportation – were discouraged or continued to be prohibited, although liberalisation was promised in view of China's application to join the WTO. A third list covers restricted sectors, including department stores, foreign trade, mining and insurance. The priority sectors continued to receive tax concessions and access to soft loans (Murray 1995).

At the beginning of 1998, the 'Industry Catalogue' was revised. The adjusted list broadened the scope of foreign investment in order to meet the demands of industrial structure adjustment, to favour the absorption of advanced technologies, and to fully promote FDI in the central and western regions. In the context of its WDS, the State Planning Commission and MOFTEC formulated a number of preferential measures to attract more foreign investment towards the inland region. Additional areas in the inland region are opened with special tax incentives, while foreign investment in agriculture, hydropower, ecology, transport, energy, engineering, environment projects, mining and tourism are encouraged. Also, more provincial cities became experimental bases for FDI in banking, retail and trade. For instance, in 1999 the Chinese government decided to open four more cities to foreign insurance companies in order to boost foreign investment in this sector. Foreign banks have been allowed to operate banking business in Renminbi, while wholly foreign owned enterprises (WFOEs) will be given permission to operate telecommunication, insurance and tourism services according to the relevant policies and regulations. Sino-foreign joint ventures were allowed to be established in accounting, legal services, engineering, design centres, rail and highway transportation and public utilities.

In June 2000, a 'List of Industries with Advantages for Foreign Investment in Central and Western China', decreed by the State Economic and Trade Commission and the Ministry of Foreign Trade and Economic Cooperation and approved by the State Council, was issued in order to enhance the LSAs of these regions with new tax incentives for FDI. The list included a number of industries or projects that are promoted in different provinces and autonomous regions in the central and western regions. The 'Industry Catalogue' on the sectoral distribution of FDI in China has to some extent affected the structure and competitiveness of Chinese industries in a very differential way, such as increasing competition in the Chinese consumer electronics as compared to the still highly protected car industry and telecommunication services (Zhang 2000). Yet, new developments have shown that the 'quality' of FDI in China has apparently improved (discussed later).

Until recently, China had neither regulatory nor incentive measures to oblige or pressure foreign enterprises to 'localise' R&D activities in China. In 1999, some fiscal incentives were issued in order to encourage FIEs to invest into local R&D activities, however. In April 2000, MOFTEC issued a notice to encourage foreign companies to establish R&D centres in China. It set forth rules on the establishment procedures for such R&D centres and stipulated the applicable preferential policies, including tax breaks on equipment imports and exemptions from corporate taxes when a R&D centre assigns technology resulting from its own R&D.

Ownership control and FDI forms

China's legal and regulatory regime has also evolved into a wider range of investment options for foreign investors seeking more flexibility and variety for their investment projects. There are five types of FDI under current Chinese law.

Equity joint-ventures

Equity joint-ventures are limited liability companies incorporated in China in which foreign and Chinese investors hold equity. Their main features are: a term period (usually 15–20 years); profit and risk sharing proportionate to capital share; minimum 25 per cent of equity capital contribution; foreign exchange control, including remittance of profits abroad, etc.

Contractual joint-ventures

Contractual joint-ventures are organised as business partnerships in which both parties operate as separate legal entities and bear liabilities independently. The main features are: no required minimum foreign contribution; participation is not necessarily in monetary value and may include labour, resources and services; profits are divided according to the contract terms and not necessarily the equity share; flexibility in the structure of the organisation; no limits on duration, etc.

Wholly foreign-owned enterprises

China permits 100 per cent ownership in industries where such investment is not prohibited and where it is conducive to economic development. The government remains relatively selective, requiring applicant companies to satisfy one of the two following criteria for the WFOEs: (a) the company must use advanced technology and equipment, develop new products, be economical with respect to energy and raw materials and upgrade and replace existing products or produce goods and services that can be substituted for imports; (b) the value of the products exported annually by the enterprise must represent more than 50 per cent of the firm's total production and the firm must balance foreign exchange receipts and payments.

Joint stock company

A legal entity[5] of which the capital stock is made up of equal value shares contributed by both domestic and foreign shareholders. The registered capital of this type of companies should be at least RMB 30 million. The total value of the shares purchased and held by the foreign shareholders should be no less than 25 per cent of the company's total registered capital (EU 1997). As compared to the EJV, CJV, WFOE and holding company, it is still quite complicated to start a limited company in China.

Holding company

The minimum registered capital for the establishment of a holding company has been increased from US\$ 10 million to 30 or even 50 million. This huge amount, to be submitted in foreign exchange, constitutes a considerable barrier to conducting competitive business (EU 1997). The holding company regulations permit to engage in a number of support and service activities for MNEs with several subsidiaries in China. It may purchase raw materials or production inputs on behalf of its subsidiaries and sell its subsidiaries' products in China and overseas; assist subsidiaries in recruiting employees and provide technical training and marketing assistance; and provide consulting services to its subsidiaries. Perhaps most importantly, the regulations will allow holding companies to integrate the financial operations of their different subsidiaries. This makes it possible for foreign investors to co-ordinate and allocate their tangible and intangible assets all over the country and to participate efficiently in extending their existing operations or in acquiring a new business portfolio within the privatisation process.

Other forms of investment

The new forms of FDI in China are becoming increasingly familiar to foreign investors, especially the acquisition of existing Chinese companies by transactions on the stock exchange, the establishment of holding companies and the use of direct investment vehicles in project finance transactions (Hickman and Mendelsohn 1998). Cross-border mergers and acquisitions (M&As) have become one of the main modes of FDI. The acquisition of existing Chinese companies through stock exchange operations, the establishment of holding companies and the use of direct investment vehicles in project finance transactions have become more and more frequent. For instance, although the regulations on M&As and alliances in China are still considered to be rather vague, imprecise and inconsistent, a preliminary framework has been put into shape since 1999. The evolution of this legal framework tends to make acquisitions of and participations in existing SOEs an increasingly important form of direct investment in China (Capener 1998; Van Den Bulcke, Zhang and Li 1999; Zaloom and Liu 1999). In the context of the recent WDS, new forms of investment have been initiated for foreign investors, such as leasing, ownership transfer, co-operative industrial investment funds, venture capital, M&As, BOT, etc. In fact, China is continuously researching for FDI measures that would allow it to optimise its benefits from the activities of foreign MNEs.

Reform of Chinese SOEs and opportunities for European MNEs

The Chinese government introduced a new programme to further the reform of SOEs at the 15th Congress of the Chinese Communist Party in September 1997. These new initiatives were intended to separate government responsibilities from enterprise activities through ownership diversification and market-oriented M&As that convert traditional SOEs into private and shareholding companies. As a result of the ongoing reform process, the following changes have been envisaged (Van Den Bulcke, Zhang and Li 1999). First, interventions by the government in enterprise activities will be reduced further, and enterprises will increasingly conduct their business activities according to market conditions. The substantial decline in the power of the central/local administration to direct or control an enterprise in different ways will improve the efficiency of SOEs, especially because of their enhanced management autonomy.

Second, it is hoped that the separation of the government from business decisions through the introduction of a 'state asset management system' will simplify corporate governance and the organisational structure of SOEs. These structures have since a long time been regarded as excessively complicated not only by foreign investors, but even by Chinese managers. On the other hand, a number of the social objectives currently carried out by these enterprises, in particular housing, pensions and other social security arrangements will have to be reallocated to the relevant publicly owned institutions.

Third, the government's effort in reforming SOEs will be aimed at the corporate re-organisation of large- and medium-sized enterprises on a sustainable development basis. For this purpose, the Chinese government decided to allocate the necessary financial resources to develop large corporations, especially in key sectors with strategic importance, such as metallurgy, chemicals, automotive, communications, etc. It tries to establish large enterprise groups with trans-regional, inter-industry, cross-ownership and trans-national operations. This trend of sectoral concentration is expected to result in an increase of competition from large Chinese corporations not only in the domestic market, but also in the regional and global market at least in the long term.

Fourth, the government promised to adapt the legal system and continue to introduce and update regulations and laws concerning bankruptcy, leasing, mergers, acquisitions, joint-stock systems and investment holdings. A set of incentives (e.g. tax reductions and favourable loans) were already set up by the central and local governments to ensure a receptive environment for the reform of SOEs.

Fifth, the employment structure will change tremendously. It is expected that numerous workers will be laid-off and the availability of unskilled human resources and low cost of labour will be increased, especially in the inland region. The training facilities that have been set up by different government institutions in the context of the reform programme should improve the skill level of workers and employees and provide more flexibility in the labour market.

Sixth, the joint-stock system and capital markets will play key roles in the reform of large- and medium-sized SOEs. A large number of state-owned key sectors will be opened to domestic as well as to foreign private investors in order to help to solve debt problems and capital shortages.

Several of the above-mentioned changes represent both opportunities and challenges for foreign and EU companies and will affect their strategic decisions to settle, operate and/or expand in China.

First, because of the improvement of the legal system with regard to business organisational aspects and economic transactions, foreign investors can look forward to more transparency in the regulations concerning the business environment. China's legal and regulatory regime is also evolving into a wider range of options for foreign investors seeking more flexibility and variety for their investment projects. There are indications that foreign investors are more frequently exploiting these opportunities than before to diversify their investments in China. That China is determined to 'privatise' its SOEs is making acquisitions an increasingly important form of direct investment in China. Partial and complete take-overs of existing SOEs are becoming preferred options among foreign investors despite the remaining uncertainties about the legal environment.

Second, the changes in the government–business relations, especially because of the elimination and/or reorganisation of the influence of Chinese ministries and government departments lowers the protection barriers for Western MNEs, in particular, early entrants that often were strongly protected. Yet, the changes in the government's administrative structure also cause problems for the MNEs established since many years that have already developed privileged linkages with these sectoral departments and bureaucracies. They have to adapt to the new situation where they can no longer rely on their usual partners or mediators.

Third, the privatisation and 'corporatisation' of SOEs present opportunities for European and other MNEs to enter into new market areas for building up global market capabilities. Yet, the creation of large national enterprise groups by the central government in the reform programme is intended to increase the competitive position of a number of SOEs vis-à-vis foreign MNEs, especially in key industrial sectors. In order to pre-empt competitive threats, MNEs might seek to participate in this process, especially through mergers, joint ventures and strategic alliances in both the domestic and international markets. This would not only allow European MNEs to confront not only strong rivals, but also to enter into alliances and partnerships for certain aspects of their value-added chain with these competitors.

Fourth, the opening up of large enterprises/complexes in the state-owned defence industries frees unused production facilities and relatively qualified human resources, especially in mechanical engineering. The development of subcontracting and joint manufacturing activities with these enterprises might allow to build up world-class production capabilities and to speed up the introduction of new products on the basis of lower production costs.

Yet, the difficulties for European MNEs to actively participate in the Chinese reform process should not to be underestimated. The ownership reform of SOEs on the one hand and the further evolution of FDI policy on the other hand will determine the further development of Chinese inward FDI in a more competitive environment. These processes not only concern new investors who are still in the negotiating stage of their projects, but also well-established foreign enterprises, because of the rapid changes occurring in their partner companies and the general business environment.

Recent developments

To prepare for WTO membership, China revised its existing legal framework regarding FDI during 2000–2001. Major revisions eliminated the requirement that FIEs balance the demand and supply of foreign exchange; abolished the provision that FIEs must join local suppliers in China for purchasing raw materials. Also, the regulation that FIEs must report their production and operation plans to supervisory government authorities and the requirement that FIEs should export to earn foreign exchange were suspended (NERI 2001). In the coming years, foreign investment will be encouraged in strategic sectors, although restrictions remain in place in many other areas. During the period 2003–2005, a gradual opening of previously protected areas of the economy should take place in line with WTO commitments.

With regard to the WTO negotiations, China signed an agreement with the European Union in which three major concessions were made (*Homeway Financial News*, 26 June 2001): (a) China will allow EU companies to freely choose their joint venture (JV) partners, especially partners in the area of telecommunications. This is a very important concession made by China because, until now EU companies only had the option of choosing from three to four partners when considering business alliances in China: (b) EU companies that have already received permission to operate in China will be allowed into the Chinese market within a maximum of two months. There should be no further delays: (c) Not only will EU companies be able to set up sales offices in China, they will also be allowed to directly market and sell their products to Chinese consumers. This will be important to the development of large business groups in the Chinese market.

As a result of changes in China's business environment in general and FDI policy in particular, the reduction of tariffs and cancellation of quotas after joining WTO will encourage MNEs to expand their R&D and production activities to China on the basis of considerations of global resource allocation. The further opening of the service sector and related industries to FDI should convince foreign financial, insurance and other service companies to invest in telecommunications, microelectronics, software development, international exhibitions, accounting, management consulting and legal services. Foreign investors are expected to shift from establishing production bases for labour-intensive products to setting up international product development bases, from building factories to developing retail branches, from the Coastal region to Western China. The entry form of FDI is likely to shift from greenfields to take-overs of established SOEs.

3 Overview of inward foreign direct investment in China

During the period 1979–2000, China approved a total number of 364,000 foreign investment projects with a cumulative foreign capital investment (contract value) of US$ 676.4 billion, of which US$ 348.4 billion was effectively invested. China consequently became the largest developing host economy in the world. The size and pattern of Chinese inward FDI have been affected by many factors, such as the strategies of MNEs, changing endowments of China's location factors and the FDI policy of the Chinese government. In this chapter, the expansion and trends of Chinese inward FDI are examined against the background of the main changes of the Chinese investment environment and the ensuing reaction of foreign-owned companies. The longitudinal analysis of FDI data is focused on the period 1979–2000 and provides a clear picture about the country of origin, sector distribution, investment form and location of China's inward FDI as well as its changing characteristics.

FDI growth and trends

Since the opening up to FDI in the late 1970s, China has undertaken bold liberalisation moves and has become one of the most dynamic economies in the world with regard to FDI and foreign trade. These changes are the outcome of the gradual liberalisation of China's FDI policy in general, and the enhancement of its location factors in particular. China's inward FDI has closely followed these shifts and has developed in several stages.

During the period 1983–2000 – although the inflows of FDI in terms of utilised value have continually increased at an averaged annual rate of growth of 30 per cent – the contract value and number of contracted FDI projects have significantly declined after the peak of 1993 (Figure 3.1).

The tremendous growth of inward FDI during the early 1980s stopped in its tracks in 1986, after foreign and especially Western investors hesitated to operate in China for market-seeking purposes. The severe difficulties to balance their foreign exchange as a result of the deficit in the Chinese balance of payments during 1985–1986 confronted those investors with the fact that China might be a risky investment. Because of structural inefficiencies and the low quality of locally sourced products, market-seeking investors had to import components

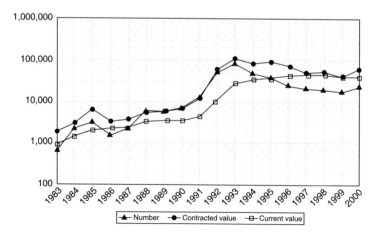

Figure 3.1 Evolution of FDI in China (1983–2000).

Source: MOFTEC (1983–2001).

Note
Logarithmic scale.

and semi-finished products and got into serious problems to balance their foreign exchange receipts and expenses. On the other hand, the growing decentralisation of the Chinese economic system and the extension of the decision-making authority from the central level to provincial and local governments resulted in increased protection of their own markets from outside competitors as all kinds of new barriers were set up by these lower-level institutions. This regional protectionism fragmented the market for both consumer and industrial goods in a serious way. However, increased protection at the provincial or regional level also meant that Western companies engaging in import substitution production were confronted with new difficulties to sell their products in other regions in China than those they were located. The 'bad' experiences of these pioneer investors negatively affected the perception about the investment situation in China by companies which had been considering to locate in China.

In order to improve the overall investment climate and to provide foreign investors with concrete measures to solve the difficulties they encountered in their daily operations, the Chinese government issued in 1986 a set of new regulations, especially the so-called 'Provisions for the Encouragement of Foreign Investment'. These measures provided foreign investors – especially those active in market-seeking production – with new possibilities to balance their foreign exchange operations through a more flexible system. The ensuing renewed confidence of the foreign investors resulted in an expansion of the contracted FDI by more than 36 per cent during 1987–1988.

The growing FDI inflows during 1987–1988 were dramatically broken off after June 1989, because of the government's military intervention against the student protests in Tiananmen Square in Beijing. Although the contracted and utilised FDI inflows during the first half of 1989 rose, respectively, by 44 and 22 per cent as compared to the same period of 1988, the growth rate for the whole year dropped to 5.6 and 3.6 per cent, respectively. The political instability, as perceived by foreign investors, especially those from Western countries, suddenly acted as a deterrent that seriously undermined the willingness to invest in China. For instance, the share of the European Union and North America in the total FDI in China went down, respectively, from 7.4 and 11.8 per cent in 1986–1988 to 5.3 and 6.8 per cent in 1989–1991.

Foreign direct investment started to flow back to China after 1991 as a result of the continued and convincing engagement of the Chinese government in the economic reform process. The opening up of new geographical areas for foreign investors and the liberalisation of previously prohibited sectors created a new wave of inward FDI in 1992. However, the approval of new FDI projects started to decline after 1993, although the real FDI inflows continued to increase. In 1996, the number of approved FDI projects in China fell further and was 33.7 per cent lower than in 1995, while the contracted equity capital dropped by 19.8 per cent. The approved FDI amounted to US$ 51 billion in 1997, indicating a drop of 30 per cent as compared to 1996. The decline of approved FDI in China during these latter four years had much to do with the stricter control of speculative real estate projects after July 1993. This sector had taken up a large proportion of the foreign investment flows during the years before the monitoring was set up. This reduction in FDI can also be partly explained by the completion of the investment wave that followed the liberalisation movement in the early 1990s and the ensuing process of consolidation. Also, China's new taxes on foreign affiliates that came into effect in January 1994 may have negatively affected FDI at that time. Of course, the government's regulations with regard to the approval process of FDI was only one aspect of the Chinese adjustment policy that included macro-economic reforms in public finance, banking system, foreign exchange management, trade and investment and pricing and distribution system.

During the second half of the 1990s, China intensified its investment promotion efforts in order to face a number of adverse factors, including the negative consequences of the Asian financial crisis of 1997 and the slowdown of its economic growth. Its previous incentive scheme for foreign investors, which had been abandoned earlier – such as exemptions of import duties and value-added tax on imports of equipment – was partially resumed, particularly for those industries listed as having a high priority for attracting FDI (UN/UNCTAD 1999). However, by 1998 FDI growth was flat, and in 1999 contracted FDI fell by 21 per cent from US$ 52 to 42 billion. Utilised FDI dropped 12 per cent. The slowdown of Chinese inward FDI was attributed to a more realistic view of foreign investors, many of whom rushed in during the mid-1990s, lured by the size of the Chinese market. Additionally, opaque investment regulations and a difficult legal and business environment tempered much of the initial enthusiasm of MNEs. Also, the Asian financial crisis weakened the position of Asian investors, as FDI from the Asian economies in China declined by 9 per cent during this period, while inflows from the United States and Europe rose by 21 and 3 per cent, respectively.

Although the trends in Chinese FDI inflows show that contracted FDI slowed down or stagnated after 1997, as a result of the more selective FDI policy, the 'quality' of FDI projects improved. The proportion of capital-intensive and hi-tech investment in the newly approved FDI projects as well as the average size of the projects went up. Whereas Hong Kong and Taiwanese companies – of which many are involved in small-scale processing activities such as textiles – initially dominated FDI in China, the world leading MNEs have been moving into China in a more extensive way. Apart from the trend towards larger projects, foreign investment has also become more spread out in a geographical sense with the inland provinces gradually taking up a larger percentage in the newly approved investment projects.

Foreign direct investment data from MOFTEC about the beginning of the new millennium showed that Chinese inward FDI has to some extent recovered from this stagnation. In the first half of 2001, China approved a total of 11,973 FIEs, up 18.5 per cent from the same period of 2000. Those firms contracted foreign investment deals for US$ 33.4 billion, up 38.2 per cent. Utilised FDI in this period reached US$ 20.69 billion, an increase of 20.5 per cent. This sudden surge of FDI to China in the first half of 2001 is considered to be linked to the steady growth of the Chinese economy on the one hand and China's entry into the WTO on the other hand.

Countries/regions of origin

As Figure 3.2 shows, FDI in China has been dominated by Asian NIEs which invested US$ 202 billion (in utilised value) between 1979 and 2000, accounting for 64 per cent of the total Chinese inward FDI. The EU countries, taken together, represented 7.5 per cent, while North America and Japan took up 9.3 and 8 per cent, respectively. The United Kingdom, Germany, France, Italy and the Netherlands constituted the main sources of EUDI in China, as together they accounted for about 92 per cent of all EU outflows. The combined relative share of FDI from the European Union, North America and Japan progressively declined over time. The share of this so-called 'Triad' economy went down from 18.5, 16 and 9.4 per cent in 1983–1985 for its three constituent parts to 8.4, 6.6 and 4.4 per cent in 1993–1995, respectively. The lowest level of these dominant economies occurred in the period 1989–1992. However, since 1992 the investment position of the European Union and North America has somewhat recovered, especially for Germany and the United Kingdom (discussed later).

Although the share of Asian NIEs in the total Chinese inward FDI stock decreased from 71 per cent in 1997 to 64 per cent in 2000 (in terms of utilised value), they still dominate Chinese inward FDI. Hong Kong invested more than US$ 170 billion in China, taking up practically half (49 per cent) of the total Chinese inward FDI. Although information on its FDI in mainland China only became available since 1990, Taiwan is ranked as the fourth largest foreign

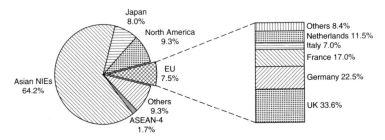

Figure 3.2 Sources of inward FDI in China (1979–2000).
Source: MOFTEC (1983–2001).

investor after Hong Kong, Japan and the United States with a share of 7.5 per cent, even without including the cumulative investments made in previous years through other channels, that is, via Hong Kong and Singapore. Singapore (5 per cent), South Korea (3 per cent) and Macau (1.2 per cent) follow at still a lower level.

Although Hong Kong is ranked as the first home base of Chinese inward FDI, the flows of the direct investment from Hong Kong are definitely overvalued in MOFTEC's statistics, on the one hand because a considerable part of Hong Kong's FDI is carried out by firms from China which reinvest in China via Hong Kong and, on the other hand because many Asian and Western investors use Hong Kong as a platform for their Chinese FDI operations. The capital flows from Taiwan to China through Hong Kong constituted a very important proportion of Hong Kong's outward FDI to China, especially during the early 1980s because of the official restrictions at that time by Taiwan's government with regard to the investment activities of their enterprises in mainland China. Yet, the exact amount of these capital movements is unknown because of their intra-firm nature. Also the 'reverse' investment[1] by Chinese companies located in Hong Kong presented a very large share of Hong Kong's FDI in Mainland China. During the first nine months of 1993, four subsidiaries of Chinese firms in Hong Kong invested about US$ 1.5 billion in China, accounting for 14 per cent of China's total utilised FDI inflows during this period (Lin 1996). According to another source (Harrold and Lall 1993), the reverse investment by Chinese companies located in Hong Kong was estimated at 25 per cent of Chinese FDI inflows in 1992. This particular type of investment has continuously expanded, as a result of the growing FDI from China to Hong Kong (Zhan 1993; Lin 1996).

The investment position of Asian NIEs in China had been strengthened significantly before the Asian financial crises in 1997, as their share in the cumulative flows (current value) rose from 51 per cent during 1983–1985 to 77 per cent during the period 1993–1994. This growth was mainly due to the substantial FDI inflows from Taiwan and Singapore. The proportion of these latter economies in the total Chinese FDI inflows consequently rose from 4.7 and 1.4 per cent in 1989–1992 to 8 and 5.4 per cent in 1995–1997, respectively. The relative share

Table 3.1 Major home economies of inward FDI in China (1979–2000)

Home country/region	Number of projects		Contracted value (US$ million)		Current value (US$ million)	
	Number	%	Value	%	Value	%
Hong Kong	192,023	52.74	327,918	50.04	170,297	48.77
Japan	20,383	5.60	38,815	5.92	27,802	7.96
Taiwan	46,624	12.81	47,816	7.30	26,159	7.49
USA	31,311	8.60	60,611	9.25	30,032	8.60
Singapore	9,122	2.51	35,380	5.40	16,993	4.87
South Korea	15,291	4.20	18,706	2.85	10,327	2.96
United Kingdom	2,815	0.77	16,975	2.59	8,748	2.51
Germany	2,421	0.66	12,235	1.87	5,852	1.68
Macau	6,851	1.88	9,657	1.47	3,983	1.14
France	1,720	0.47	5,472	0.84	3,792	1.09
All countries	364,070	100.00	655,295	100.00	349,169	100.00

Source: MOFTEC (1983–2001).

of Hong Kong went down from 62 to 50 per cent during the same period. Yet, the increasing share of FDI from Taiwan, on the one hand, and the decline of Hong Kong's FDI position, on the other hand, can be explained by the introduction of a more liberal FDI policy by the Taiwanese government in the early 1990s. This new policy allowed Taiwanese companies to invest officially in China, meaning that they no longer had to use Hong Kong as an indirect conduit for their investment operations in Mainland China (Table 3.1).

In reviewing the FDI inflows during 1979–2000, several conclusions can be drawn. First, a large part (about 70 per cent in terms of utilised value) of Chinese inward FDI came from Chinese and Overseas Chinese owned companies located in Taiwan, Hong Kong, Singapore and other Southeast Asian countries. This proportion has continually increased over time and to a certain extent formed the basis for the economic integration of the region, which is sometimes referred to as Greater China, especially for export-oriented manufacturing and trade. The specific locational factors of China for low-cost production activities allowed Asian investors to sharpen their competitiveness in export markets for labour-intensive products. Yet, FDI from these economies has declined since 1996 and this trend has been accentuated as a result of the Asian financial crises in 1997, by which Asian investors got into financial difficulties and became involved into heavy restructuring in their home bases. The data available for the period 1998–2000 show that Asian countries and regions, including Japan, accounted for only 54 per cent of the newly contracted US$ 156 billion FDI. The Western countries (i.e. Europe and North America) therefore took up 28 per cent, as compared with only 10 per cent during the period 1989–1992. The strong expansion of EU and American MNEs in Chinese inward FDI at the end of the 1990s allowed China to offset the decline of FDI from the Asian countries that were struck by the financial crisis of 1997–1998.

Second, the United States and Japan were the largest home base of FDI in China from industrialised countries. Together they accounted for about 17 per cent of the total Chinese inward FDI. The position of the European Union in Chinese inward FDI was quite weak. Not only did the EU countries account for a very small part in the total Chinese inward FDI, only a few of their MNEs have engaged in far-reaching FDI activities in China. The upsurge of FDI from the EU countries in China after 1992 was mainly the result of the significant liberalisation of the access of local markets and the improved economic performance of China. The new dynamism in China's domestic sector opened up new opportunities, including easier backward linkages and co-operation possibilities. Besides, the continuing investment by the Chinese government in its infrastructure also attracted Western companies to invest in high-technology and capital-intensive industries, such as, for example, energy, transportation and telecommunications.

Location

China's inward FDI is highly concentrated in the Eastern region, that is, the 12 coastal provinces (including two coastal cities – Shanghai and Tianjin – and Beijing that have special administrative status as centrally controlled cities), which accounted for about 86 per cent of the total Chinese FDI inflows in terms of current value, 87 per cent in contracted value and 82 per cent in terms of the number of projects (Table 3.2). Two leading provinces, Guangdong and Fujian, attracted nearly 45 per cent of the total FDI (in utilised value) in China between 1979 and 2000. This high concentration reflects the location advantages of these provinces and cities as they benefited from the early opening and their faster

Table 3.2 Geographical distribution of inward FDI in China (1983–2000)

Host regions	Number of projects		Contracted value (US$ million)		Current Value (US$ million)	
	Number	%	Value	%	Value	%
Eastern region	298,277	81.97	587.30	86.87	298.56	85.71
Fujian & Guangdong	134,410	36.94	281.03	41.57	158.26	45.43
Western region	18,091	4.97	25.09	3.71	10.84	3.11
Central region	45,896	12.61	52.50	7.76	30.49	8.75
Central government	1,601	0.44	11.20	1.66	8.46	2.43
Total	363,865	100.00	676.08	100.00	348.35	100.00

Source: MOFTEC (1983–2001).

Note
Eastern region: Beijing, Tianjin, Hebei, Liaoning, Shanghai, Jiangsu, Zhejiang, Fujian, Shangdong, Guangdong, Guangxi and Hainan; Central region: Shanxi, Inner Mongolia, Jilin, Heilongjiang, Anhui, Jiangxi, Henan, Hubei, Hunan; Western region: Sichuan, Chongqing, Guizhou, Yunnan, Shaanxi, Gansu, Qinghai, Ningxia, Xinjiang.

pace in the transition towards the market economic system. Although the FDI flows to certain provinces in Central and Western China have increased since the opening up of inland regions in the 1990s, the relative share of these regions in the Chinese inward FDI is still quite small, that is, only 8.8 and 2.4 per cent, respectively, in terms of utilised value.

The location pattern of FDI in China significantly changed over time. Before 1992, the ten leading FDI provinces and cities received 80 per cent of the total Chinese FDI inflows (in utilised value), that is, Guangdong (35 per cent), Fujian (9 per cent), Jiangsu (7 per cent), Beijing (7 per cent), Shanghai (6 per cent), Shandong (5 per cent), Liaoning (5 per cent), Hainan (3 per cent), Zhejiang (2 per cent) and Tianjin (2 per cent). Since 1992, the location of FDI in the Eastern region has undergone important changes, because of industrial restructuring and the rising labour costs in the early opened provinces, such as Fujian and Guangdong. A growing number of foreign and domestic enterprises, in textiles, clothing and electronics assembly, have relocated their labour-intensive activities into the inland region. Although Guangdong is still ranked as the most important location of FDI, its share in the total FDI inflows in the country has declined from 31 per cent in the 1980s to 27 per cent during the period 1996–2000. By contrast, the proportion of Jiangsu went up from 2.4 to 13.9 per cent, which puts it in second place in this ranking of the provinces. The rapid growth of FDI flows into Jiangsu pushed up the proportion of the Eastern region in the total Chinese inward FDI from 71 per cent during the 1980s to 86 per cent between 1996 and 2000.

Since the opening up of the eighteen inland provincial-capital cities and five cities along the Yangtze river in 1992, more foreign investors have started to locate in the inland region. The cumulative flows of FDI directed towards the Central region went up to 10 per cent of the total utilised FDI in China during the period 1996–2000 as compared to only 3.6 per cent in the 1980s. It is interesting to notice that the FDI, which was contracted directly by the various ministries of the central government (e.g. MOFTEC, Ministry of Finance), declined from 21 per cent in the 1980s to less than 1 per cent during 1996–2000 as a result of the decentralisation of the Chinese economic system.

Modes of entry

As was explained before, four forms of FDI are largely used in China, that is, CJVs, EJVs, WFOEs and JEs. By the end of 2000, 57 per cent of the approved inward FDI projects in China were EJVs, 29 per cent WFOEs, 14 per cent CJVs and less than 1 per cent joint oil exploration projects (Table 3.3). In terms of utilised value, EJVs represent 42 per cent of cumulative inward FDI, while WFOEs and CJVs account, respectively, for 29 and 19 per cent. The modes of inward FDI to penetrate the Chinese market have significantly evolved over the years (Figure 3.3), as a result of the changes incurred in the Chinese investment regulations, the business environment and consequently the strategic positioning of foreign owned companies.

Table 3.3 Entry forms of inward FDI in China (1983–2000)

Investment forms	Number of projects		Contracted value (US$ billion)		Utilised value (US$ million)	
	Number	%	Value	%	Value	%
EJVs	206,747	56.79	290.48	42.95	160.02	42.29
CJVs	49,779	13.67	148.74	21.99	71.42	18.87
WFOEs	107,352	29.49	231.99	34.30	109.89	29.04
JEs	177	0.05	4.82	0.71	6.64	1.75
Total	364,055	100.00	676.37	100.00	378.40	100.00

Source: MOFTEC (1983–2001).

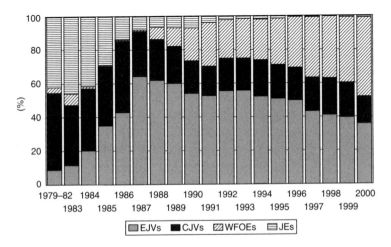

Figure 3.3 Changing patterns of inward FDI forms in China (in utilised value) (1979–1997).

Source: MOFTEC (1983–1999).

At the early stage of the liberalisation of FDI in China, CJVs were the principal form of foreign entry, because it allowed foreign investors to minimise investment risks by using flexible arrangements in resource sharing and management commitment. Between 1979 and 1985, CJVs represented 30 per cent of total Chinese inward FDI in terms of utilised value, while the EJVs that involve more resource and management commitment only took up 17 per cent. With the introduction of the so-called 'twenty-two' regulations in 1986, the incentive measures for FDI became more geared towards long-term investment projects with a high resource commitment, however. As a result, EJVs became the most important form of FDI in China: their share in the total FDI rose to 49 per cent from 1986 to 1988, while the proportion for the CJVs went down to 25 per cent. Because the wholly owned enterprises were strictly regulated at that time and were only admitted on a case by case basis by the government authorities, this mode of investment remained limited to 1.8 per cent.

After the early 1990s, the foreign-ownership conditions were further liberalised and the strategies of foreign investors in China gradually became more long-term oriented. The WFOE became a major mode of entry, as foreign investors expected it to provide a higher investment return, more guarantees for the protection of their transferred technology and better control over the corporate strategic orientation of the subsidiaries. The proportion of WFOEs in terms of current value increased from 3 per cent in 1986–1988 to 20 per cent in 1989–1992 and 37 per cent in 1996–2000. Although EJVs were most used as a vehicle for foreign entry into China, their proportion in the total Chinese inward FDI was overtaken for the first time by WFOEs in 2000, that is, the capital investment by WFOEs in terms of current value was 30 per cent higher than that of EJVs.

Sector distribution

Table 3.4 shows the sectoral distribution of inward FDI in terms of the number of projects and the contracted equity capital. Between 1979 and 2000, FDI in manufacturing amounted to US$ 412 billion in contracted value, accounting for 61 per cent of the total inward FDI in China. Real estate was the second largest sector for foreign investors, as it received 24 per cent of the cumulative contracted FDI.

Table 3.4 Sectoral distribution of inward FDI in China (1979–2000)

Sector	Number of projects		Contracted value (US$ billion)	
	Number	%	Value	%
Agriculture, forestry and fishing	10,355	2.85	12.31	1.82
Manufacturing	265,609	72.99	411.53	60.87
Construction	9,059	2.49	19.69	2.91
Transport and communications	4,027	1.11	16.39	2.42
Commerce and retailing services	18,410	5.06	23.40	3.46
Real estate and public utility services	37,252	10.24	159.54	23.60
Health, sport and social welfare	1,030	0.28	4.77	0.71
Education and culture	1,336	0.37	2.12	0.31
R&D and technological services	2,510	0.69	2.12	0.31
Other services	14,297	3.93	24.22	3.58
Total	363,885	100.00	676.10	100.00

Source: MOFTEC (1983–2001).

Because there was a lack of a specific sectoral policy vis-à-vis foreign investors, at least at the early stage of China's liberalisation of FDI, the inflows in the early 1980s were highly concentrated in the service sectors, especially in tourism-related activities, such as hotels, restaurants and taxi services. Between 1983 and 1984, foreign investors contracted for more than US$ 1 billion in the tourism sector, which took up 21.6 per cent of the country's cumulative FDI during that period. Foreign investment in the manufacturing sector reached only 29 per cent between 1983 and 1985.

After the Chinese government decided in 1986 to stimulate FDI in import-substitution activities, export-promotion and advanced technology production, inward FDI increasingly moved into manufacturing, especially into export-oriented production. FDI in the manufacturing sector reached 56 per cent in the period 1986–1988 and 64 per cent between 1989 and 1992. The growth of man-ufacturing FDI declined afterwards, especially during the period 1993–1994 as result of the opening up of certain additional service sectors for foreign investors in 1992. Yet, manufacturing maintained its dominant position in Chinese inward FDI. The newly admitted FDI in infrastructure and service sectors, such as trans-port, communication, energy, banking and insurance, continued to increase, while FDI in real estate dropped. The liberalisation of service sectors, such as business-related services and retail trade will intensify these trends even more.

With regard to the distribution of FDI within the manufacturing industry itself, even the incomplete data reveal some changes over time. FDI in China used to be concentrated in labour-intensive export activities that took advantage of lower labour costs. Yet, with the improved access to the Chinese market and the rising income of its consumers, more and more foreign investors are focusing on the local market. As a result, they have increased their investment in capital- and technology-intensive sectors. This will be illustrated in Chapter 4 on the basis of more detailed information from a large and special database on FDI projects.

Although China did not explicitly apply sectoral requirements before the introduction of its 'Industry Catalogue' in 1995, the administrative measures, such as the approval process of FDI projects, combined with tax incentives, mon-itored the sectoral orientation of FDI even before that date. The third industrial survey (1995) clearly showed that these measures were effectively implemented. The subsectors – such as leather, clothing, sport goods and electronics – that were largely opened to FDI within the context of the export-promotion policy became dominated by foreign-owned companies that generated more than 50 per cent of total sales in those industries. In the context of the import substi-tution policy, FDI was also encouraged in basic chemicals, pharmaceuticals, machinery and transportation equipment. Consequently, the presence of foreign companies in these industries rose substantially. However, in the so-called strate-gic sectors, such as energy, mining and water and gas supply, FDI was marginal mainly because of the restrictions that were still applicable (Table 3.5).

It can be concluded that the changing patterns of FDI in China were signifi-cantly affected by the Chinese FDI policy that has progressively implemented

Table 3.5 Share of foreign invested enterprises in subsectors of the Chinese economy (1995)

Sector	Number of companies			Sales (CNY billion)		
	Foreign	Total	%	Foreign	Total	%
Coal mining	29	11,953	0.24	0.25	111.86	0.22
Petroleum and natural gas	5	134	3.73	2.40	136.72	1.76
Metal ores	12	2,141	0.56	0.02	10.17	0.19
Non-ferrous metal ores	40	3,774	1.06	0.18	30.00	0.61
Non-metallic minerals	250	11,820	2.12	1.12	33.26	3.36
Forestry and logging	3	1,237	0.24	0.00	16.50	0.01
Food processing	1,893	30,711	6.16	60.58	286.40	21.15
Food manufacturing	1,909	16,130	11.84	28.33	92.94	30.48
Soft drinks and bottling of mineral waters	1,202	14,719	8.17	28.50	108.76	26.20
Tobacco	10	423	2.36	0.56	99.45	0.56
Textiles	4,218	25,686	16.42	76.13	425.70	17.88
Wearing apparel	5,965	20,007	29.81	68.41	134.64	50.81
Tanning and dressing of leather	2,513	10,468	24.01	48.29	89.20	54.14
Manufacture of wood products	1,270	15,480	8.20	9.96	36.53	27.27
Furniture	741	8,760	8.46	6.17	20.10	30.67
Pulp, paper and paperboard	1,079	13,890	7.77	16.39	96.36	17.01
Publishing and printing	860	15,436	5.57	7.06	38.68	18.26
Sport goods	1,188	5,564	21.35	17.78	35.07	50.71
Refined petroleum products	133	2,734	4.86	2.89	204.74	1.41

Basic chemicals and chemical products	2,625	28,371	9.25	45.34	359.21	12.62
Pharmaceuticals	868	5,388	16.11	16.50	90.27	18.28
Man-made fibres	363	1,333	27.23	9.91	78.30	12.65
Rubber products	470	4,663	10.08	14.72	58.94	24.98
Plastic products	3,038	19,255	15.78	34.59	104.67	33.05
Non-metallic mineral products	2,548	61,278	4.16	31.64	277.44	11.40
Basic iron and steel	380	7,299	5.21	23.46	376.38	6.23
Basic precious and non-ferrous metals	459	4,621	9.93	16.11	128.72	12.51
Fabricated metal products	2,371	30,728	7.72	40.38	151.56	26.64
General purpose machinery	1,450	29,631	4.89	31.94	220.21	14.50
Special purpose machinery	1,303	18,701	6.97	14.71	164.33	8.95
Transport equipment	1,409	19,445	7.25	80.32	318.55	25.21
Electrical machinery and apparatus	2,230	19,671	11.34	59.93	247.90	24.17
Electronics and telecommunication equip.	2,900	7,997	36.26	147.42	242.46	60.80
Instruments and office appliances	999	5,637	17.72	16.18	41.67	38.83
Electricity, steam and hot water supply	229	12,600	1.82	32.95	307.58	10.71
Gas supply	17	372	4.57	0.50	9.15	5.49
Water supply	17	5,147	0.33	0.02	17.71	0.13
Total	49,559	510,381	9.71	1,011.63	5,293.62	19.11

Source: Third industrial survey, 1995.

a set of liberalisation measures with regard to the location, ownership and sectoral requirements for foreign investors. All these measures combined with the progress made in the implementation of market mechanisms in the Chinese economic system constitute the driving force of the 'guided scenario' of Chinese inward FDI during the last two decades of the twentieth century and have significantly affected the patterns and extent of FDI in China.

4 Salient and evolving features of EU direct investment in China

This chapter[1] attempts to survey the extent and patterns of EUDI in China during the last two decades on the basis of both firm and country level data. Its main objective is to deal with questions such as: what are the salient characteristics of EU-invested enterprises in China; how have these features evolved over time and to what extent are the EU enterprises different from firms from the US, Japan and Asian NIEs. The section 'Importance of EUDI in China' will give an overview of the origin and development path of EUDI in China against the background of the changing Chinese investment environment. In the section 'Characteristics of EV enterprises in China', the major operational characteristics of EU-invested enterprises in China – such as investment size, industrial specialisation, location, ownership and contract duration – will be examined on the basis of an extensive statistical analysis. The section on 'Comparative analysis' will compare and contrast the features of the European-owned enterprises over time and with other foreign-invested companies in China. In the concluding section, the patterns of EUDI will be discussed from the perspective of the implications for the future development of Chinese FDI policy and the strategic reactions of MNEs.

Importance of EUDI in China

The European Union is the largest home region, as well as the largest recipient, of FDI in the world. The cumulative EU outward FDI amounted to US$ 1,652 billion, accounting for 35 per cent of the world's FDI stock in 1999. During 1995–1999, the average annual outflows of FDI from the European Union reached more than half (53 per cent) of the world's FDI outflows, as compared to 5 and 22 per cent for Japan and the United States, respectively (UN/UNCTAD 2000).

The largest share of EUDI goes to countries within the European Union itself. In 1999, the intra-EUDI represented 52 per cent of the region's total outward *FDI flows*. Excluding intra-EUDI, the United States has become the most important destination of EU investment and accounted for 67 per cent of EUDI outflows outside of the European Union. Asia as a whole absorbed 6.5 per cent of EUDI outflows to the rest of the world, while Japan, NIEs and China had a share of 6.47, 0.29 and 0.37 per cent, respectively. During the 1980s, EU MNEs focused mainly on the opportunities offered by the European integration process and, to some extent, the United States. Since the beginning of the 1990s, the attention by European investors has turned to the so-called 'emerging markets' that are gaining increasing importance in EUDI. During the period 1992–1998, emerging markets received more than 27 per cent of all outward EU flows. However, within emerging markets, EU MNEs have been focusing less on the traditional four Asian NIEs and more on Central and Eastern Europe and Latin America. Between 1992 and 1998, the CEE and Latin America received more than 80 per cent of total EUDI in emerging markets, while Asian NIEs had only a share of about 1 per cent (European Commission 2001).

The volume of the EU's outward *FDI stock* in Asia is still relatively small, especially when compared with its presence in North America and Latin America. As far as the EU outflows of FDI to Asian countries are concerned, large countries, such as China and India, received less European FDI than relatively small economies such as South Korea, Singapore and Taiwan. The greater attractiveness of the latter countries for European FDI is partly related to their relatively advanced level of economic development, illustrated by their higher per capita incomes and lower shares of agriculture in GDP. Their earlier and greater openness of some of them to FDI, as compared to some of the larger economies, is also an important contributory factor (EU/UNCTAD 1996).

Table 4.1 China in the cumulative outward FDI of EU countries (1999)

Home country	Outward FDI stock (US$ million)		
	World (1)	*China[a] (2)*	*(2)/(1)*
Austria	17,522	201	1.15
Belgium/Luxembourg	159,461	402	0.25
Denmark	42,035	300	0.71
Finland	31,803	155	0.49
France	298,012	3,582	1.20
Germany	420,908	4,811	1.14
Greece	783	2	0.26
Ireland	15,096	19	0.13
Italy	168,370	1,623	0.96
Netherlands	306,396	2,201	0.72
Portugal	9,605	30	0.31
Spain	97,553	194	0.20
Sweden	104,985	467	0.44
United Kingdom	664,103	7,584	1.14
EU total	2,336,631	21,570	0.92
United States .	1,131,466	25,648	2.27
Japan	292,781	24,886	8.50

Sources: UN/UNCTAD (1999) and MOFTEC (1983–1999).

Note
a Cumulative FDI current value.

Following the generally weak position of the EU countries in Asia and South-East Asia, it should not be too much of a surprise to learn that EU MNEs have not engaged themselves relatively more in China, and this despite China's enormous market size and rapid growth. China had only received 0.9 per cent of the total outward EUDI stock at the end of 1999, while the relative proportions for the United States and Japan were, respectively, 2.3 and 8.5 per cent (Table 4.1). Among EU member countries, the United Kingdom, Austria, France, Italy and Germany attached relatively more importance than the other EU countries to China as a location for their outward investment. Yet, the proportion of China in the total outward FDI stock of 1.4 per cent for the United Kingdom was still less than the relative share of the United States.

Nevertheless, the European Union reinforced its investment position in China during the second part of the 1990s. The share of China in the EU outward *FDI flows* increased from 0.13 per cent in 1990 to 0.45 per cent in 1995, 0.84 per cent in 1997 and 0.92 per cent in 1999. By the end of 2000, the United Kingdom was the largest EU investor country in China with accumulated FDI flows of US$ 7,584 million, followed by Germany with US$ 4,811 million, France with US$ 3,582 million, the Netherlands with US$ 2,201 million and Italy with US$ 1,623 million.

Historical perspective

Before the liberalisation of FDI at the end of the 1970s, China had already opened its coastal cities to foreign direct investors in the 1890s under the 'Treaty of Shimonoseki' as a result of its defeat in the Chia-Wu War against Japan (1894). Between 1885 and 1936, about 210 foreign affiliates and JVs were established by companies from Western Europe with a total foreign investment of US$ 1,200 million (Shen 1994: 283). At that time, the United Kingdom was the first home base among the European countries with US$ 990 million invested in 155 enterprises in China, followed by Germany (twenty-three enterprises with US$ 103 million), Belgium (five enterprises with US$ 82 million), France (eighteen enterprises with US$ 12 million) and Italy (five enterprises with US$ 6 million). As compared to the British companies, which had engaged in a large number of business activities in most of Chinese regions, German FDI was mainly directed towards the Shandong Province and concentrated in railway construction and mining extraction. French companies were predominantly located in Shanghai and Guangdong and mostly operated in textiles and trading. Although at that time a number of large European companies, such as Siemens, Philips, Fiat, Agfa, AEG, Unilever, Wagons-Lits and P&O, had already established a manufacturing or service presence in China, most of them were only active in marketing and sales activities (Table 4.2).

The European countries lost their predominant position in China during and after the First World War, when Japan replaced them as the most important home base for FDI in China by setting up 151 enterprises and taking over of a number of local and foreign enterprises in the three North-eastern provinces (Cao 1991).

Table 4.2 Large European enterprises operating in China before 1949

Name	Year of entry	Location	Activities
Fiat	1925	Shanghai, Tianjin	Representative office
Philips	N/A	Shanghai	Sales
Wagons-Lits	1912	Tianjin, Shanghai, Beijing	Branch
P&O	1844	Wuhan, Tianjin, Chongqing	Agency
Agfa	1901	Shanghai, Tianjin	Sales and production
AEG	1929	Shanghai	Sales
Siemens	1923	Shanghai, Tianjin, Guangdong	Sales
Imperial Chemical Industries	1920	Shanghai, Tianjin, Guangzhou, Wuhan, Beijing	Sales
Lloyd's	Before 1861	Xiamen, Fuzhou, Shanghai, Guangzhou, Wuhan,	Branch
GEC	1908	Wuhan, Tianjin, Dalian, Beijing	Sales
Lever Brothers (Unilever)	1913	Shanghai, Guangzhou, Wuhan, Jinan	Production, sales
General Accident	1913	Shanghai, Zhengjiang, Fuzhou, Tianjin, Beijing, Guangzhou	Branch
Bayer	1914	Shanghai, Wuhan, Changsha, Tianjin, Chongqing	Sales

Source: Huang (1995).

In the aftermath of the Second World War, American affiliates were the dominating foreign presence in China. Yet, all foreign firms were nationalised after 1949, when the Communist Party took over the country and the government. Although the early investors from Western countries had been out of China for about thirty years, that is, until the re-opening of the Chinese economy to foreign direct investors at the end of the 1970s, their historical reputation and experience allowed them to return to the Chinese market more rapidly than the newcomers. This catching up is clearly illustrated by the case of Unilever. Like some other multinationals, Unilever's Chinese roots go back many years. Lever Brothers, Unilever's British 'arm', built a factory in Shanghai in the early 1920s. It became China's largest production unit for soap for laundry and personal use, but was nationalised in 1951. After the plant was taken over by the state, Unilever's famous Lux brand lay dormant for many years. When the Chinese government deregulated FDI and began to re-admit foreign investment in 1979, Unilever came back to its old Lever Brothers site and set up a JV with local partners for re-introducing its Lux brand and launching a new product range. In 1998, Unilever controlled twelve separate business activities in China with a combined turnover of US$ 300 million (Unilever 1999).

Evolution of EUDI in China after 1979

After China liberalised FDI in 1979, a number of European investors returned with a renewed interest. The cumulative FDI inflows from the EU-15 countries to China reached US$ 50 billion in contracted value and US$ 26 billion in utilised value at the end of 2000, accounting, respectively, for 7.46 and 7.48 per cent of all Chinese contracted and current inward FDI during this 20-year period. The United Kingdom became the largest European home basis of EUDI in China with a share of 34 per cent (in utilised value), followed by Germany (22 per cent), France (17 per cent), the Netherlands (12 per cent), Italy (7 per cent), Sweden (2.4 per cent) and Belgium (1.6 per cent). Together the rest of the EU countries take up less than 5 per cent (Table 4.3).

Although Denmark has higher contracted investment in China than Belgium, the amount of its real investment is smaller. This might be explained by the differences in the timing of its investment cycle, meaning that Denmark started to invest later than Belgium in China. Many of its investment projects were only recently approved so that most of their real capital commitment still needs to be carried out. With regard to the number of approved projects, Italy, Belgium, Sweden, Denmark, Finland, Austria and Spain have a higher share in the total EUDI as compared to their relative position in terms of contracted and current flows of capital. This shows that the investment size for individual projects by firms from these countries is smaller than other EU countries, especially the United Kingdom.

Reviewing the EUDI flows to China, several phases can be distinguished (Figure 4.1). During 1979–1985, the EUDI accounted for about 10 per cent of the total Chinese inward FDI in terms of current value. Such a relatively strong

Table 4.3 EUDI in China by countries of origin (1979–2000)

Home country	Number of projects		Contracted investment (US$ million)		Current investment (US$ million)	
	Value	%	Value	%	Value	%
United Kingdom	2,815	24.73	16,975	33.66	8,748	33.55
Germany	2,421	21.26	12,235	24.26	5,852	22.45
France	1,720	15.11	5,747	11.40	4,435	17.01
Netherlands	824	7.24	7,484	14.84	2,990	11.47
Italy	1,495	13.13	2,711	5.38	1,833	7.03
Sweden	418	3.67	973	1.93	626	2.40
Belgium	340	2.99	802	1.59	417	1.60
Denmark	173	1.52	1,210	2.40	349	1.34
Finland	118	1.04	449	0.89	241	0.92
Spain	464	4.08	788	1.56	228	0.87
Austria	422	3.71	510	1.01	220	0.84
Luxembourg	58	0.51	320	0.63	65	0.25
Portugal	52	0.46	78	0.15	30	0.12
Ireland	36	0.32	90	0.18	21	0.08
Greece	29	0.25	57	0.11	15	0.06
Total	11,385	100.00	50,430	100.00	26,072	100.00

Source: MOFTEC (1983–2001).

FDI position of the European Union in the early 1980s was related to two factors. First, several EU chemical companies, notably BP and Elf, participated in large joint oil exploration projects in the South China Sea. Second, a number of leading European MNEs concluded JV agreements with the Chinese government for setting up large-scale manufacturing subsidiaries, such as Pharmacia (US$ 6 million in 1982), Alcatel-Bell (US$ 39.5 million in 1983) and Pilkington (US$ 29.9 million in 1983).

Since the mid-1980s, the FDI flows from the European Union to China slowed down as compared to those coming from elsewhere. The decline of the growth rate of EUDI in China (Figure 4.1) resulted in a drop of its share in the total Chinese inward FDI from 10.4 per cent in 1984 to 4.2 per cent in 1988 (in current value) and reached an all time low level of 2 per cent in 1987. Although the drop in the relative position of the European Union in the total inward FDI in China in the second half of the 1980s could be attributed to the general economic recession that affected most of the industrial countries, some specific problems related to the Chinese business environment in general and the market transition process in particular were also responsible for this decline (see Chapter 2).

The expansion of FDI from the European Union as well as from other Western countries was dramatically broken off after June 1989 due to the government's military intervention against the student activists in Tiananmen Square and the resulting hesitation of foreign firms to engage in new projects and even to continue with projects that had already been launched. The newly perceived

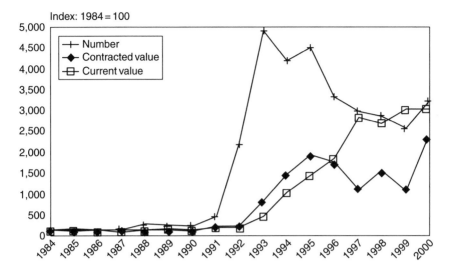

Figure 4.1 Evolution of EUDI in China (1984–2000).
Source: MOFTEC (1983–2001).

political instability by Western investors suddenly became a deterrent that seriously affected their investment plans. The proportion of the European Union in the total contracted FDI in China decreased from 8.3 per cent in the period of 1986–1988 to 2.7 per cent between 1989 and 1992. American and European MNEs may to some extent have switched their investment to the new 'single European market' and other alternative locations such as the newly opened Central and Eastern European markets, while Japanese firms focused their efforts on conquering American and European markets.[2] At the same time, FDI from Asian NIEs to China expanded very strongly and went up from US$ 7.4 to 63.6 billion, increasing their share from 62 to 77 per cent of the total Chinese inward FDI.

In the aftermath of the post-Tiananmen confidence crisis, the political and economic 'isolation' measures taken by Western countries slowed down FDI inflows from the European Union to China. Yet, several Western MNEs that had already established a presence in the Chinese market were able to strengthen their 'insider position' in this strongly 'imperfect' Chinese market (Van Den Bulcke and Zhang 1994b). The competition for these firms from outside China was quasi-non-existent, while demand significantly increased because of the improvement of the country's overall economic performance (real growth rate of GDP of 13 per cent in 1992) and increasing levels of per capita income.

As a result of the continued engagement of the Chinese government in economic reform on the one hand and the relaxation of investment regulations on the other hand, the decline of FDI stopped after 1992. Although the recovery of the EU's FDI position started later in China than for the United States and Japan after the drop of 1989, it caught up and reached a higher growth rate, especially after 1994. During the short period of 1993–1994, the contracted value of EU MNEs amounted to US$ 8.8 billion, that is, almost double the total investment from the same origin during the period 1979–1992. The expansion in newly contracted FDI projects from the European Union countries lasted until 1996, when a decline (9 per cent) was recorded as compared to 1995. The fall in contracted FDI flows from the European Union after 1996 can be regarded as a move towards consolidation. The decline of inward FDI from Asian countries after 1994 was mainly related to the new difficulties encountered in the real-estate sector because of the stricter measures introduced by the Chinese government after July 1993 in order to control the speculative development in this type of projects. By contrast, the reason for the slowdown of contracted FDI from the 'so-called' Triad countries was quite different. It was much more linked to the completion and ensuing process of consolidation of projects, as there was a continuous increase in current FDI inflows.

During the Asian financial crisis, the investment position of the European Union in China was reinforced as compared to not only Asian economies, but also the United States (Figure 4.2). Outward FDI from the European Union to China rose both in absolute value and relative share in the EU total outward investment. From 1997 to 2000, the European Union invested US$ 4.3 billion in China each year, as compared to about US$ 3.9 billion from the United States. It has to be noted that the accumulated FDI flows from the European Union to China during the ten-year period of 1984–1993 amounted only to US$ 2.15 billion.

The annual growth rate of utilised EUDI to China reached 86 per cent between 1996 and 2000 – and went up from US$ 2.1 billion in 1995 to US$ 4.5 billion in 2000 – as compared to 24 per cent for the United States. Consequently,

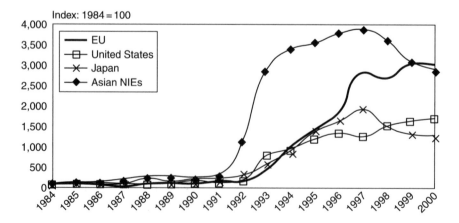

Figure 4.2 Evolution of EUDI in China as compared to other regions of origin (1984–2000).

Source: MOFTEC (1983–2001).

Table 4.4 Direct investment by EU member countries in China as compared to their economic size (1999)

Home country	Per cent in EU GDP (1)	Per cent in total EU outward FDI in China (2)	Ratio (2)/(1)
Austria	2.53	0.93	0.37
Belgium/Luxembourg	2.97	1.86	0.63
Denmark	2.09	1.39	0.67
Finland	1.53	0.72	0.47
France	17.31	16.61	0.96
Germany	25.30	22.30	0.88
Greece	1.47	0.01	0.01
Ireland	1.00	0.09	0.09
Italy	14.11	7.52	0.53
Netherlands	4.55	10.20	2.24
Portugal	1.31	0.14	0.11
Spain	6.73	0.90	0.13
Sweden	2.71	2.16	0.80
United Kingdom	16.41	35.16	2.14
Total	100.00	100.00	1.00

Sources: Eurostat (2001) and MOFTEC (2001).

the share of the European Union in the total Chinese inward FDI flows increased from 5.68 per cent in 1995 to 6.56 per cent in 1996, 9.22 per cent in 1997, 8.75 per cent in 1998 and more than 11 per cent in both 1999 and 2000.

Importance of China in EU outward FDI

The FDI position of a particular EU country in China can be determined both by its overall propensity for outward FDI and its economic size. The first aspect was already presented in Table 4.1. The second aspect, that is, the share of a member country in the total EUDI in China to its share in the total EU's GDP in 1999, shows the country's investment position as compared to its economic size. This analysis emphasises that the Netherlands (with a ratio of 2.24) and the United Kingdom (ratio of 2.14) have a relative stronger FDI position in China than the other EU countries with regard to their relative economic size in the European Union. On the contrary, Greece, Portugal, Ireland and Spain are practically absent in China, while Denmark, Belgium, Finland and Austria are weakly positioned among EU member countries with regard to their FDI operations in China as their ratio varies between 0.8 and 0.37 (Table 4.4). France and Germany are situated in a higher intermediate range and have a ratio that oscillates around 0.9.

Characteristics of EU enterprises in China

Although FDI from the European Union into China is less important than from other major home countries both in terms of the number of approved projects and the capital flows, it has been shown that the EU subsidiaries in China are quite competitive vis-à-vis foreign affiliates from other countries. They are relatively more concentrated in capital and technology intensive sectors, have a large investment size and a high local-market orientation (Van Den Bulcke and Zhang 1994b, 1998). In this section, the main characteristics and features of the EUDI projects in China will be analysed and compared to those from other regions or countries.

The comparison of European-invested firms in China is based on the statistical analysis of the 8,077 FIEs approved by MOFTEC during 1979–1996. Initially, this database covered only foreign equity JVs. However, since 1993, a number of WFOEs (i.e. about 10 per cent of the sample) have also been included for reasons that have not been explained by MOFTEC. This sample represents 2.9 per cent of all approved FDI projects in China during the period 1979–1996 and 11.7 per cent in terms of the total foreign equity contributions. The European Union sample consists of 470 firms and accounts, respectively, for 6.4 and 16.3 per cent of EUDI in China in terms of the number of projects and contracted value. Although the criteria, which were used by MOFTEC to select the sampled companies, were not explicitly mentioned, most of the important and 'promoted' FDI projects are included in this database. This extensive sample is therefore assumed to provide a good insight into the evolution of European MNEs in China in general and their specific characteristics in particular. The data set contains information about the country of origin of the investor, the type of business activity, the size of the project in terms of total investment and the foreign equity contribution, the ownership structure and the location and duration of the project.

The principal statistical method used here to identify differences between subsidiaries in terms of project size, foreign equity contribution, ownership structure and duration is the one-way analysis of variance (ANOVA). Cross-tabulations are used to examine the patterns of foreign subsidiaries according to the country of origin, geographic location, sectoral distribution and period of establishment. The standardised residuals – showing the difference between the observed value and the expected value – should allow to highlight the main differences between companies from different origins and their changes over time.

Size of investment

On the basis of the information available in the database, the size of a project can be measured by the amount of the total investment and/or foreign equity contribution. The first measure provides information about the total cost of the project, while the second one reflects the resource commitment by the foreign investors. On average, the total investment of EU-invested subsidiaries in China amounted to US$ 17 million per project, while the equity contribution from the European parent companies reached US$ 9.6 million. The size of the European subsidiaries is clearly much larger than for the other countries of origin, as the average investment and foreign equity commitment for the whole sample (including the European Union) only reached US$ 11.2 and 6.4 million (Tables 4.5 and 4.6).

Table 4.5 Size of EU subsidiaries (total investment) (1979–1996)

Home country	Total investment (US$ million)			Size categories (% of number of projects)				
	Mean	SD	No.	<1 US$ million	1–2.9 US$ million	3–4.9 US$ million	5–9.9 US$ million	10 US$ million or over
Austria	8.41	11.06	6		33.33	33.33		33.33
Belgium	16.65	23.93	15		13.33		40.00	46.67
Denmark	33.31	67.23	12	16.67	16.67		16.67	50.00
Finland	11.94	9.81	2				50.00	50.00
France	16.66	24.76	84	11.90	16.67	4.76	21.43	45.24
Germany	22.63	76.64	109	10.09	9.17	7.34	14.68	58.72
Ireland	20.00	—	1					100.00
Italy	9.12	8.61	63	11.11	12.70	14.29	25.40	36.51
Luxembourg	29.40	—	1					100.00
Netherlands	19.98	17.55	34	11.76	2.94	5.88	11.76	67.65
Spain	13.44	11.06	11	9.09	18.18		18.18	54.55
Sweden	7.57	7.54	19	15.00	20.00	15.00	10.00	40.00
United Kingdom	16.54	16.64	111	8.93	11.61	7.14	8.93	63.39
EU total	17.14	41.51	468	10.21	12.34	7.66	16.38	53.40
North America	10.13	13.36	1,068	14.45	22.46	9.04	17.43	36.63
Japan	12.25	23.82	621	19.10	22.47	7.70	12.52	38.20
Asian NIEs	10.38	21.27	4,991	16.34	24.36	8.36	16.78	34.17
Total sample	11.17	22.26	7,607	15.66	22.64	8.29	16.39	37.03

Source: MOFTEC database of FIEs in China (1983–1998).

Table 4.6 Size of EU subsidiaries in China (foreign equity investment) (1979–1996)

Home country	Foreign equity investment (US$ million)			Size categories (% of number of projects)				
	Mean	SD	No.	<5 US$ million	0.5–0.99 US$ million	1–2.9 US$ million	3–4.9 US$ million	5 mil US$ million or over
Austria	6.11	10.55	6	16.67	50.00			33.33
Belgium	8.10	10.33	15		13.33	20.00	26.67	40.00
Denmark	31.28	67.79	12	25.00		16.67	8.33	50.00
Finland	3.36	2.62	2			50.00		50.00
France	8.84	13.90	84	14.29	10.71	21.43	11.90	41.67
Germany	11.39	31.40	109	12.84	6.42	15.60	11.01	54.13
Ireland	8.00	—	1					100.00
Italy	4.28	5.24	63	15.87	12.70	31.75	12.70	26.98
Luxembourg	5.33	—	1					100.00
Netherlands	14.04	16.52	34	11.76	2.94	11.76		73.53
Spain	6.08	6.34	11	18.18		36.36		45.45
Sweden	3.77	4.19	19	15.79	5.26	42.11	10.53	26.32
United Kingdom	9.72	10.29	111	12.61	3.60	18.92	7.21	57.66
EU total	9.62	21.09	468	13.46	7.48	20.94	9.62	48.50
North America	5.70	7.62	1,068	21.72	11.99	22.47	10.77	33.05
Japan	7.78	14.82	622	24.28	13.67	16.72	6.43	38.91
Asian NIEs	5.72	13.88	5,003	24.33	13.61	22.89	9.87	29.30
Total sample	6.38	14.00	7,620	22.83	12.61	21.90	9.53	33.12

Source: MOFTEC database of FIEs in China (1983–1998).

The subsidiaries from Asian NIEs are generally the smallest ones: their average size both in terms of the total and foreign equity investment is only half as high as for the EU ventures.

Almost three-quarters (70 per cent) of the EU subsidiaries are concentrated in the large-sized categories, that is, those for which the average investment per project amounted to at least US$ 5 million. The relative proportion in the same size category was only 54 per cent for North America and 51 per cent for both Japan and the Asian NIEs. Among EU countries, the subsidiaries established by firms from Belgium, the Netherlands, Germany and the United Kingdom tend to be concentrated more often in the larger-sized categories.

As far as foreign equity investment is concerned, almost half (48.5 per cent) of the EU companies contributed on average at least US$ 5 million in the equity capital of their subsidiaries in China. As this proportion reached only 33 per cent for North America, 39 per cent for Japan and 29 per cent for Asian NIEs (Table 4.6), this in a certain way confirms that EU-invested enterprises are more capital intensive than their foreign counterparts. The subsidiaries of the Netherlands, Germany and the United Kingdom are slightly more present in the larger sized categories as compared to those from Austria, Italy and Sweden, which are to be found relatively more in the small-sized categories of less than US$ 1 million. Ranked by the amount of foreign equity investment, the largest EU ventures in China before 1997 were set up by Volkswagen with US$ 316.4 million in 1990, followed by the wholly owned subsidiary of Novo Nordisk, which invested a total of US$ 243 million as equity capital in 1994.

Sectoral pattern

More than 86 per cent of the EU subsidiaries in the database are manufacturing companies (Table 4.7). They are highly concentrated in chemicals (18 per cent), metal products and machinery (13 per cent), electrical equipment (11 per cent), food (9 per cent), non-metallic mineral products (8 per cent) and textiles (7 per cent). In terms of the amount of foreign equity investment the same distribution is found, except that the investment in transport equipment is much higher (13 per cent) than its relative share in the total number of EU subsidiaries (only 6 per cent). The high share of this latter sector in the total EU investment in China is a result of the large investments of European leading companies in the automotive industry, such as Volkswagen, Mercedes-Benz, Volvo, Peugeot, Citroën, Renault and Fiat. A number of large producers of automotive components have also moved into China, such as Lucas, GKN and Robert Bosch.

The trading and service companies together account for 11 per cent of the total number of EU establishments in China, with communication and transport services taking up 4 per cent. EU investment in China is less oriented towards the service sector as compared to its overall outward FDI in other parts of the world. The tertiary sector reached 56 per cent in the total EU outward FDI stock in 1998, while the manufacturing sector accounted only for 37 per cent (European Commission 2001). Even in Asian developing economies, the EUDI in services

Table 4.7 Sector distribution of EU subsidiaries in China (1979–1996)

Sector categories	Number		European investment	
	No.	*%*	*(US$ million)*	*%*
Agriculture, forestry and fishing	9	1.91	94.74	2.10
Mining	4	0.85	38.55	0.86
Manufacturing	406	86.38	3,758.22	83.47
Food	42	8.94	346.25	7.69
Textiles and clothing	34	7.23	184.52	4.10
Paper and wood products	17	3.62	192.39	4.27
Chemicals, rubber and plastics	85	18.09	892.53	19.82
Leather	19	4.04	23.42	0.52
Non-metallic minerals	39	8.30	361.10	8.02
Basic metals	11	2.34	160.34	3.56
Metal products, machinery and equipment	61	12.98	484.54	10.76
Electrical and electronic industries	52	11.06	483.86	10.75
Transport equipment	27	5.74	597.36	13.27
Toys, measuring equipment and related industries	19	4.04	31.92	0.71
Services and trade	51	10.85	610.91	13.57
Transport and communication	20	4.26	316.48	7.03
Construction	8	1.70	52.03	1.16
Finance, insurance and real estate	10	2.13	168.04	3.73
Other services	13	2.77	74.36	1.65
Total	470	100.00	4,502.43	100.00

Source: MOFTEC database of FIEs in China (1983–1998).

amounted to 41 per cent of its total stock, while FDI in manufacturing took up 33 per cent (EU/UNCTAD 1996). The lower proportion of EUDI in the Chinese service sectors, at least as compared to the United States (11.3 per cent) and Japan (8.9 per cent), shows that EU companies are more interested in China as a manufacturing base than as a location for service activities. Although more and more EU service companies are investing in China, their presence is still limited. The weak position of EU service companies in the Chinese market can only be partly explained by the restrictive policy of the Chinese government for the FDI in this sector, especially with regard to retail trade, banking, insurance, legal services, consulting and transport and communication. Yet, the gradual liberalisation of service sectors at the end of the twentieth century and the new impetus by the WTO agreement, for example, in banking and insurance, have convinced a number of EU companies to invest in China.

The manufacturing subsidiaries of EU companies in China are largely concentrated in the so-called 'scale-intensive industries' and 'specialised-supplier industries'[3] (Table 4.8). The scale-intensive industries, which include mainly chemicals and motor vehicles, account for 28 per cent of the total number of EU subsidiaries in China, while the relative proportion is 24 per cent for North America

Table 4.8 Industrial distribution of EU subsidiaries in China (1979–1996)

Home country	N	Resource-intensive industries (%)	Labour-intensive industries (%)	Specialised supplier industries (%)	Scale-intensive industries (%)	R&D-based industries (%)
Austria	6	16.67	50.00	16.67	16.67	
Belgium	10	50.00		30.00	10.00	10.00
Denmark	9	11.11	22.22	11.11	33.33	22.22
Finland	2	50.00			50.00	
France	75	38.67	16.00	14.67	26.67	4.00
Germany	97	16.49	12.37	25.77	34.02	11.34
Ireland	1			100.00		
Italy	58	27.59	34.48	12.07	20.69	5.17
Luxembourg	1	100.00				
Netherlands	26	7.69	19.23	38.46	23.08	11.54
Spain	9	44.44	33.33		22.22	
Sweden	18	11.11	16.67	27.78	27.78	16.67
United Kingdom	94	28.72	17.02	21.28	29.79	3.19
EU countries	406	25.86	18.72	20.69	27.59	7.14
North America	885	27.57	16.16	20.68	24.41	11.19
Japan	547	23.77	23.22	22.30	19.38	11.33
Asian NIEs	4,112	25.61	25.54	17.29	25.97	5.59
Total sample	6,327	26.39	23.06	18.24	25.32	6.99

Source: MOFTEC database of FIEs in China (1983–1998).

and 19 per cent for Japan. The relatively high share of Asian NIEs (25 per cent) in these sectors is linked to their strong presence in paper, rubber and plastics manufacturing that are part of this industrial category. Yet, their technological level and scale of production is often below international industrial standards.

A second EU industrial sector that is strongly represented in China consists of the specialised-supplier industries, such as non-electrical and electrical machinery, communication equipment and electronic components like semiconductors. However, the subsidiaries from Japan and the United States have a comparable position in these sectors.

The share of R&D-based industries – aerospace, computers, pharmaceuticals and scientific instruments – in the total sampled EU subsidiaries is 7 per cent. The higher share of Japanese and American companies in these sectors greatly contrasts with the weak position of the European Union. The stronger presence of the United States and Japan in these Chinese industries reflects to a certain extent their global competitiveness in industries that rely on specific technological and innovatory capabilities. Yet, a number of European companies did successfully penetrate into these sectors and do actively engage in competition and/or participate in alliances with their American and Japanese counterparts, especially in pharmaceuticals.

The EU enterprises in the database are less concentrated in the industries that are resource and labour intensive as compared to those from Japan and in particular from Asian NIEs. Because of the geographical distance and the past difficulties in the foreign exchange market, few EU companies invested in China for sourcing their home production or export back to the home market. As a matter of fact, the opening up of Central and Eastern Europe (CEE) provided West European companies sometimes with better offshore conditions than in faraway China, especially for the immediate neighbours such as Germany and Austria. Given the geographical proximity and the cultural similarity between Western and Eastern Europe and the real difference in production costs, many EU enterprises were enticed to shift certain routine activities or labour-intensive production processes into CEE. Besides the so-called 'delocalisation' in the context of the 'structural changes' of the EU industry, a number of companies established production bases in CEE in order to substitute their outsourcing and subcontracting operations located in low-wage countries in South-East Asia for efficiency-seeking purposes (Van Den Bulcke and Zhang 1997). China was apparently not all that attractive yet for EU MNEs for outsourcing and cost-oriented investment. Even if these latter motivations apply, they are often combined with market-oriented investment. In a sense, cost-oriented or resource-seeking FDI in China is mostly related to the attraction of China's market itself. There are few EU companies that invested in China for offshore operations as such. Although it has to be mentioned that a large number of Italian trading enterprises have invested in the Chinese textile industries for sourcing, most of them are owned by Overseas Chinese living in Italy.

As far as resource-intensive industries are concerned, the location of production facilities in China by European companies can to a large extent be explained by the cost structure of their resource-intensive production, that is, the relevance of the level of their transportation costs for sourcing and distribution purposes. The proximity to both suppliers and consumers for the selection of the production location was quite important, especially for companies operating in basic metals and construction materials. This can be illustrated by the multiple-location strategy of Pilkington in China. Pilkington was one of the first Western companies to invest in China. In 1983, the company signed a JV agreement to install China's first 'float glass' manufacturing plant. Located in Shanghai, the JV, that is, Yaohua Pilkington Glass (SYP), was in the enviable position of not being able to produce enough glass to meet demand. In 1993, SYP invested in Changchun Pilkington Safety Glass Co. Ltd. In 1994, the company signed two other JV agreements, one in Guilin, Guangxi province, and another in Wuhan, Hubei province. These three plants were designed to supply automotive glass to domestic and foreign car makers, such as the First Auto Works, Volkswagen, Citroën, etc. (*Financial Times*, 7 November 1994). In 2000, SYP acquired 40 per cent of the equity capital of Shanghai Fuhua Glass Co. Ltd (SFH). The acquisition of SHF was another major move of SYP into automotive glass after its investments in three autoglass JVs in Changchun, Wuhan and Guilin during the period between 1995 and 1997. SYP also purchased 75 per cent of the shares of Guangdong Float Glass Co. Ltd. This latter acquisition made SYP into the most advanced and largest glass company in China (SYP 2001).

The specific industrial characteristics of EU MNEs operating in China can equally be illustrated by the technological profile of their subsidiaries (Figure 4.3). By using the four-digit SIC of business activities as a classification, the manufacturing subsidiaries in the database are divided into four categories according to their technological nature and capital intensiveness, namely labour intensive and low technology, labour intensive and high technology, capital intensive and low technology and capital intensive and high technology. This method of classification was developed and used by Dunning (1979), Lee (1983) and Schroath, Hu and Chen (1993).[4] The standardised residual (higher than 1) derived from the cross-tabulation demonstrates the concentration of enterprises from a specific home country/region in a particular technological category.

The subsidiaries controlled by Asian NIEs are highly specialised in the industries that are characterised by low technology and high labour input, for example, textiles and clothing and electrical and electronic assembly operations. In comparison with Asian NIEs, EU, US and Japanese firms are more concentrated in the high-tech industries. Yet, there are differences among these three outward investors. EU companies in China are strongly concentrated in the capital intensive industries with a high level of technology, such as construction materials, transportation and telecom equipment, metal products, chemicals and

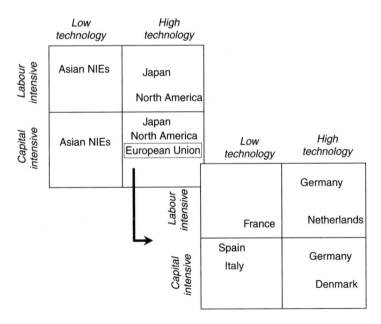

Figure 4.3 Technological level of foreign invested enterprises (per cent of number) (1979–1996).

Source: MOFTEC database of FIEs in China (1983–1998).

Table 4.9 Technological level of EU subsidiaries in China (1979–1996)

Home country	Number	Labour intensive and low technology (%)	Labour intensive and high technology (%)	Capital intensive and low technology (%)	Capital intensive and high technology (%)
Austria	6	66.67	16.67	0.00	16.67
Belgium	10	40.00	30.00	10.00	20.00
Denmark	9	22.22	11.11	11.11	55.56
Finland	2	100.00	0.00	0.00	0.00
France	75	42.67	17.33	14.67	25.33
Germany	97	28.87	30.93	10.31	29.90
Ireland	1	0.00	100.00	0.00	0.00
Italy	58	39.66	13.79	32.76	13.79
Luxembourg	1	0.00	0.00	100.00	0.00
Netherlands	26	34.62	42.31	0.00	23.08
Spain	9	33.33	0.00	44.44	22.22
Sweden	18	27.78	33.33	11.11	27.78
United Kingdom	94	32.98	24.47	18.09	24.47
EU countries	406	35.22	23.89	16.26	24.63
North America	885	37.29	24.97	15.59	22.15
Japan	547	41.50	27.61	10.97	19.93
Asian NIEs	4,112	46.78	19.96	17.17	16.10
Total sample	6,327	44.44	21.35	16.25	17.97

Source: MOFTEC database of FIEs in China (1983–1998).

allied products, while those from North America and Japan are more strongly represented in the high-tech and labour-intensive sectors (e.g. machinery and equipment).

As far as the European Union is concerned, enterprises from Germany and Denmark have a high technological level with an intensive capital input, while those from France, Italy and Spain are likely to be more present in the labour-intensive industries with a lower technological level as compared to other EU subsidiaries. The investments from the Netherlands and Germany also occur more frequently in labour-intensive, but high-tech industries. The enterprises originating from Belgium, Sweden and the United Kingdom are close to the average of the EU sample (Table 4.9).

Ownership pattern

About 40 per cent of the EU subsidiaries in the sample are minority owned, that is, their European parent companies hold less than half of the equity capital. This relative proportion is higher than the EU average in the case of Austrian and Italian firms. The proportion of minority participation in the EU sample is relatively lower than in the other non-European ventures located in China: the minority JVs account for 45 per cent of the total North American companies and 51 per cent of those from Asian NIEs. Yet, the minority participation occurred less frequently in the Japanese subsidiaries. There is a strong Japanese presence in the category of the equally owned JVs: 23 per cent as compared with the average of 15 per cent for the European Union (Table 4.10).

The companies from the so-called Triad regions make somewhat more use of equal ownership arrangements than the Asian investors who rely more on minority participations in establishing their subsidiaries in China. Among the Triad economies, Japanese subsidiaries are more frequently present in the category of equal JVs as they account for nearly a third of their total sample. As far as European EJVs are concerned, equal ownership is most relied on by parent companies from Denmark (25 per cent), France (23 per cent) and Sweden (20 per cent).

More than two-fifths (43 per cent) of the European and Japanese subsidiaries in the sample are majority or wholly owned from abroad, while the relative share is slightly lower for American (38 per cent) in China. Among EU countries, the Netherlands has the largest share of majority-owned subsidiaries (62 per cent), followed by Sweden (60 per cent), the United Kingdom (46 per cent) and Germany (45 per cent). The least represented European country in the category of majority-owned subsidiaries is Italy with a share of only one-fifth. The investors from the Asian NIEs are significantly different from enterprises

Table 4.10 Ownership patterns of EU subsidiaries in China (1979–1996)

Home countries	Foreign equity share (%)			Ownership categories (% of number of projects)			
	Mean	SD	No.	5–49	50	51–94	95–100
Austria	48.67	25.63	6	66.67	0.00	33.33	0.00
Belgium	47.80	16.13	15	40.00	13.33	46.67	0.00
Denmark	69.00	27.74	12	33.33	25.00	0.00	41.67
Finland	28.80	1.70	2	100.00	0.00	0.00	0.00
France	53.12	21.26	84	33.33	22.62	35.71	8.33
Germany	51.05	21.01	109	39.45	15.60	38.53	6.42
Ireland	40.00	—	1	100.00	0.00	0.00	0.00
Italy	42.98	16.45	63	63.49	15.87	19.05	1.59
Luxembourg	45.00	—	1	100.00	0.00	0.00	0.00
Netherlands	63.35	24.61	34	20.59	17.65	38.24	23.53
Spain	46.73	15.05	11	36.36	18.18	45.45	0.00
Sweden	54.15	15.80	20	20.00	20.00	60.00	0.00
United Kingdom	54.44	23.30	112	40.18	13.39	37.50	8.93
EU countries	52.26	21.68	470	40.21	16.60	35.11	8.09
North America	50.95	22.21	1,071	44.91	16.53	30.91	7.66
Japan	56.57	22.86	624	33.65	23.08	29.65	13.62
Asian NIEs	50.02	23.25	5,022	51.93	13.62	24.23	10.22
Total sample	51.35	23.23	7,647	47.67	15.06	26.77	10.50

Source: MOFTEC database of FIEs in China (1983–1998).

from other home countries with regard to the degree of ownership. The majority JVs and wholly owned companies account only for one-third of the total number of the Asian NIEs' subsidiaries in China. If one considers the wholly foreign-owned subsidiaries separately by country, Denmark and the Netherlands have the highest proportion of this type of enterprises in their investment operations in China.

The strong presence of EU companies in the majority-owned subsidiaries is determined by their FSAs and strategic choices. Because many EU MNEs invested in China for market-seeking motives, they were especially concerned with the accessibility of the Chinese domestic market (distribution network and market information) and the relationship with the host government. The potential contribution from local partners, in order to enjoy good political connections, efficient links with the bureaucracy and full benefits from administrative facilities, is therefore regarded by the EU MNEs as an important factor that might favourably influence their market entry and business results. Therefore, these MNEs often preferred JVs to wholly owned subsidiaries, especially in the early years when the concern with the culturally different and complex institutional and bureaucratic environment in China was very high. Also, the Chinese government applied a restrictive regime about the establishment of wholly foreign-owned subsidiaries until the end of the 1980s.

The situation changed towards a more frequent use of wholly and majority-owned subsidiaries as a result of the improved performance of the Chinese market mechanism, the decreasing dependence of MNEs on the Chinese government for marketing support, the diminishing reliance on Chinese partners because of the acquired experience and more entrenched position by the foreign investors and especially the relaxation of the foreign ownership regulations by the Chinese government in the 1990s. The high equity stakes by European MNEs are also related to the technological character of many of their operations. The wholly or majority-owned subsidiaries provide more certainty to the investors for the appropriation of the economic rent and guarantee better protection against technological erosion. Especially those foreign investors who are engaged in the transfer of sophisticated technology (e.g. telecommunications and pharmaceuticals) insisted on more influence on and continued control of their operations in China. These developments confirm the theoretical predictions and empirical findings of previous studies (e.g. Beamish 1988). The transfer of technology by MNEs to their subsidiaries in China undoubtedly is often the most important bargaining item in the negotiation process with the Chinese government and the potential partners. The larger the stream of economic rents to be generated by the transferred technology (i.e. capital- and technology-intensive operations), the more likely it will be that the MNEs will try to obtain, either a more significant equity stake, a longer duration of the agreement, or a stronger management control. Of course, the MNEs' technological strengths are counterbalanced by their need for a local partner with strong political links and good local-market connections. The ensuing negotiations often resulted in an equal equity (50:50) position in the early years of the Chinese open door policy.

Duration of joint venture contract

The determination of a time period for JV contract was originally introduced by the Chinese government to promote FDI in high-tech industries and projects with long investment cycles. Although there is no formal limit on the duration of FIEs, the promoted projects can more easily obtain a longer period of joint operations than the less-valued ones that are characterised by a combination of a low investment level with a high profit rate. The average contract period for EU FIEs is 25 years and somewhat longer than for firms from other countries, in particular those from Asian NIEs (20 years) and North America (21 years) (Table 4.11). The strong presence of EU FIEs in the categories of longer contract duration indirectly reflects their higher resource commitment in terms of technology and capital.

As far as the European Union is concerned, subsidiaries established by firms from the Netherlands, the United Kingdom and Germany generally obtained longer periods of operation (on average between 30 and 27 years) than those from other EU countries, in particular those from Finland (14 years), Italy and Luxembourg (17 years). The subsidiaries from the former group of countries are highly concentrated either in resource-intensive industries (the Netherlands) or scale-intensive industries (the United Kingdom, Germany and the Netherlands)

Table 4.11 Duration of the investment contract of subsidiaries located in China (1979–1996)

	Duration (year)			Categories (% of number of projects)				
	Mean	SD	No.	<10 years	10–15 years	16–20 years	21–30 years	>30 years
Austria	18.67	7.12	6	0.00	33.33	50.00	16.67	0.00
Belgium	22.80	10.05	15	0.00	26.67	26.67	40.00	6.67
Denmark	24.36	13.49	11	0.00	27.27	45.45	9.09	18.18
Finland	13.50	2.12	2	0.00	100.00	0.00	0.00	0.00
France	25.48	14.05	83	0.00	42.17	10.84	25.30	21.69
Germany	26.82	15.49	108	0.93	42.59	7.41	20.37	28.70
Ireland	20.00	—	1	0.00	0.00	100.00	0.00	0.00
Italy	17.05	9.15	63	0.00	69.84	15.87	9.52	4.76
Luxembourg	17.00	—	1	0.00	0.00	100.00	0.00	0.00
Netherlands	31.12	16.12	34	0.00	23.53	8.82	29.41	38.24
Spain	26.09	13.90	11	0.00	36.36	9.09	36.36	18.18
Sweden	20.95	11.71	20	0.00	50.00	25.00	15.00	10.00
United Kingdom	27.25	13.81	112	1.79	22.32	21.43	29.46	25.00
EU countries	25.03	14.05	467	0.64	39.19	15.85	22.91	21.41
North America	20.83	12.65	1,072	0.93	51.59	20.80	14.74	11.94
Japan	23.36	14.43	623	0.64	48.80	14.13	17.66	18.78
Asian NIEs	19.89	13.37	4,998	2.28	58.10	16.51	10.80	12.30
Total sample	21.02	13.67	7,619	1.75	53.97	16.93	13.19	14.16

Source: MOFTEC database of FIEs in China (1983–1998).

and R&D-based industries (Germany), while firms originating from Italy and Austria are more strongly represented in labour-intensive industries.

Location of EU subsidiaries in China

Almost one-third of the EU subsidiaries in China are located in the fourteen coastal cities (30 per cent), while about half (49 per cent) have set up their activity in the Eastern region. About 5 per cent of the EU firms are based in the SEZs (Table 4.12). As far as the coastal cities and Eastern region are concerned, almost two-thirds of EU subsidiaries in China are located in seven cities and provinces, namely Jiangsu, Shandong, Shanghai, Beijing, Tianjin, Zhejiang and Guangdong. All these cities and provinces are highly ranked in the Chinese economy in terms of size and growth, as they accounted for about 45 per cent of the total Chinese GDP in 1999 and recorded a higher growth rate than the national average. Some of these cities and provinces, notably Shanghai, Shandong and Jiangsu, emerged after 1992 as the fastest growing locations for FDI within the context of the geographical restructuring of the Chinese economy.

On the basis of the industrial agglomerations, the Eastern region can be divided into the Yangtze Delta (Shanghai, Zhejiang and Jiangsu), the Pearl River Delta (Guangdong) and the Bohai Rim (Beijing, Tianjin, Shandong and Liaoning). The location patterns of EU FIEs are similar to the American ones, but contrast strongly with those of the Japanese affiliates (Figure 4.4).

Table 4.12 Location pattern of EU subsidiaries in China (1979–1996)

	Coastal cities	Central region	SEZ	Eastern region	Western region	Rest of Fujian and Guangdong
Austria	33.33	0.00	16.67	33.33	16.67	0.00
Belgium	26.67	6.67	6.67	53.33	6.67	0.00
Denmark	33.33	0.00	25.00	25.00	0.00	16.67
Finland	50.00	0.00	0.00	0.00	50.00	0.00
France	32.14	15.48	3.57	45.24	1.19	2.38
Germany	32.11	11.01	8.26	43.12	3.67	1.83
Ireland	0.00	0.00	0.00	100.00	0.00	0.00
Italy	15.87	11.11	1.59	63.49	6.35	1.59
Luxembourg	0.00	0.00	0.00	100.00	0.00	0.00
Netherlands	32.35	5.88	2.94	55.88	0.00	2.94
Spain	9.09	27.27	0.00	54.55	0.00	9.09
Sweden	35.00	0.00	0.00	55.00	10.00	0.00
United Kingdom	33.93	6.25	5.36	50.00	4.46	0.00
EU countries	29.79	9.57	5.32	49.36	4.04	1.91
North America	25.16	9.23	7.08	50.23	5.41	2.89
Japan	45.03	5.77	4.65	39.74	3.37	1.44
Asian NIEs	22.16	11.34	13.65	35.16	3.16	14.52
Total sample	25.10	10.51	11.09	39.10	3.50	10.70

Source: MOFTEC database of FIEs in China (1983–1998).

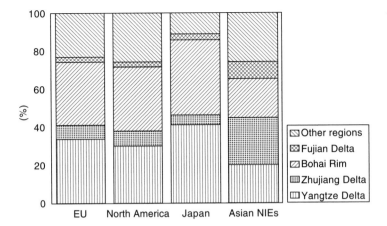

Figure 4.4 Regional distribution of foreign subsidiaries in China (1979–1996).
Source: MOFTEC database of FIEs in China (1983–1998).

European-invested enterprises are relatively more concentrated in the Yangtze and Bohai Rim region, where the major Chinese industries are based and infrastructure is relatively well developed. The specific location patterns of European MNEs are strongly related to their market-seeking options. The extensive and densely populated urban areas, the easy access to a relatively well-developed industrial infrastructure and the more efficient transportation and communication systems are considered as crucial, especially because the vast Chinese market is relatively fragmented. As local governments increasingly introduced protectionist measures to isolate their regional or provincial markets, MNEs have been prompted to abandon their centralised approach to distribution and marketing and decided to establish their own networks in the different regions around the country (Van Den Bulcke and Zhang 1994a).

The European investment in the Bohai Rim is strongly represented in the resource-intensive (28 per cent), labour-intensive (20 per cent) and scale-intensive (20 per cent) industries, such as food processing, textiles and clothing, chemicals and machinery and equipment. The MNEs from France, Germany, Sweden and the Netherlands have a higher presence (30–40 per cent) in this region. In the Pearl River Delta, only enterprises from Belgium, Sweden and the United Kingdom have established a relatively important presence (about 10 per cent). The location patterns of Dutch, German, Italian and British enterprises are more diversified as compared to other EU companies, as more than 20 per cent of their subsidiaries are located outside of the above-mentioned three industrial regions.

Comparative analysis

In this section, the specific characteristics of EU-invested enterprises are compared with those from other home countries on the one hand and on the basis of time periods on the other hand. The measure used for this comparison is the standardised residual value (SR) that is derived from the cross-tabulation. The presence of a particular group of enterprises – as compared to the whole sample – in a specific category is measured as higher (SR > 1), lower (SR > −1) or around average (SR between −1 and +1).[5]

Changing patterns of EU subsidiaries in China

The changing patterns of European subsidiaries in China are clearly apparent from Table 4.13 with regard to their size, sector distribution, regional location, foreign equity share and duration of the projects over the period 1979–1996.

The amount of investment by European parent companies in their subsidiaries increased over time, especially after 1993. The European subsidiaries that were established during the 1980s and early 1990s were highly concentrated in the smaller-sized categories, especially during the early years when many foreign investors considered the investment climate in China as unstable and risky. The small project size and the low equity participation that characterised European subsidiaries during the 1980s perfectly illustrated the 'testing the water' attitude of EU MNEs in the early years of the Chinese open door policy. Since 1993, a growing number of leading EU MNEs have engaged into large-scale FDI projects in China.

The sector distribution of EU investment in China has remained relatively unchanged over the period 1979–1996. Yet, the EU investment in services and specialised-supplier industries has slightly increased during 1995–1996, while the proportion of labour-intensive industries in the total investment projects was reduced. This increase of EUDI in these latter sectors is strongly related to the more liberal sectoral policy measures and the enlarged market access granted by the Chinese authorities. Interestingly, during the period 1989–1992, EUDI in R&D-based industries was less important as compared to the other periods. As already mentioned, this probably reflected the negative perception of the political situation of foreign investors in high-tech and longer-term oriented projects at that time.

With regard to the geographical distribution of European FDI in China, the first European investors had a preference to locate in the Zhujiang and Fujian Delta, in the early opened provinces of Guangzhou and Fujian. After 1992, the European companies accelerated their investment activities in the Yangtze Delta and Bohai Rim, which resulted in a decline in the SEZs. Because of the increasing liberalisation of the Chinese economy and the extension of economic decision-making authority to local governments, foreign investors got more alternatives to locate and organise their value-added chain in China and to do so in a more efficient way. Several European MNEs as well as investors from

Table 4.13 Changing characteristics of EU subsidiaries in China according to sub-periods (1979–1996)

	1979–1989	1989–1992	1993–1994	1995–1996
Size (Foreign equity investment in US$ million)				
<0.5	**5.1**	**2.9**	−4.6	−3.4
0.5–0.99	**3.1**	**1.1**	−3.1	−0.9
1–2.9	0.2	1.0	0.4	−1.8
3–4.9	−2.0	−1.9	**1.9**	**1.9**
5 or over	−4.0	−2.3	**3.2**	**3.2**
Sector distribution				
Agriculture, forestry and fishing, mining	0.6	−0.1	−0.8	0.3
Manufacturing	0.1	0.9	0.5	−1.2
Services	−0.5	−2.6	−1.0	**3.1**
Industrial specialisation				
Resource-intensive industries	0.1	−1.7	1.1	0.2
Labour-intensive industries	0.8	**2.7**	−0.7	−2.1
Specialised-supplier industries	−1.3	−0.1	−0.5	**1.7**
Scale-intensive industries	0.2	0.3	0.1	−0.5
R&D-based industries	0.5	−1.5	−0.4	**1.1**
Location				
Yangtze Delta	−0.6	**1.5**	−1.2	0.5
Zhujiang Delta	**3.7**	−1.2	−2.8	0.3
Bohai Rim	−0.4	−0.2	**1.2**	−0.6
Fujian Delta	**3.7**	−0.5	−1.0	−1.8
Other locations	−2.1	−0.8	**2.0**	0.5
Ownership (%)				
5–49.9	**3.2**	0.8	**1.5**	−4.6
50	**4.7**	**2.0**	−2.4	−3.2
51–94	−5.2	−1.0	−0.1	**5.2**
95–100	−3.0	−2.5	0.3	**4.0**
Duration (years)				
Less than 10	**1.6**	−0.7	−0.9	0.0
10–15	**5.7**	1.0	−0.6	−4.9
16–20	0.0	1.0	0.0	−0.8
21–30	−3.1	0.5	−0.3	**2.5**
More than 30	−4.8	−2.6	**1.2**	**4.7**

Source: MOFTEC database of FIEs in China (1983–1998).

Notes
The standardised residual value in bold means: strong presence; regular: moderate presence; italic: weak presence.

other countries gradually shifted or expanded their operations from the initially opened areas to the inland region in order to capture new business opportunities and benefit from special incentives in these 'newly emerging markets' located within China.

The average duration of the contract of European-invested enterprises as well as the degree of the ownership by European parent companies rose significantly since the beginning of the 1990s. The minority and equally owned JVs were strongly preferred in the period when the investment climate was still considered to be extremely risky, that is, before 1992. The majority and wholly owned firms were chosen more frequently after 1993 as a result of the introduction of the more liberal Chinese FDI policy with respect to ownership on the one hand and the consequent changes in the strategic options of European parent companies with regard to their Chinese operations on the other hand.

European Union versus Asian economies and other old industrial countries

A comparative analysis shows that the characteristics of European-invested enterprises in China were quite distinct from those of other countries of origin in resource commitment, industrial specialisation, location, ownership and contract duration.

European Union versus Asian NIEs

The MNEs from the European Union as well as from the United States and Japan mainly invested in China for market-seeking purposes. The EU subsidiaries are largely concentrated in the specialised-supplier and scale-intensive industries, such as telecommunications, chemicals, pharmaceuticals and the automotive sector. These industries are characterised by a high degree of technology and are quite capital intensive. The availability of skilled labour, the size and growth of the local market and the presence of reliable industrial infrastructure are important factors for their locational decisions. As compared to Asian firms, a higher proportion of EU subsidiaries are indeed located in the Yangtze Delta and Bohai Rim, regions that have a long established tradition in manufacturing and are among the fast growing regions in China.

The resource commitment by European parent companies to their manufacturing plants in China is also much higher than for the Asian NIEs, as they are highly present in the large-scale and high-tech manufacturing production. With regard to ownership, European MNEs prefer majority-owned JVs. This high degree of ownership by European parent companies of their Chinese subsidiaries is strongly related to the nature of their operations in China. Wholly or majority-owned firms are assumed to allow them a more appropriate return of their invested tangible and intangible assets and to better protect their transferred technology. Yet, because of their needs for local partners to guarantee market access, European investors often accept local equity participation mostly by SOEs or government institutions. This 'balancing' between the preference to 'internalise' technology and the need for local partners to increase market access often resulted in equally owned JV agreements (e.g. 50–50).

In contrast to the European subsidiaries, the firms from the Asian NIEs, especially from Taiwan and Hong Kong are mostly resource (especially cheap labour) seekers in China. A great number of this latter group of firms gradually moved all or a part of their export-processing activities to China in order to benefit from the supply of unskilled and abundant labour. The FSAs of these Asian firms are mainly linked to their small-scale production know-how and their specialised skills and capabilities in the labour-intensive and export-oriented activities. The high concentration of Asian export-processing and resource-seeking investors in South China (especially in the SEZs and Guangdong and Fujian provinces) is strongly influenced by locational factors. The proximity of the Chinese sub-sidiary to the home bases in Taiwan and Hong Kong present additional advantages as it limits transport and communication costs. Of course, tax and tariff reductions and favourable administrative import and export procedures also may consist of attractive incentives for export-processing investors, because their competitiveness in the international market is mainly based on lower-priced products (Table 4.14).

As compared to European investors, companies from Asian NIEs have accepted a lower equity position and control of their operations in China in a less formal way. Firms from NIEs are still often at the early stage of multina-tionalisation. They have rather limited financial and technological capabilities, are more dependent on the local resources and consequently also less powerful in their negotiations with the Chinese authorities and potential partners. Therefore, they are less likely to obtain a high equity stake. Also, as the labour-intensive export-processing activities of Asian firms are often influenced by the rapid changes in the export markets, non-equity arrangements (e.g. contractual JVs and subcontracting) or minority-owned EJVs may be preferred to the less flexible, majority EJVs and wholly owned subsidiaries. The specific activity of the subsidiary and the degree of its integration within the value chain of the par-ent company can also affect ownership. Since many firms from Hong Kong and Taiwan 'delocalised' practically all their manufacturing activities to China and only kept their trade and marketing activities in the 'home' bases, they do not necessarily need full ownership to control and co-ordinate the intra-firm pro-duction integration between the 'offshore' processing activities of the subsidiaries and the parent company's value added chain (i.e. often a trade–manufacturing link across borders) (Van Den Bulcke and Zhang 1998).

European Union versus the United States and Japan

Several substantial differences were found among the investors from 'old' indus-trialised countries. European-invested enterprises in China generally benefit from a higher equity contribution from their parent companies as compared to Japanese and American ones. They negotiated a longer contract duration and more often obtained majority ownership in their JVs than their counterparts. These differences between MNEs from different older industrialised countries with regard to their FDI operations in China are often related to divergences in their global competitiveness and strategic positions. As compared to their Japanese and American rivals, European investors are highly concentrated in the scale-intensive industries, such as the automotive sector and chemicals in which

Table 4.14 Characteristics of European subsidiaries in China as compared to Asian NIEs, the United States and Japan (1979–1996)

	EU versus other OICs[a]			EU versus Asian NIEs[a]	
	EU	North America	Japan	EU	Asian NIEs
Size (foreign equity capital in US$ million)[b]					
<0.5	−2.9	0.4	**1.9**	−3.6	1.0
0.5–0.99	−2.2	0.2	**1.5**	−2.7	0.8
1–2.9	0.7	1.2	*−2.1*	0.2	*−0.1*
3–4.9	0.6	**1.2**	*−2.1*	0.3	*−0.1*
5 or over	**3.2**	*−2.4*	0.4	**5.4**	*−1.6*
Sector distribution					
Agriculture, forestry and fishing, mining	−0.2	0.9	*−1.0*	**2.1**	*−0.6*
Manufacturing	0.4	−0.8	0.8	1.0	−0.3
Service	−0.9	**1.8**	*−1.6*	*−2.9*	0.9
Industrial specialisation					
Resource-intensive industries	−0.1	0.9	*−1.1*	0.1	0.0
Labour-intensive industries	0.0	*−1.8*	**2.4**	*−2.5*	0.8
Specialised-supplier industries	−0.2	−0.3	0.6	**1.5**	*−0.5*
Scale-intensive industries	**1.6**	0.5	*−2.0*	0.6	*−0.2*
R&D-based industries	*−2.0*	0.8	0.7	**1.2**	*−0.4*
Location					
Yangtze Delta	−0.1	*−2.2*	**3.0**	**5.7**	*−1.8*
Zhujiang Delta	0.4	0.9	*−1.5*	*−6.9*	**2.1**
Bohai Rim	−0.8	−0.8	**1.7**	**5.2**	*−1.6*
Fujian Delta	−0.5	−0.3	0.9	*−4.5*	**1.4**
Others	1.1	**3.4**	*−5.4*	*−1.0*	0.3
Ownership (%)					
5–48.9	−0.1	**2.2**	*−2.7*	*−3.3*	1.0
50	−0.9	*−1.5*	**2.7**	**1.6**	*−0.5*
51–94	**1.4**	−0.3	−0.8	**4.3**	*−1.3*
95–100	−1.0	*−1.9*	**3.4**	*−1.3*	0.4
Duration (years)					
Less than 10	−0.4	0.5	−0.4	*−2.2*	0.7
10–15	*−2.8*	**1.6**	0.2	*−5.0*	**1.5**
16–20	−1.0	**2.3**	*−2.2*	−0.3	0.1
21–30	**2.9**	*−2.0*	0.2	**7.0**	*−2.1*
More than 30	**3.0**	*−3.3*	1.8	**5.0**	*−1.5*
Period of entry					
Before 1989	*−2.2*	0.1	**1.8**	*−4.1*	**1.3**
1989–1992	*−2.6*	**2.2**	−0.6	*−2.6*	0.8
1993–1994	**1.7**	0.1	*−1.5*	**1.1**	*−0.3*
1995–1996	**3.1**	*−2.2*	0.1	**7.1**	*−2.2*

Source: MOFTEC database of FIEs in China (1983–1998).

Notes
a The sample consists of EU subsidiaries and those from OICs.
b The sample includes subsidiaries from European Union and Asian NIEs.
The standardised residual value in bold means: strong presence; regular: moderate presence; italic: weak presence.

European MNEs have a strong competitive position or benefit from their early entry advantages in China. Among the 38 major MNEs that invested in the Chinese automotive industries, 16 (42 per cent) have an EU basis, while 10 come from the United States and 9 from Japan (Huang 1995). In the chemical industry, among the 25 largest (with more than US$ 10 million per project) FIEs between 1993 and 1995, 11 had been established by EU MNEs as compared to only three by US firms and one by a Japanese company. Nine other firms were controlled by other European (but non-EU), that is, Swiss and Norwegian companies.

Although there are some crucial differences between European- and American-invested enterprises in China, the most important ones were found between European and Japanese firms. Japanese investment in China was characterised by a smaller scale and lower equity contribution from the parent companies. The equity participation by the Japanese parent companies was also lower than for their European and American rivals. In fact, Japanese FDI in China is mainly carried out by two types of enterprises, that is, the Sogo Shosha or trading companies and the industrial groups. Japanese Sogo Shosha invested more in labour-intensive enterprises to supply their home base or export markets. Because of geographical proximity, these investors rely on their Chinese subsidiaries to produce at lower costs and tend to vertically integrate their Chinese 'offshore' operations into the trading activities of the parent companies. The investment behaviour of the Japanese Sogo Shosha is rather similar to that of the Asian so-called 'mobile exporters'. Yet, most of the Japanese industrial groups showed a different pattern in their investments in China and invested more in supply activities and R&D-based industries, especially in automotive parts and electronics. The investment motives of large Japanese industrial groups are quite similar to those of the 'global players' from the European Union and United States, although many Japanese firms only moved in later.

This analysis demonstrates a number of differences between, on the one hand, EU-invested enterprises and those from other countries of origin and, on the other hand, among EU-invested enterprises according to the period during which they entered China. Investors coming from different countries and/or at a different time were responsive to China's changing FDI policy and the upgrading of the locational factors. First, EU FIEs gradually attached less and less importance to the preferential status introduced by the Chinese government to the SEZs and relied more and more on their appreciation of the evolution of the political situation and the overall economic system of the country. These changing attitudes by the investors are reflected in the decline of EUDI during the period 1989–1991 and its later relaunched expansion. Second, EU FIEs have become more concerned with 'created' rather than 'natural' locational factors. The location patterns of EU MNEs clearly show their growing preference for regions with good industrial infrastructure and distribution facilities. Third, the extent and patterns of EU FIEs have become more influenced by the extension of the transition process towards the market system rather than 'artificial' export-promoting or even import-substituting measures. Real market access, rather than the FDI incentives as such, is of special importance for EUDI in high-tech and long-term projects.

These observations also have implications for the Chinese government at a time it is carrying out its renewed FDI policy, especially at the crucial stage of its 'inland' extension programme. First, the Chinese central government as well as local authorities should concentrate their efforts on the liberalisation of market access and the creation of a favourable market environment rather than overestimating their location-bound factors, such as cheap unskilled labour, abundant natural resources and underdeveloped markets. Since the economic system in the Chinese inland regions is still strongly dominated by the SOEs and affected by government interventions, progress towards a market system and the changes of the government's attitude will be important determinants of the attractiveness of the inland region. Second, as was the case during the launching of the FDI promotion programme in the coastal region, the Chinese government needs to invest more in infrastructure in order to improve the conditions for foreign investors who want to engage into resource intensive and related processing industries. Apart from these physical shortcomings, the monopolistic position of a number of central government controlled SOEs in resource-intensive industries (e.g. coal mining and processing in the Northern part of Shaanxi) have to be removed in order to give more initiative to local governments and to allow for a more diversified ownership structure of the economy. The introduction of such measures will provide a more efficient use of resources and create a more vigorous competitive environment.

The introduction of a three-year reform programme for the SOEs in 1997 should allow EU MNEs to play a more specific role. First, as compared to small- and medium-sized Asian enterprises active in export-processing industries, the capital-intensive and high-tech character of EU enterprises provides them with more opportunities to enter into deals with the Chinese government for the privatisation and/or restructuring programme, especially of the large SOEs. The long-term impact of EU MNEs on the employment structure in the SOEs might be significant. The high-tech and capital-intensive character of the European subsidiaries in China should invigorate the training efforts for dismissed employees from the restructured SOEs. Second, a number of large EU MNEs have already started to restructure their operations in China. This should provide opportunities for Chinese inland provinces to be integrated in the value-added chain of EU MNEs in China and possibly in the Asian region.

The changes in the Chinese FDI environment in general and the introduction of the privatisation programme for SOEs in 1997 in particular also present new challenges for EU MNEs. Although EU MNEs have been very well positioned in certain Chinese industries, such as automotive, pharmaceuticals and telecommunications, the competition from their rivals from the United States and Japan has become more severe. The buyouts of Guangzhou Peugeot by Toyota and Wuxi Agfa by Kodak demonstrates that the handicap by the decision by some large companies to invest into China at a late stage can be alleviated with the support of the Chinese government. Such a decision may affect the position of the early European movers in a detrimental way. Yet, the introduction of the new reform programme for SOEs combined with the WDS provides European MNEs with both opportunities and challenges in China. This will be of crucial importance not only for their competitive position within China, but also for their global competitiveness vis-à-vis their counterparts in the rest of the world.

The combination of a relatively lower EUDI position in China as compared to the US and Asian economies with the strong competitiveness of European companies in the Chinese market is to a certain extent the reflection of a particular investment behaviour and strategic attitude of the EU MNEs within the Chinese economic and institutional environment. The motivation and managerial aspects of EU MNEs with FDI operations in China will be discussed in the subsequent chapters.

Part II

Characteristics of EU MNEs with FDI activities in China

5 Operational and strategic characteristics of EU parent companies with investment operations in China

The previous chapters showed that European subsidiaries in China are characterised by a large size, a high level of technology and an intensive capital input. These specific features of EU-invested enterprises are largely determined by the FSAs and strategic options of their EU parent companies. In this chapter, operational and strategic characteristics of EU MNEs that have engaged into FDI activities in China are studied. The section on 'Characteristics of EU parent companies' analyses the specific characteristics of EU parent companies with FDI operations in China. The sectoral patterns and industrial specialisation of these firms are pictured against the overall structure of European industries. This section also deals with operational characteristics of EU MNEs, especially with regard to their size, performance, degree of multinationality and the importance of China in their Asian operations. The section on 'Strategic issues and motivations' studies managerial and strategic aspects of EU MNEs' investment operations in China. Issues, such as motivation, market entry process and location decisions, are also taken up.

Characteristics of EU parent companies

The data used in this section were collected on the basis of a survey via embassies, trade organisations and business associations of the EU member countries in China during the period 1996–1997. This intensive data collection process allowed to identify 741 European companies that wholly or partly owned 1,214 manufacturing, trade and service subsidiaries, representative offices/branches and regional headquarters in China. The business and financial data of about 300 of 741 European parent companies were collected from their annual reports and/or web sites, publications of business associations, local business directories and the CD-ROM AMADEUS (1994).

Two preliminary aspects have to be mentioned before delving deeper into these data sets, however. First, as compared to MOFTEC's data on registered FDI projects as used in the previous chapters, this sample covers companies that already started their operations in China. Therefore, it provides a more realistic picture of EU investment in China than the registration data by MOFTEC. Second, this database covers a larger number of EU companies than are included in the list of foreign subsidiaries published by MOFTEC that is limited to 405

Table 5.1 EU parent companies and their subsidiaries in China according to nationality (1996, 1997)

Country of origin	Parent companies		Subsidiaries in China	
	Number	%	Number	%
Germany	194	26.18	332	27.35
France	158	21.32	245	20.18
Italy	108	14.57	138	11.37
United Kingdom	86	11.61	144	11.86
Netherlands	52	7.02	117	9.64
Sweden	34	4.59	93	7.66
Belgium	32	4.32	42	3.46
Austria	29	3.91	35	2.88
Denmark	18	2.43	25	2.06
Spain	13	1.75	14	1.15
Finland	10	1.35	17	1.40
Other Western European countries	7	0.94	12	0.98
Total	741	100.00	1,214	100.00

Source: Survey of embassies, trade organisations and business associations of the EU member countries in China (1996/1997).

registered by EU companies in China. Among the 741 sampled EU parent companies included in the survey database, more than one-fourth (26 per cent) come from Germany, one-fifth (21 per cent) from France, 15 per cent from Italy, 12 per cent from the United Kingdom and 7 per cent from the Netherlands. The proportion of each country in this sample is relatively similar to the data from MOFTEC both at the country and company level, except that the United Kingdom is rather underpresented in the survey database. Table 5.1 indicates the home countries of the EU companies that are included in the sample and the number of their subsidiaries in China.

The EU parent companies in the sample realised on average two FDI projects in China, while 16 per cent of them established two or more subsidiaries. Some leading MNEs even control more than 20 subsidiaries in China (Figure 5.1). At the end of 1997, the 66 top European companies owned 345 subsidiaries in China, that is, each of them having on average more than five subsidiaries. The largest investors in China at that time were Siemens (45 subsidiaries), Akzo Nobel (37), AEG (33), BOC Group (32), Philips (17), Alcatel Alsthom (16), Bayer (15), ABB (12), Air Liquide (11), Henkel (11) and Unilever (11). The total investment of 225 EU companies in their 422 Chinese subsidiaries reached US$ 7,733 million, that is, an average investment per project of US$ 34.4 million. The available – but very limited – data for 23 EU firms showed that these companies created 62,807 jobs in China and employed on average 2,731 persons in 1997.

Sectoral patterns

European Union MNEs that established subsidiaries in China are mostly manufacturing firms. In the sample of 741 EU parent companies, 80 per cent are in

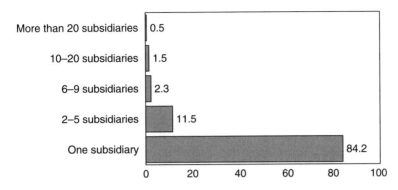

Figure 5.1 Presence of EU MNEs in China (number of subsidiaries) (1996, 1997).
Source: Company reports, web sites and AMADEUS database (1996/1997).

manufacturing, 18 per cent in service activities and 2 per cent in mining exploration and extraction. EU manufacturing MNEs in the sample are highly concentrated in chemicals (19 per cent of all sampled companies), machinery (13 per cent) and electronics and electric industry (13 per cent), while EU multi-national service companies in China are mainly operating in wholesale trade and supermarkets (8 per cent). EU financial companies have a very low involvement (less than 1 per cent) in China, which is only partly due to the restrictions of the Chinese government on FDI in the financial sector. Indeed, American and Japanese firms are not as hesitant about these barriers and are more strongly represented in the service sectors.

In order to situate the industrial concentration of EU MNEs operating in China against the industrial structure of all EU companies included in the CD-ROM AMADEUS database, a concentration ratio was calculated for two- to four-digit SIC codes. The industries that register a ratio higher than one are considered as relatively more involved in FDI activities in China, while the sectors with a ratio below one are regarded as weakly presented as compared to their relative importance in the total EU industrial structure.

The results show that the EU industries in which companies have a higher propensity to invest in China are refined petroleum products (8.3), motor vehicles and parts (5.9), electrical machinery (5.9), chemicals (5.6) and machinery and equipment (3.9) (Table 5.2). The high concentration of EU MNEs in these capital-intensive and high-tech industries in China is probably related to the global competitiveness of European companies and the competitive pressures to which they are exposed to.

European Union investment in the Chinese chemical industry, for instance, followed and was linked to significant operations of European petroleum firms that acquired a substantial presence in China since the early 1980s. Several leading European petroleum companies entered China shortly after the very beginning of FDI liberalisation in China. For instance, Shell and Elf started offshore

Table 5.2 Sector concentration of EU multinational parent companies with FDI in China (1996, 1997)

Industries	ISIC code	EU companies with FDI in China[a] (1)		All EU based companies[b] (2)		Ratio (1)/(2)
		Number of companies	%	Number of companies	%	
Refined petroleum products and other energy	23	6	2.28	350	0.27	8.30
Motor vehicles and parts	34	13	4.94	1,060	0.83	5.94
Electrical machinery and apparatus	31	17	6.46	1,399	1.10	5.88
Chemicals and chemical products	24	41	15.59	3,554	2.79	5.58
Machinery and equipment	29	38	14.45	4,689	3.68	3.92
Electricity, gas, steam and hot water supply	40	6	2.28	808	0.63	3.59
Office, accounting and computing machinery	30	4	1.52	591	0.46	3.28
Radio, television and communication equipment	32	11	4.18	1,646	1.29	3.24
Medical, precision and optical instruments	33	14	5.32	2,143	1.68	3.16
Fabricated metal products	28	15	5.70	2,554	2.01	2.84
Pharmaceuticals and medicinal chemicals	2,423	19	7.22	3,554	2.79	2.59
Non-metallic mineral products	26	8	3.04	1,593	1.25	2.43
Total manufacturing		263	100.00	127,321	100.00	1.00

Notes
a Survey of embassies, trade organisations and business associations of the EU member countries in China (1996/1997).
b All companies included in the AMADEUS database.

oil activities in China in the early 1980s and later extended into refinery, manufacturing and trade. In 1997, Shell had already invested US$ 1 billion and provided jobs to more than 600 employees. It established twenty oil and chemical manufacturing JVs and sixteen offices around the country. Shell participated in the Nanhai chemical complex with a 50 per cent share in the venture's equity capital. This latter petrochemical complex is a central element of Shell's global chemical strategy in China. Elf has followed a similar entry process by investing US$ 300 million in fourteen downstream chemical projects, five of which became operational in 1998. Total,[1] another French oil company, entered into a JV with China's West Pacific Petroleum Company in 1991 to build the Dalian refinery that started its operations in 1996. Next to the downstream investment by petroleum firms in basic chemical manufacturing, the European leading chemical and pharmaceutical companies also established a strong position in China's upstream chemical industries.

European MNEs are also well established in the Chinese automotive industry, especially in passenger car production and luxury bus assembly activities. European-invested JVs produced 65 per cent of all passenger cars 'made' in China in 1995, while the other third was taken up by American jeeps and Japanese mini-cars. European FDI in the Chinese automotive industries is mainly carried out by German and French car producers and their domestic and European suppliers. Companies from Italy, the United Kingdom and Austria also entered into the Chinese automotive industry in the early 1980s, but they mainly concluded licensing or co-production arrangements and concentrated on, for example, dump trucks and light trucks. The first step towards the strong market position by European automotive MNEs in China was taken in 1985, when Volkswagen established its first automotive JV in Shanghai. The early European entrants have changed the market and industrial structure in the Chinese automotive sector. They clearly contributed to the agglomeration of the passenger car and component industry and shaped the future development of the industry, especially in the area of Shanghai. The large-scale investment by European MNEs at a later stage allowed them to quickly acquire a dominant position in the Chinese car market. The proportion of European car models, such as the Santana, Audi, Jetta, Peugeot 405 and Citroën ZX, in the total Chinese car fleet rose from less than 7 per cent in 1989 to 62.4 per cent in 1993. In 1997, Shanghai VW sold 200,000 Santana cars, accounting for 52 per cent of total passenger car sales in China, while the market share for its Jetta was 10 per cent.

In the electrical and machinery industry, a number of EU MNEs, such as ABB and Siemens, also established a leading position in the Chinese market. Siemens entered China in 1982 by opening a representative office in Beijing. In 1985, it signed a memorandum with the Chinese ministries in charge of mechanical engineering, electrical and electronics industries, which was the foundation for its future development in China. The company planned to establish more than 50 JVs in China with a total employment of about 30,000 people. In 1994, Siemens set up its holding company in Beijing to support its JVs and wholly owned companies with capital, marketing expertise, general services, personnel man-agement and purchasing as well as financial and foreign currency management. Until 1998, Siemens had established a total of forty-five JVs in China in different business sectors. Total employment and sales of Siemens in China reached, respectively, 27,000 people and DM 3.5 billion in 1998. Its main investment in manufacturing activities was concentrated in communication, energy and industrial automation.

Size

The EU parent companies with FDI operations in China are on average large sized when measured in terms of sales and employment. The average worldwide employment of the European parent companies with FDI in China amounted to 21,719 persons in 1997, while their consolidated sales averaged US$ 4,109 million per company. The top ten EU MNEs employed 2.5 million people in 1997, which accounted for about 40 per cent of the total employment of the sam-pled companies. The comparative figures for all EU enterprises included in the AMADEUS database were only 501 persons and US$ 114 million sales per com-pany in 1994. Sixty-six of EU MNEs operating in China are among the top 500 EU companies in 1997. Table 5.3 shows some business characteristics of EU MNEs with FDI operations in China.

The breakdown by size categories shows that 38 per cent of the sampled EU companies have 1,000 or more employees, while the comparable proportion for all EU companies incorporated in the AMADEUS database reached only 1.3 per cent. Sales figures demonstrate the same trend: 60 per cent of EU MNEs with FDI in China recorded US$ 1 billion or more of sales in 1997, while the comparative proportion for all the companies that reach such a level of turnover is only 7 per cent. While it is clear that large EU companies have more tangible and intangible assets to organise their value-adding activities on a worldwide

Table 5.3 Some general characteristics of EU parent companies with FDI activities in China (1996, 1997)

	Number of sampled companies	Mean	SD
Age of European group (year)	257	57	41
Sales worldwide (US$ million)	302	4,109	10,190
Number of employees worldwide	287	21,830	51,124
Number of employees in China	31	2,140	3,402
Number of overseas subsidiaries	38	101	154
Number of subsidiaries in Asia	28	11	8
Number of subsidiaries in China	742	2	3
Investment in China (US$ million)	225	35	205

Source: Survey of embassies, trade organisations and business associations of the EU member countries in China (1996/1997).

Table 5.4 Size of EU MNEs with FDI operations in China as compared to the total sample of European companies (1994, 1997)

Size categories	European MNEs with FDI in China[a]		All EU-based companies[b]	
	N	%	N	%
Categories by number of employees worldwide				
<10	50	17.24	8,009	7.52
10–19	12	4.14	33,250	31.20
20–49	22	7.59	37,220	34.93
50–199	31	10.69	20,652	19.38
200–999	63	21.72	6,072	5.70
1000 & over	112	38.62	1,368	1.28
Total	290	100.00	106,571	100.00
Categories by sales worldwide (US$ million)				
<150	8	2.65	49,311	53.90
150–249	21	6.95	16,207	17.72
250–499	42	13.91	13,092	14.31
500–999	55	18.21	6,523	7.13
1000–4999	63	20.86	5,247	5.74
5000 & over	113	37.42	1,104	1.21
Total	302	100.00	91,484	100.00

Notes
a Survey of embassies, trade organizations and business associations of the EU member countries in China (1996/1997).
b All companies included in AMADEUS database (1994).

scale in general and in expanding into the Chinese market in particular, SMEs are clearly more risk averse when expanding abroad, especially into 'Far East' countries such as China (Table 5.4).

Degree of internationalisation and 'Asianisation'

The EU MNEs included in the database are mostly 'global players' as they are characterised by a high degree of internationalisation as measured by the ratio of foreign sales to total sales and foreign employment to total employment. The foreign sales of seventy-eight EU companies with FDI in China accounted on average for 68 per cent of their total sales. The highest ratios of foreign to total sales are mainly recorded in the basic metal industry (79 per cent), petroleum (78 per cent), non-metallic minerals (76 per cent) and machinery (71 per cent). The total foreign employment of a sample of thirty-two EU companies with FDI in China for which information could be obtained amounted to 2,034,336 in 1997, representing 61 per cent of their total employment. The companies with a high ratio of foreign employment are also the ones that operate in petroleum (78 per cent), mining (75 per cent) and metal products (71 per cent). As far as the number of subsidiaries

Table 5.5 Market orientation and degree of internationalisation of selected European MNEs operating in China (1996, 1997)

Name	Home country	Foreign sales as % of total sales	Asian sales as % of total sales	Employment abroad as % of total employment	Employment in Asia as % of total employment
Andritz-Sprout-Bauer	Austria	96.00	23.00	58.00	–
Ericsson	Sweden	95.50	22.40	55.00	–
Nokia	Finland	95.00	22.00	54.00	10.80
Molins	United Kingdom	91.00	29.00	–	–
Spirax Sarco	France	86.00	23.00	69.80	–
Unilever	Netherlands/UK	85.92	15.00	89.90	27.50
Schering	Germany	84.25	17.00	–	–
Valmet Paperikoneet	Finland	79.60	–	35.00	20.59
Alcatel Alsthom	France	77.64	13.00	–	6.00
Philips Electronics	Netherlands	77.01	17.50	83.40	24.90
Schindler Elevator	Switzerland	76.00	17.00	86.00	24.00
Zetex	United Kingdom	75.00	28.00	–	–
Beiersdorf (Nivea)	Germany	67.00	13.50	59.10	18.00
Siemens	Germany	66.00	11.00	49.10	6.99
Akzo Nobel	Netherlands	66.00	5.00	75.00	–

Source: Company reports, web sites and AMADEUS database (1996/1997).

is concerned, the available data of 38 companies show that they control on average 101 domestic and overseas subsidiaries, of which 11 are based in the Asian and Pacific region (Table 5.5).

The Asian region occupied an important and increasing proportion in the corporate portfolio of the surveyed EU MNEs. The share of Asia in the total sales of these companies amounted on average to 14 per cent, while their share in the total employment reached a similar level. The companies in machine production have the highest proportion (18 per cent) of employment and sales in Asia.

When one examines the characteristics of EU parent companies with FDI operations in China, two major conclusions can be drawn. First, most of EU parent companies that have substantial investment operations in China are active in competitive EU industries. These firms are large sized and have a high degree of internationalisation and involvement in Asia. Yet, recently a number of EU SMEs started to invest in China as 'followers' of leading MNEs in order to maintain their supplier relationship. Second, EU MNEs attributed more functional and strategic importance to their subsidiaries in China as compared to their operations in other Asian developing economies. This is, for example, reflected by their investment in R&D activities and regional management facilities (regional headquarters/offices) in China (discussed later). Yet, although EU companies consider China as a very important part of their Asian regional strategy, many of their operations in China are still 'stand alone' subsidiaries as compared to Japanese and US companies that have succeeded in integrating their Chinese operations more into their cross-border production networks.

Strategic issues and motivations

On the basis of qualitative data that was mainly collected by a questionnaire survey of twenty-seven EU parent company operating forty-one subsidiaries in China, the motivations, location factors, entry routes and strategic behaviour of EU parent companies are analysed in the following subsections.

Importance of China

The questionnaire survey of twenty-seven EU parent companies shows that about 7 per cent of their total sales were realised in China in 1996, while the proportion of China in their total investment and personnel accounted for, respectively, 14 and 5 per cent (Table 5.6). Ninety-four per cent of the surveyed companies reported that their sales in China were expected to increase, 82 per cent of them planned to expand their investment and 91 per cent planned to bring the number of their employees to a higher level in that year.

The importance of the Chinese subsidiaries in the Asian/global strategy of EU companies can be documented not only by their share in the total sales, employment and new investments of the EU parent companies, but also by their changing functional roles in the group as a whole. As compared to other Asian countries, China is no longer only a target market for or production basis of EU companies, but also gets more involved into R&D activities of EU MNEs.

Table 5.6 Geographical distribution of the corporate portfolio of a sample of European MNEs with investments in China (%) (1996)

	Sales (N = 22)		Investment (N = 12)		Personnel (N = 13)	
	Mean	*SD*	*Mean*	*SD*	*Mean*	*SD*
Home country	35.59	27.08	57.25	26.91	62.33	19.50
Other EU countries	30.36	16.88	8.92	8.85	13.49	11.66
Rest of Europe	5.61	4.70	5.40	9.42	4.24	7.41
North America	9.26	9.97	11.62	15.88	8.07	12.60
Japan	1.50	3.76	0.38	1.39	2.67	8.53
China	6.66	9.24	13.88	25.59	4.93	9.99
Asia (excl. Japan and China)	5.14	5.43	0.38	1.39	0.55	1.05
Other regions	5.88	6.64	2.17	5.50	3.72	6.41
Total	100.00		100.00		100.00	

Source: Survey of EU parent companies with FDI operations in China.

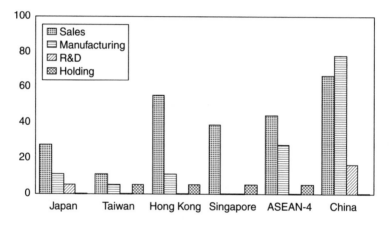

Figure 5.2 Business activities of EU MNEs in Asia (per cent of number of companies) (1996).

Source: Survey of EU parent companies with FDI operations in China.

Among 18 EU companies that established 114 subsidiaries in Asia including China, 14 (78 per cent) of them set up production facilities in China, 12 (67 per cent) opened sales offices and 3 (17 per cent) started local R&D facilities (Figure 5.2). By contrast, the investment of these same companies in ASEAN is mainly concentrated in manufacturing and sales activities. Apart from China, only Japan hosted some R&D facilities of EU companies in Asia.

Market-entry process

A number of previous studies of the so-called Uppsala or Scandinavian School about the internationalisation process of MNEs have stated that firms tend to follow a number of intermediate stages – direct export, local agent, sales subsidiary, etc. – before they set up a production subsidiary in a particular country (Johanson and Vahlne 1977). Each stage provides for a learning process and prepares for the next phase. The analysis of the investment routes of twenty-three EU MNEs in China shows a rather mixed result (Figure 5.3). Only one of the surveyed EU parent company went through all intermediate stages before investing in production activities in China (route D), while seven firms directly established local production facilities without passing through any of the previous stages of the 'learning process' (route A). Twelve other firms started to produce in China after exporting and establishing a representative office/sales subsidiary (route E) and two firms penetrated the Chinese market through the establishment of representative offices and production facilities without having any prior experience with exports to China. Two of these companies also extended their production activities into headquarters and/or holding functions.

Several observations can be made on the basis of the entry modes of these companies, despite the limited size of the sample. First, the companies that followed route A – directly started production without following any previous stages – are generally much larger than those having taken other preparatory steps before establishing production facilities (route E). The sales of this first group reached US$ 9.2 billion on average in 1996, while the number of their employees averaged 44,000, and the average size for the second group amounted, respectively, to US$ 4 billion of sales and 23,000 employees. The differences in

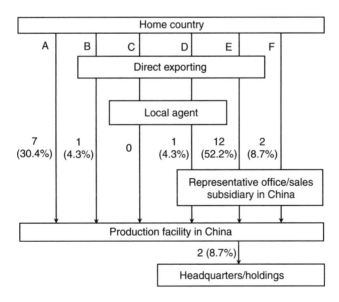

Figure 5.3 Routes followed by EU MNEs for investing in production facilities in China (*N* = 23).

Source: Survey of EU parent companies with FDI operations in China.

size and the previously acquired experience in other international markets might explain the variations in these entry patterns. Second, few companies used a local agent before launching into production activities in China. This may be due to the underdevelopment of the agency system in China. However, five companies that entered the Chinese market through route E used local agents based in Hong Kong. Third, most EU companies penetrated the Chinese market through a gradual process (route E), going from direct exports, local agent (in Hong Kong), representative offices and production facilities. Such a gradual approach reflects that more than half of these firms needed to accumulate local know-how in order to reduce the investment risks and followed the so-called 'establishment chain', which has lost much of its lustre in the developed countries, however. Competition has become so hectic, that firms wanting to enter new foreign markets hardly have the time to follow the stage approach and therefore proceed more often by acquiring existing companies. In a sense they buy into the local market in order to be able to proceed more quickly. To the extent that mergers and acquisitions will become more common in China the same phenomenon is likely to occur.

To conclude, most European MNEs entered the Chinese market through a gradual process in order to acquire the necessary and specific knowledge about the Chinese business environment. However, with the improvement of the Chinese market system and the build-up of a more transparent legal infrastructure, more firms tend to directly move into the Chinese market without going through the traditional stages.

Investment determinants

On the basis of the analytical framework that was developed in Chapter 2, a number of factors were presented to the surveyed EU parent companies in order to identify their motivations for producing in China and to examine their locational choices within the country. The relative importance of each factor is measured on a five-point Likert scale in order to assess the impact of different factors on the motivations and locational decisions of EU MNEs in China. These different factors are also gathered into four groups according to the framework that was developed in Chapter 2, that is, strategic asset seeking, market seeking, cost/supply orientation and efficiency seeking. The importance of each group was measured by using the average of the Likert scale of all factors that are included in the category.

It was found that the investment decisions by EU MNEs in the Chinese manufacturing industry are principally based on their market-seeking motive (3.71 on a scale of 1–5) and strategic-asset-seeking motive (3.43), while the reasons for cost/supply (2.90) and efficiency seeking (2.76) score relatively less important.

Strategic-asset seeking

As already mentioned, strategic-asset-seeking investment in an emerging market is linked with the objective to establish a broader multi-regional or national presence. Defensive strategy, such as avoiding or reducing competition, is also quite important for a company willing to enter into a new market. Yet, both of these two options (i.e. offensive and defensive) may intend to reach long-term strategic objectives. Most of surveyed EU companies considered their investment in China as part of their long-term strategic objectives for creating and sustaining competitiveness in the Asian emerging market. The most important motive for these firms – first movers as well as latecomers – for investing in China is to build a broader multi-regional and national presence (4.16 on the Likert scale), as 47 per cent of the surveyed companies considered this factor as the most important reason for establishing and intensifying their business activities in China. The opportunities offered by the Chinese open door policy at the end of the 1970s attracted a number of EU MNEs that have since then established a prominent position in the Asian region. The decision to move into China for these leading investors is not so much to exploit specific cost or marketing factors, but to add to the firm's existing global and Asian portfolio of assets. This can be illustrated by Unilever's strategic entry into the Chinese market in the 1980s. Unilever was already well positioned with established operations in many Asian countries. Since its presence in some of these countries goes back many years, for instance, to India in 1933, the Philippines in 1927, China in 1920, Thailand in 1932 and Indonesia in 1933, it has acquired useful local knowledge and a leading position in the Asian regional market. After the opening up of the Chinese market, Unilever came back to China in order to relaunch its brands in a massive but as yet underexploited market and to regain 'first mover advantage'. Since its first JV with Shanghai Soap Factory in 1986, it established a total number of eleven JVs with 6,000 employees, manufacturing and marketing over twenty major brands (Unilever 1997).

The 'follow the leader' behaviour is also typical for EU MNEs, meaning that they reacted to the increasing presence of their competitors in the Chinese market (3.34). Almost one-third (31 per cent) of the companies mentioned this factor as the most influencing determinant in their investment decision. Another important reason for an EU company to position itself adequately in China, besides exploiting the given market potential, is to learn from emerging market/competitors. The business basics are often quite different in the major world regions, and it is imperative for a globally operating company to understand and respond to those differences as adequately as possible and to be able to manage their business accordingly. For instance, although Hoechst already acquired strong footholds in Asia due to its strengths in specific technologies and marketing, it still considered its move into China as part of a learning process (Hoechst 1997).

Market determinants

As far as the market seekers are concerned, the main reasons for their investment in the Chinese manufacturing industries are explicitly related to the setting up of a foothold in the Chinese market (4.58 on the Likert scale), the expansion into a new market for the parent company (4.55), the acquisition of a dominant market share in that market (3.81) as well as the promotion of the parent company's exports (3.13). The proportion of companies that considered the above-mentioned factors as extremely relevant for their investment in China are, respectively, 70, 64, 38 and 19 per cent. Although trade protection (e.g. tariffs and quotas) is often considered as the main reason for MNEs to produce in a foreign market, it is not highly ranked by European MNEs in their decisions for investing in China (2.66). Only about one of five companies reported that tariffs, quotas and other trade barriers are among the most influential determinants of their investment decision.

Cost-reduction motives

The cost/supply related factors are clearly less important than the market and strategy related ones for EU MNEs to invest in the Chinese manufacturing industry. Only 7 per cent of the surveyed companies ranked production costs as a crucial factor affecting their investment decision in China. Although low production costs attracted a number of EU investors to build up a production basis in China, the products of these companies are usually for export to neighbouring markets (3.22 on the Likert scale). This practice is quite different from the traditional cost/supply-oriented offshore operations, of which the products are often shipped back to the home market or other subsidiaries of the group. The most important influence on the cost/supply-oriented investment of EU MNEs in China for one-fourth of the surveyed companies consisted of the development of substantial local sourcing capability in the Chinese market (3.00). Yet, this motivation is mainly related to the market-oriented investment operations of EU MNEs and/or to the pressure of 'localisation' (local content) requirements by the Chinese government in certain industrial sectors. The recent entry of European component manufacturers into the Chinese automotive industry has been influenced by a similar motive. For instance, twenty-seven German parts and accessories producing firms have established forty-five JVs in China to continue or extend their supplier linkage with Volkswagen's production units in Shanghai and Changchun (Table 5.7).

Efficiency seeking

The efficiency-seeking investment by EU MNEs in China is strongly related to the market expansion and/or product diversification (3.2 on the Likert scale of 5) and the learning experiences from producing in a new business environment (2.91). To achieve economies of scale by investing in China is only of minor relevance as less than 4 per cent of the companies mentioned this factor as a most important motive for their investment in China. The efficiency-seeking FDI is often intended to take advantage of differences in the availability and costs of traditional factor endowments in different countries. As such, it is much more linked with the resource-intensive activities and the existence of specialised

Table 5.7 Motivations for EU MNEs to invest in China (1997)

Motives	N	Mean	SD	Ranking
Strategic presence (combined)	28	3.43	1.04	
To build a broader multi-regional or national presence	32	4.16	1.05	3
To strategically respond to avoid or reduce competition	29	3.34	1.61	5
To follow key customers to maintain relations	31	2.97	1.52	10
Market seeking (combined)	30	3.71	0.72	
To gain a foothold in the Chinese market	33	4.58	0.75	1
To extend the geographical market of the parent company	33	4.55	0.67	2
To secure dominant share of the market within specific sector	32	3.81	1.33	4
To advance exports of parent company	31	3.13	1.38	8
To avoid tariffs, quotas and other forms of protection	32	2.66	1.58	13
Cost/supply orientation (combined)	29	2.90	1.21	
To create an export base for neighbouring markets	32	3.22	1.56	6
To develop substantial local sourcing capability	32	3.00	1.70	9
To reduce production costs	30	2.87	1.31	12
Efficiency seeking (combined)	25	2.76	0.97	
Product/market diversification	30	3.20	1.47	7
To learn about market and business management in China	32	2.91	1.49	11
To shape industry structure and norms	28	2.39	1.34	14
Economies of scale in production	29	2.31	1.39	15

Source: Survey of EU parent companies with FDI operations in China.

spatial firm/industry clusters (Dunning 1997). Since EU MNEs are mostly specialised in technology and capital-intensive industries and their operations in China are often of a 'stand alone' nature, economies of scale in production are less urgent for these firms. However, recent developments have shown that more and more MNEs try to rationalise their Chinese or even Asian business from China by creating integrated management tools and structures, for instance, by the establishment of holding companies and/or regional headquarters (Table 5.8).

The comparative analysis revealed that the motives for EU MNEs to invest in China to some extent vary according to their specific firm and location characteristics (Table 5.9). MNEs from EU small open economies such as Belgium, Denmark and Finland are likely to be more strategic and market oriented as compared to those from the larger European countries, such as Germany and Italy. The firms from the small open economies of the European Union have a higher degree of multinationality and a greater propensity to engage into cross-border value-added activities due to the limited size of their domestic market (Dunning 1997). This specific feature provides MNEs from these countries with a more 'outward looking' character. The investment in China by these firms might possibly be considered as a way to avoid or reduce the competitive pressures from their rivals. Also, the promotion of exports of the parent company and the avoidance of market protection (tariffs and quotas) are cited more often by MNEs from small open economies than those from the larger ones. The difference between MNEs from these two groups of countries is significant (level 0.05) with regard to factors such as strategic response to avoid or reduce competition, advancing exports of parent company and avoiding trade protection. However, the difference between firms from these two groups of EU countries should not be exaggerated as they are almost all global players with comparable strategic

Table 5.8 Selected holding companies and/or headquarters of EU MNEs in China (1996)

Holding companies	Parent company	Location	Year	Number of subsidiaries
Henkel China	Henkel	Beijing	1995	12
Siemens China	Siemens	Beijing	1994	36
Ericsson China	Ericsson	Beijing	1994	9
Hoechst	Hoechst	Guangzhou	1994	25
Philips China	Philips	Beijing	–	–
Shell Companies in Greater China[a]	Shell	Beijing	1997	16
Novo Nordisk China	Novo Nordisk	Beijing	–	–
Alcatel China	Alcatel	Shanghai	1994	17

Source: Companies annual reports and other corporate information.

Note

a Number of offices. At that time Shell had four operational JVs, another five JVs and two wholly owned subsidiaries under construction.

Table 5.9 Differences among EU MNEs in the motivations for investing in China (1997)

	Number of companies	Strategic presence		Market seeking		Cost/supply orientation		Efficiency seeking	
		Mean	SD	Mean	SD	Mean	SD	Mean	SD
Country of origin									
Small open economies	14	3.74	0.84	4.05	0.67	2.87	1.27	3.06	0.78
Large economies	14	3.12	1.15	3.46	0.66	2.92	1.20	2.48	1.08
Location									
Coastal region	21	3.40	1.15	3.73	0.79	2.85	1.30	2.92	0.98
Inland region	7	3.52	0.66	3.66	0.49	3.05	0.91	2.25	0.82
Type of industry									
Resource-intensive industries	4	3.20	0.96	3.15	0.82	2.33	1.36	2.95	1.15
Specialised-supplier industries	10	3.73	0.66	3.92	0.62	3.19	0.84	2.68	0.79
Scale-intensive industries	12	3.22	1.41	3.75	0.66	2.86	1.42	2.75	0.98
R&D-based industries	4	3.42	1.13	3.65	1.00	2.92	1.34	2.69	1.41
Technology level[a]									
LI–LT	2	3.67	0.94	3.60	0.85	2.50	1.65	1.88	0.88
LI–HT	11	3.79	0.65	3.89	0.60	3.23	0.80	2.81	0.82
KI–LT	3	3.33	1.22	3.27	1.10	2.89	1.71	3.63	0.48
KI–HT	14	3.06	1.28	3.69	0.75	2.71	1.38	2.57	1.08
Period of entry									
Before 1994	9	3.74	1.21	3.88	0.76	3.19	1.33	3.39	0.69
1994–1997	19	3.28	0.94	3.65	0.72	2.80	1.18	2.51	0.97
Type of subsidiary									
First subsidiary	12	3.44	1.15	3.78	0.87	2.48	1.19	2.77	0.84
Largest subsidiary	9	3.63	0.92	3.80	0.63	3.30	1.13	3.03	1.05
Most recent subsidiary	7	3.14	1.07	3.50	0.60	2.96	1.30	2.38	1.15

Source: Survey of EU parent companies with FDI operations in China.

Note
a LI–LT = Labour intensive and low technology; LI–HT = Labour intensive and high technology; KI–LT = Capital intensive and low technology; KI–HT = Capital intensive and high technology.

targets and market orientations. The detected differences are likely to be less related to the 'country of origin effect' than to the specific characteristics of their particular investment projects in China.

The survey results also show that the investment operations by MNEs in the coastal region are apparently more related to strategic-asset- and efficiency-seeking motives, while firms with investments in the inland region more often opt for resource-seeking activities. The early strategic moves of EU MNEs were largely concentrated in the coastal cities – especially Tianjin and Shanghai. During the 1990s, the efficiency-seeking investment also tended to be directed to these cities because of their better industrial and transport infrastructure. This illustrates the locational attractiveness of the different Chinese regions. Yet, the statistic test (one-way ANOVA) did not reveal any significant difference between firms investing in these two regions with regard to their motivations. The market-seeking motive was quoted with equal importance by firms investing in the inland as well as in the coastal region.

The ranking of the motives for EU MNEs to invest in China is not significantly affected by their industrial orientation. Although firms operating in resource-intensive industries are likely to be more efficiency seeking and those in specialised-supplier industry are more driven by market seeking, the statistic test did not detect significant differences. However, when the differences in technological orientation are taken into account, it is found that firms operating in labour-intensive industries with a low technological level are less concerned with the strategy to gain a foothold in the Chinese market, while firms operating in the labour-intensive industries with high technology, for example, electronic assembly, are more – as is to be expected – concerned with labour costs.

The motivations for EU MNEs to invest in China did not change much over time. The comparative analysis did not show any significant differences between firms entering into China in different time periods. Yet, most of the surveyed companies (70 per cent) went into the Chinese market only after 1994. Some difference was found between different types of subsidiaries, that is, the first, the last and the largest investment project. The decision for the 'first-time' investment in China seems to have been more affected by strategy-related factors, especially as compared to the most recent investment operation. The market factors are considered by first-time investors as more important. By contrast, the investment in the largest projects of the group are more linked with the cost/supply and efficiency-seeking motives. However, the difference found in the average was not confirmed by the one-way ANOVA analysis.

Choice of location within China

The location factors within China are classified into four groups, namely market size and access, production costs, infrastructure and FDI incentives. The responses from the survey show that the locational choices of EU MNEs in China are less related to production costs (2.49) and FDI incentives (2.39) than to market size and access (3.74) and industrial infrastructure (3.35) (Table 5.10).

Table 5.10 Location factors for EU MNEs investing in China (1997)

	N	Mean	SD	Ranking
Market size and access (combined)	29	3.74	0.96	
Proximity to major customers	30	3.57	1.33	5
Size and growth of local market	31	4.00	0.89	1
Production costs (combined)	31	2.48	1.19	
Cheap and abundant labour	32	2.84	1.22	8
Cheap raw materials	31	2.16	1.34	12
Infrastructure and linkages (combined)	29	3.35	0.74	
Availability of skilled labour	31	3.52	1.36	6
Transport links and communication facilities	31	3.97	1.11	2
Availability of local sourcing	31	3.58	0.99	4
Presence of local partners	32	3.81	1.18	3
Living conditions (quality of education, housing, etc.)	29	2.24	1.38	11
FDI incentives (combined)	29	2.39	1.05	
Simplicity of process to obtain building and operating permits	31	2.97	1.58	7
Special administrative procedures for market access	31	2.52	1.23	10
Availability of regional or local investment incentives	31	2.58	1.50	9
Tax and other incentives for R&D	29	1.97	1.05	13

Source: Survey of EU parent companies with FDI operations in China.

These results confirm the market- and strategic-asset-seeking motivations of EU MNEs that have already been discussed.

The highest ranked locational factor is the size and growth of the local market (4.00). It is considered by one-third of the surveyed firms as one of the most important location factors. Transport links and communication facilities were only slightly less acknowledged as a relevant factor (3.97), although the proportion of firms that placed this factor among the most important ones reached 39 per cent. The presence of local partners (3.81), the availability of local sourcing (3.58), the proximity to major customers (3.57) and the availability of skilled labour (3.52) rank also quite high in the location decisions of EU MNEs in China. It has to be noted that the tapping into Chinese industry clusters by EU MNEs through JVs with Chinese partners – especially in the automotive and chemical industries – makes the presence of local partners into one of the dominant factors. Almost one-third of the EU subsidiaries of the surveyed companies was strongly influenced by the presence of local partners, especially for the automotive and chemical companies located in Shanghai and its neighbouring region. By contrast, the existence of cheap raw materials (2.16), the living conditions (2.24) and the tax incentives for R&D (2.52) had less of an impact on the location of the EU subsidiaries in China. Only, respectively, 13, 10 and 3 per cent of EU MNEs considered these aforementioned factors as having strongly influenced their locational choices in China.

Table 5.11 Locational choices of EU MNEs in China according to some different characteristics (1997)

	Number of companies	Market size and access		Production costs		Infrastructure and linkages		FDI incentive	
		Mean	SD	Mean	SD	Mean	SD	Mean	SD
Country of origin									
Small open economies	14	3.64	1.05	2.21	0.85	3.24	0.95	2.68	0.98
Large economies	14	3.83	0.90	2.71	1.39	3.45	0.47	2.12	1.08
Size (by foreign invested funds)									
Small sized (<US$ 10 million)	10	3.93	1.06	2.56	1.18	3.43	1.09	2.50	1.22
Medium sized (10–99 million)	13	3.95	0.88	2.17	1.30	3.07	0.70	2.39	1.09
Large sized (US$ 100 and more)	6	2.80	0.76	2.30	0.76	3.76	0.41	2.55	0.91
Type of industry									
Resource-intensive industries	5	3.60	1.08	2.70	0.84	3.28	0.41	2.45	0.94
Specialised-supplier industries	14	3.72	0.79	2.82	1.38	3.58	0.95	2.56	1.24
Scale-intensive industries	13	3.95	0.96	2.23	1.21	3.27	0.74	2.25	1.07
R&D-based industries	4	3.38	1.38	2.00	0.91	3.15	0.64	2.31	1.03
Technology level[a]									
LI–LT	2	4.00	0.00	2.50	0.71	3.30	0.14	3.13	0.18
LI–HT	15	3.75	0.75	2.67	1.42	3.60	0.89	2.60	1.18
KI–LT	4	3.75	1.44	2.88	0.85	3.05	0.64	1.75	0.96
KI–HT	15	3.69	1.09	2.19	1.13	3.26	0.69	2.31	1.02
Period of entry									
Before 1994	11	3.63	1.13	2.56	1.24	3.93	0.45	2.88	1.00
1994–1997	25	3.79	0.92	2.45	1.19	3.13	0.72	2.20	1.04
Type of subsidiary in China									
First subsidiary	15	3.79	1.03	2.42	1.24	2.87	0.68	1.83	0.84
Largest subsidiary	11	3.56	0.98	2.45	1.28	3.78	0.46	2.72	1.11
Most recent subsidiary	10	3.88	0.92	2.63	1.13	3.60	0.71	2.84	1.01

Source: Survey of EU parent companies with FDI operations in China.

Note

a LI–LT = Labour intensive and low technology; LI–HT = Labour intensive and high technology; KI–LT = Capital intensive and low technology; KI–HT = Capital intensive and high technology.

The statistical tests did not show any substantial difference among EU MNEs involved in different-sized FDI projects. However, the ranking of factors showed that the firms with large investment projects, that is, with an investment of US$ 100 million or more are likely to pay more attention to factors such as transport and communication infrastructure, availability of skilled labour and local sourcing capability. By contrast, the firms with small- and medium-sized projects (respectively, less than US$ 10 and 100 million investment) depend more on the size and growth of the local market and the proximity of their major customers (Table 5.11).

Performance evaluation

The performance of EU subsidiaries in China was evaluated by their European parent companies in the survey in terms of profitability and cost reduction, acquisition of marketing knowledge and market position as well as strategic significance. Half of the surveyed EU parent companies stated that they failed to reach their performance targets in China in terms of profitability expectation and cost reduction, while only 15 per cent of them reported that their performance had surpassed their original expectations. Yet, EU parent companies are more satisfied about the performance of their Chinese subsidiaries with regard to the strategic achievements, the accumulation of local knowledge and acquisition of market share. More than two-thirds of EU parent companies reported that they reached or exceeded their strategic targets in China, while about 90 per cent were satisfied with the market share they had acquired in China as compared to their initial marketing plan.

Table 5.12 shows the assessment by EU parent companies of their operations in China on a five-point Likert scale in terms of performance evaluation and

Table 5.12 Performance evaluation and major difficulties of EU subsidiaries in China (1997)

	N	Mean	SD
Performance evaluation – exceeded expectations			
Profitability	18	2.61	1.0369
Cost reduction	18	2.50	0.9852
Accumulated marketing knowledge	18	2.78	1.2154
Strategic positioning	18	3.06	1.0556
Market share	17	2.65	0.9963
Main obstacles			
Underdeveloped local logistics and business services	17	3.41	0.8703
Lack of reliable local enterprises for sourcing and distribution	17	3.18	1.0146
Lack of patent/trademark protection	16	2.81	1.2230
Barriers to create cross-border intra-firm linkages	17	3.06	0.8993
Unfamiliar business environment, culture and ethics	17	3.82	0.8828

Source: Survey of EU parent companies with FDI operations in China.

expected degree of difficulty. As already mentioned, European parent companies were relatively more satisfied with the strategic positioning and market knowledge accumulation, while the expectation about profitability and cost reduction scored somewhat lower. The main obstacles that EU companies encountered in China are mostly related to the unfamiliar business environment (3.8 on the Likert scale), underdeveloped local logistics and business services (3.4) and lack of reliable local sourcing capabilities (3.2). Yet, these factors are regarded as crucial for market-seeking investors.

The above analysis showed that European MNEs are clearly oriented towards the domestic Chinese market. The potential growth of its market size also encouraged European firms to establish a strategic presence in China. As a result of local-market considerations and long-term oriented investment options, European MNEs considered location factors – such as market size and access, presence of local partners, transport and communication facilities and local sourcing – as most important determinants for their decision to locate within China. The evaluation by EU MNEs about their ongoing operations in China confirmed that their primary objectives for investing in China, that is, establishing a strategic presence and local-market dominance, were reached. Yet, some difficulties still prevented EU MNEs from successfully operating in China. These aspects will be examined in more detail in Part III of this study, that is, on the basis of the questionnaire survey of European subsidiaries operating in China.

Part III

Characteristics of EU subsidiaries in China

6 Characteristics of EU subsidiaries in the Chinese manufacturing sector

In the first section of this chapter, about the specific characteristics of EU manufacturing subsidiaries in China,[1] a framework is established to analyse the interaction among FSAs, LSAs and the operation of EU MNEs in China. In particular, the impact of two factors, that is, the size of parent companies and the timing of their entry into the Chinese market are discussed. The section on 'Major operational characteristics' reports about the major operational aspects of EU subsidiaries, that is, their ownership structure, partnerships, size of operation, location, sector distribution, R&D and market orientation. This analysis confirms the statistical results of Chapter 4 and provides complementary information about the specific characteristics of EU subsidiaries as compared to those from other origins. In the section on 'Comparative analysis', the characteristics of EU manufacturing subsidiaries are compared according to their period of entry (i.e. first movers versus latecomers) and to the size of their parent companies (large versus small MNEs). The comparative analysis tries to give an accurate explanation to the changing patterns of EU subsidiaries in China. The data that are used in this chapter were collected from 311 EU subsidiaries located in seven Chinese provinces and cities (see Chapter 1). After a descriptive analysis, statistical tests are carried out to verify the results.

Analytical framework

The operational aspects of EU subsidiaries in China are analysed according to the timing of their entry into the Chinese market and the size of their European parent companies. Caves and Mehra (1986) found that the internationalisation of MNEs was influenced by a variety of industry and firm-specific factors, including firm size, advertising intensity, research intensity, industry growth and industry concentration. In this study, determinant factors that influence the operations of MNEs within the host country are classified according to two key elements, that is, FSAs and LSAs (Dunning 1992a; Rugman and Verbeke 1992). Because of the dynamic patterns and changing interactions of these firm- and country-related factors, changes in the strategies and operations of MNEs occur over time (Caves and Porter 1977; Thomas *et al.* 1994), especially when the host economy is involved in a rapid transformation process (McMillan 1993). The differences and changes in LSAs can be traced to the time of entry by MNEs into

	Early mover	Latecomer
Large MNEs	• JV for sharing risks with a 'testing the water' attitude • Low resource commitment • Partnership with government institutions and SOEs for market access • Presence in strategic location • Local-market orientation with export option	• High ownership control for efficiency and strategic assets seeking • High resource commitment • Partnership with SOEs that are local competitors or suppliers • Presence in booming market • High local-market orientation
Small/ medium-sized MNEs	• Minority JV for reducing risks with a 'wait and see' attitude • Low resource commitment • Partnerships with SOEs and private SMEs for subcontracting • Presence in low-cost location • High export orientation with offshore as dominant option	• High ownership control for efficiency-seeking purposes • High resource commitment • Partnerships with government institutions/SOEs for market access • Presence in booming market • High local-market orientation with offshore option

Figure 6.1 Strategic positioning and operations of MNEs in emerging markets according to size and time of entrance.

a particular host country, while the FSAs are partly related to their size and competitive position in the global market. Figure 6.1 attempts to put forward a framework for analysing different strategies and operations of MNEs in the emerging market economy of China.

Large MNEs as early movers

The basic motivation behind the strategy of early movers is related to the so-called 'testing the water' attitude of wanting to be present in an emerging market. Yet, the resource commitment by foreign firms in the early stage of the emerging market is often quite limited given the high investment risks and limitations of the market. On the one hand, the still limited size of the local market does not yet allow to use large-scale production processes and sophisticated product technologies in which MNEs usually have competitive advantages. On the other hand, because there are many uncertainties, for example, the possible erosion of technological advances, the early movers may prefer to set up small-scale facilities and only transfer their standard production processes and product technologies.

The early strategic-asset seekers and market seekers were especially concerned with the access to the local market, the relationship with the government and the official requirement to accept partial local ownership. Therefore, the involvement of local partners into JVs, especially government institutions and SOEs with monopolistic positions in related industries, allows these foreign firms to have better political links, improved bureaucratic accessibility and possibly more favourable administrative decisions. The early movers will also prefer to locate in the larger cities where national or regional centres of decision-making are located and the highest purchasing power can be found.

Small- and medium-sized MNEs as early movers

As compared to the large MNEs, small- and medium-sized MNEs are more often confronted with resource constraints for their international expansion. When these firms lack tangible and intangible assets in terms of technological capability and organisational knowledge, they are often in a 'wait and see' position. The above-mentioned investment risks are more serious for them because mistakes may sometimes even threaten the chances for survival of the parent companies themselves. At this stage, many small- and medium-sized MNEs hesitate to take such crucial investment decisions, especially when they do not benefit from particular geographical and cultural proximity with the host economy that is under consideration for direct investment.

The early moves of small MNEs – because of high production costs in their home base – to emerging markets may be related to the strategy of cost minimisation. Production abroad by these companies will then often take the form of offshore processing activities, that is, with high inputs from abroad and strong export orientation, mainly from and to the parent company. The low costs of production, the availability of cheap or specific resources and transport and communication facilities as well as tax privileges and tariff incentives in special zones are the main determining factors for their location decisions. The technology that these small- and medium-sized MNEs transfer abroad for offshore activities will be rather limited and is generally oriented towards a labour-intensive production process.

Large MNEs as latecomers

The LSAs of emerging economies will normally change over time and are bound to become more positive from the point of view of foreign investors. First, the location factors that are initially related to the natural resources of the country will become enhanced by an 'upgrading' of factors – or even by the creation of new ones – such as, for example, human resource development, industrial infrastructure and better regulated business environment (Dunning and Narula 1994). Second, when the economic system of these countries gradually transforms from a central planning to a more market-oriented system, the needs of foreign MNEs for local partners become less urgent, as their access to the local market and their treatment by the bureaucratic system will have improved.

As a result of changes in LSAs, large MNEs that were not yet present in the market decide to follow in the steps of their immediate competitors. They prefer majority-owned JVs or wholly owned subsidiaries. Their market-entry costs will be higher as compared to those who moved in at an early stage, for example, because of the competitive strengths developed by the early movers, while the country investment risks themselves are likely to have diminished. They may have to carry out projects that are more capital and technology intensive in order to compete with the early movers and acquire sufficient market share or create new demand. Increasing demand and economies of scale in production will allow to achieve lower costs and prices and lead to an expansion of the domestic market. At this stage, the reliance on subcontractors and related industries to achieve efficiency by these MNEs will increase and should bring the industry in the emerging economy closer to the world production system.

The operations of early movers are also likely to be affected by substantial changes in the LSAs of the host country. With the upgrading of the LSAs, MNEs tend to reinforce their upstream and downstream integration into the local economy and to engage in long-term activities, higher technology oriented and organisational intensive operations. They tend to upgrade the technological level of their subsidiaries through transferring more advanced production processes and products and get involved in local R&D activities. They also try to increase their share in the equity capital of the subsidiary in order to exert more control and reduce discussions with local partners as to the strategic orientation of the subsidiary within the multinational group. The growth of the market position of established MNEs in the local economy and the integration of local production into the global value-added network increases their competitive position and may also allow them to build up a leading position in related industries.

Small- and medium-sized MNEs as latecomers

The investment by small- and medium-sized MNEs at a late stage is often the result of a 'follow-the-leader' attitude, meaning that they establish local production activities to acquire or safeguard an existing supplier's relationship with the large MNE in the host country. In other words, the realisation of economies of scale by large MNEs can lead to 'follow-up' investment by suppliers from the home country, for example, of components or semi-finished products.

The early movers of small- and medium-sized MNEs also tend to adjust their strategies and operations over time according to the changing LSAs. This means that their supply/cost-oriented options could be switched or extended to market-oriented perspectives when the demand in the local market becomes stronger.

Major operational characteristics

European Union manufacturing subsidiaries in China that participated in the questionnaire survey have on average US$ 115 million of assets, employ 316 persons and

Table 6.1 Some major characteristics of surveyed European manufacturing subsidiaries in China (1996)

	Number	*Mean*	*SD*
Assets (US$ million)	215	114.96	529.52
Number of employees	229	316.38	834.20
Sales (US$ million)	190	105.24	494.39
Foreign equity share (%)	231	61.19	22.80
R&D expenditure to sales ratio (%)	155	4.54	6.78
Advertising expenditure to sales ratio (%)	161	4.35	5.93
Exports to sales ratio (%)	171	26.89	33.31
Market share (%)	147	26.96	27.95

Source: Survey of EU subsidiaries in China (1997).

realised US$ 105 of sales in 1996. The size of EU manufacturing subsidiaries is much larger than the average of Chinese manufacturing companies, especially in terms of sales and assets.[2] Yet, the size of EU subsidiaries is very heterogeneous, as the value of the standard deviation for their sales, employment and assets is very high (Table 6.1). The equity share held by EU parent companies in their subsidiaries in China reached on average 61 per cent, reflecting the dominant position of EU parent companies in the ownership of their operations in China. EU subsidiaries also have a relatively large market share in their specific sector of activity, as it was estimated to average 27 per cent in 1996. Exports accounted for only about one-fourth of the sales of EU subsidiaries, confirming the local-market-oriented strategy of EU MNEs in China.

Equity participation

The share in the total equity capital of the subsidiary is usually interpreted as being a good measure for the ownership and control by MNEs. According to the ownership degree, ownership at the time of entry can be classified into minority-owned JVs (25–49 per cent), equally owned JVs (50:50), majority-owned JVs (51–94 per cent) and WOFEs (95–100 per cent). The choice of the entry form by MNEs, for example, joint venture versus wholly owned subsidiary, and the degree of control in the JVs not only reflect the FSAs, strategic choices and bargaining strengths of MNEs and the partner companies, but also in a certain way the influence of host countries, the specific government regulations with regard to the entry modes of foreign-owned firms. The need for specific assets – such as human resources, capital, market access, government/political support and technological know-how – are reasons for MNEs to look for partners and to select a JV as a mode of entry instead of a wholly owned subsidiary (Beamish 1988). As compared to the fully controlled subsidiary, a JV is assumed to offer a 'mutual hostage' position by creating a superior monitoring mechanism and alignment of incentives to reveal information, share technology and guarantee performance on the part of both the foreign and the local firm (Kogut 1988). Beamish's study on JVs in developing countries (1988) showed that JVs of MNEs are sometimes more efficient than wholly owned subsidiaries, because of the indigenous partner's better understanding of the general and specific local economic, political and cultural situation and business practices. The 'costs' for the MNEs that are mainly associated with the JV form are related to the loss of flexibility and mobility for business restructuring and changes in strategic orientation, the possible technological erosion and the additional costs for co-ordination and administration of the organisational structure.

Among the 231 subsidiaries in the study that provided information about their ownership structure, 42 (18 per cent) were wholly owned by EU parent companies at the end of 1996, 101 (44 per cent) EU majority-owned JVs, while 34 (15 per cent) were equally owned ventures and 54 (23 per cent) EU minority owned (Table 6.2). Compared to the initial ownership structure, that is, at the moment when the company was established, it is found that 14 per cent of the EU parent companies increased their participation in the equity capital of their JVs after the start-up (Figure 6.2). This resulted in an increase in the number of wholly owned and majority-owned subsidiaries in the total sample. The evolution towards wholly owned and majority-owned ventures was expected to become even stronger, as 22 per cent of the EU companies mentioned in the questionnaire that they anticipated a rise in their ownership share in the near future. However, the acquisition of additional shares by foreign companies in their ventures in China has recently become a relatively important concern for their local Chinese partners – which are mainly governmental institutions or SOEs – as they see this as a loss of control, especially in certain strategic sectors. However, it is doubtful that the Chinese government might try to counteract this tendency, as it would be giving a wrong signal to Western investors. Also, in many cases the increased capital participation of the foreign company is often the result of the inability of the local partner to follow-up on a capital increase in order to carry out the necessary expansion.

Yet, there are other explanations for the mounting participation of EU parent companies in their ventures' equity capital. First, the Chinese regulation on

Table 6.2 Ownership control of surveyed EU subsidiaries in China (1996)

Foreign equity share	At beginning		In 1996	
	Number	%	Number	%
<24.9	4	1.65	0	0.00
25–48.9	66	27.27	54	23.28
50	39	16.12	34	14.66
51–94	95	39.26	102	43.97
95–100	38	15.70	42	18.10
Total	242	100.00	232	100.00

Source: Survey of EU subsidiaries in China (1997).

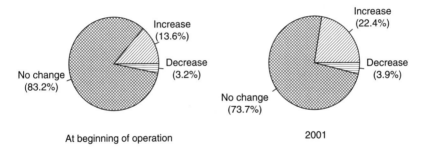

Figure 6.2 Changes in the ownership structure of surveyed EU subsidiaries in China (1996).

Source: Survey of EU subsidiaries in China (1997).

ownership control of foreign-invested companies became more relaxed after 1994 as a result of the ongoing liberalisation of the FDI policy in general. Second, the EU companies that entered early, that is, the so-called 'early movers', gradually acquired more local knowledge, which made them less dependent on local partners. Third, because of the rising resource commitment to the subsidiaries in China, especially in terms of technology and strategic choices, EU firms tended to strengthen their control in order to better protect their technology and to gain more autonomy in decision-making.

Local-partner selection

Partner choice has been identified as an essential element to the success of the JV (Beamish 1988; Geringer 1988, 1991; Blodgett 1991). The choice of the JVs partners will determine the resources that have to be contributed and what will be made available by the partners. How well the partners work together will ultimately depend on the mutual trust that will develop between them. In integrating pools of resources, attention must be paid to the compatibility, capability and commitment of the partners. In the case of a JV in a developing economy, MNEs usually contribute technology, while local partners provide local marketing knowledge, supplier relationships, political influences and relations with bureaucracy.

The JV partners of the European companies in China can be divided into four types according to their ownership, that is, SOEs, collective enterprises (including the more recent private businesses), government institutions with foreign-business-related activities, and other new corporate forms such as shareholding companies. Because of the specific economic and business environment of China, these companies have followed separate development paths and have acquired different characteristics with regard to their FSAs, such as their intra- and inter-firm relations for their supply, production and distribution arrangements, their market position and their connections with the national and local

Table 6.3 Partners of surveyed EU subsidiaries in China (1996)

	Number	%
State-owned enterprise	169	64.50
Collective-owned enterprise	34	12.98
Government institution	8	3.05
Others	17	6.49
No local partner	34	12.98
Total	262	100.00

Source: Survey of EU subsidiaries in China (1997).

government (Boisot and Child 1996; Zhang and Van Den Bulcke 1996). The involvement of different types of local partners in the JV arrangements reflect the specific needs of the EU MNEs or the changing government policies or conditions.

In establishing JVs in China, EU parent companies have shown a clear preference for Chinese SOEs as their local partners. Two-thirds of the surveyed EU companies entered into partnership with central and/or local government controlled enterprises. As mentioned in Chapter 5, EU MNEs mainly invested in China for market and strategic seeking purposes. This indicates that EU MNEs especially want to access the Chinese local market (e.g. information and distribution) and develop a relationship with the government to be granted specific treatment and protection. The involvement of SOEs is supposed to facilitate political contacts and bureaucratic accessibility, to guarantee more favourable administrative decisions and to diminish the entry and operating costs. The participation in the equity capital by Chinese government institutions and SOEs allows JVs to involve the Chinese policy-makers into their affairs in a more direct way, at least if they consider this as a priority. However, the declining position of SOEs in the Chinese economic system because of the steady progress of the market system and the acquisition of more local knowledge by the EU parent companies have reduced the need to co-operate with SOEs. An increase in the number of wholly and majority-owned subsidiaries by MNEs and a more frequent collaboration with non-SOEs has been the result (Table 6.3).

Size of operation

The top five EU subsidiaries realised 65 per cent of total sales of sampled EU subsidiaries in 1996 and their employment accounted for 31 per cent. About 15 per cent of EU subsidiaries in China realised at least US$ 100 million of sales and more than about one-fifth employed 300 or more persons in 1996. These relatively large subsidiaries are mostly concentrated in the automotive and electronic industries. One-fifth of EU manufacturing subsidiaries can be considered as small sized, as their sales reached less than US$ 1 million, while their employment

Table 6.4 Size categories of surveyed EU subsidiaries in China (1996)

In terms of sales			In terms of employment		
Categories (US$ million)	Number	%	Categories	Number	%
<1	41	23.30	<30	44	19.21
1–5	49	27.84	30–49	30	13.10
5–9	18	10.23	50–99	47	20.52
10–99	42	23.86	100–299	56	24.45
100 or over	26	14.77	300 & over	52	22.71

Source: Survey of EU subsidiaries in China (1997).

averaged less than thirty persons. The small EU companies are mostly active in the paper- and wood-related products and measuring equipment (Table 6.4).

Four out of five (82 per cent) of the surveyed EU subsidiaries reported that their sales had significantly expanded during the last five years, while three out of five (63 per cent) recorded an increase in the number of jobs. Since most of these companies are still at the beginning stage of their operations in China, they expected to expand even more in the near future. For the next five years, 92 per cent of the surveyed companies were confident that their sales would continue to rise and 73 per cent of them also anticipated an increase in their employment.

Sectoral distribution

The sectoral analysis of EUDI in China in Chapter 4 has already shown that EU firms tend to concentrate in a limited number of industries that are characterised by high capital investment and technology transfer. The questionnaire survey of EU subsidiaries confirmed these earlier findings. About one-fourth of the surveyed EU companies in China are in chemicals, one-fifth in electrical engineering and 14 per cent in mechanical engineering. The presence of EU manufacturing companies in the food sector and transport equipment industry is also quite strong, as each accounted for about 10 per cent of the total number of the surveyed firms (Table 6.5).

Industrial specialisation and technological level

A four-digit SIC classification is used to measure the industrial specialisation and technological level of the products/processes of the surveyed firms. The industrial specialisation of these firms is classified into five groups on the basis of the method developed by the Organisation for Economic Co-operation and Development (OECD). The resource-intensive industries include food, beverages and tobacco; wood products; petroleum refining; non-metallic mineral products and non-ferrous metals. The labour-intensive industries cover textiles, apparel and leather; metal products and other manufacturing. The specialised-supplier industries consist of non-electrical machinery, electrical machinery and

Table 6.5 Sector distribution of surveyed EU manufacturing subsidiaries in China (1996)

Sector	Number	%
Food	28	10.94
Textiles and apparel	15	5.86
Paper and wood	14	5.47
Chemicals, rubber and plastics	61	23.83
Leather	3	1.17
Non-metallic mineral products	10	3.91
Basic metals	1	0.39
Metal products, machinery and equipment	35	13.67
Electrical and electronic products	50	19.53
Transport equipment	24	9.38
Toys, measuring equipment and other industries	15	5.86
Total	256	100.00

Source: Survey of EU subsidiaries in China (1997).

communication equipment and semiconductors. The scale-intensive industries include paper and printing, chemicals (excl. pharmaceuticals, rubber and plastics), iron and steel, shipbuilding, motor vehicles and other transportation, while the R&D-based industries are composed of aerospace, computers, pharmaceuticals and scientific instruments.

The surveyed EU manufacturing subsidiaries in China are concentrated in the scale-intensive industries and specialised-supplier industries. Thirty-two per cent of the surveyed EU manufacturing subsidiaries in China are operating in the scale-intensive industries, especially in chemicals, while 29 per cent of them are active in the specialised supplier industries. The share of R&D-based industries accounts for 11 per cent of the surveyed EU companies that are very well established in the Chinese pharmaceutical industry (Van Den Bulcke, Zhang and Li 1999) (Table 6.6).

The EU enterprises in the sample are less present in the labour-intensive industries (only 9 per cent), which mainly consist of processing manufacturing. As mentioned before, because of geographical distance and difficulties in the foreign exchange management, few EU companies invested in China for sourcing for their home market or export back to the country of origin.

The relatively high concentration of EU companies in resource-intensive industries (19 per cent) can be mainly explained by their strong presence in food processing activities. The presence of European market seekers in the Chinese food industry is closely linked to the cost structure of production and the nature of products. The high level of transportation and inventory costs and the necessity of product adaptation to the local market obliged many food companies to enter into local production as an alternative to exports.

The surveyed EU subsidiaries are also highly specialised in the capital-intensive industries with a high level of technology (37 per cent), such as construction

Table 6.6 Industrial specialisation and technological level of surveyed
EU subsidiaries in China (1996)

	Number	%
Industrial specialisation		
Resource-intensive industries	48	18.82
Labour-intensive industries	24	9.41
Specialised-supplier industries	73	28.63
Scale-intensive industries	81	31.76
R&D-based industries	29	11.37
Technological level		
Labour intensive and low technology	66	25.88
Labour intensive and high technology	78	30.59
Capital intensive and low technology	17	6.67
Capital intensive and high technology	94	36.86
Total	256	100.00

Source: Survey of EU subsidiaries in China (1997).

materials, transportation and telecom equipment, metal products, chemicals and allied products (Table 6.6), while 26 per cent of companies operate in the industries with high labour input and low technology, such as food and textiles.

R&D activities

Seventy per cent of EU-invested companies reported that they have conducted R&D activities in China from the very beginning of their operations in the country. The proportion of companies with R&D activities increased to 80 per cent in 1996 (Table 6.7). The expenditures for R&D accounted on average for about 4.4 per cent of the total sales of these companies, of which 45 per cent spent at least 5 per cent of their sales figures for R&D purposes.

The importance of R&D activities of the EU subsidiaries in China is measured on a scale from 1 (very limited) to 5 (very important) in Table 6.8. The R&D activities of EU companies focus mainly on product development and product adaptation to the Chinese market, while product innovation for the worldwide market and basic research for the innovation of product and production process are of relatively little significance for their R&D activities in China. Since most EU MNEs invested in China for reasons of market penetration and expansion and promotion of the exports from their parent companies or the multinational groups, they need to adapt their products to the specific conditions of the Chinese market and take the necessary steps to engage in local engineering in order to carry out a successful transfer of technology and install an appropriate after-sales services. The sectoral analysis shows that the ratio of R&D expenditure to sales is higher (5.3 per cent) in the so-called specialised-supplier industries – that is, mechanical and electric engineering – and resource-intensive industries (5.5 per cent) – for example, food processing – while firms in labour-intensive

Table 6.7 R&D expenditures as percentage of sales of surveyed EU subsidiaries in China (1996)

	At the beginning		In 1996	
	Number	%	Number	%
No R&D	40	30.77	31	20.13
With R&D, of which	90	69.32	123	79.87
<5%	49	54.44	68	55.28
5–10%	27	30.00	44	35.77
>10%	14	15.56	11	8.94
Total	130	100.00	154	100.00

Source: Survey of EU subsidiaries in China (1997).

Table 6.8 Type of R&D activities by EU subsidiaries in China (1996)[a]

Function	N	Mean	SD
Development of new products for local market	209	3.82	1.20
Adaptation of existing products to local market	201	3.62	1.21
Technical customer service	194	2.99	1.50
Development of new products for worldwide market	195	2.63	1.47
Basic research	192	2.38	1.36

Source: Survey of EU subsidiaries in China (1997).

Note
a Measured on a scale from 1 to 5.

(textiles, leather and metal products) and R&D-based industries (computers, pharmaceuticals and scientific instruments) register lower relative expenditures for R&D activities.

The factors mentioned by EU companies to engage in R&D in China are mainly linked with the need for product adaptation and development for the local market (Table 6.9). Almost two-thirds (63 per cent) of the surveyed companies reported that their local R&D activities have as a major target the development of new products for the domestic market. Half of them mentioned that they are engaged in or plan to start R&D activities in China for providing technical services to their production units in China and intend to modify their product standards for its market. One-third of the surveyed companies launched their local R&D activities because of the market growth and the increasing pressure from their competitors. Few companies started R&D activities in China to develop products for other markets. The lower salaries for professional researchers were also not considered as significantly important to undertake local R&D.

Table 6.9 Motives for EU subsidiaries to undertake local R&D activities in China (1996)[a]

Motives	Percentage of companies with positive response
To help develop new products for local market	63.40
Need to provide technical service to local production unit	50.00
To help modify/standardise products for local market	48.70
A large and growing local market where R&D is seen to be crucial	38.80
To match local R&D of competing firms	37.50
To help develop new products for overseas markets	22.40
Favourable salaries for researchers	19.00

Source: Survey of EU subsidiaries in China (1997).

Note
a Several motives may apply for one firm.

Table 6.10 Market orientation of surveyed EU subsidiaries for finished products (1996)

Market orientation	Mean (N = 217)	SD
Sales in China	78.38	
Sales to immediate local market (province or city)	30.35	34.92
Sales to regional markets (neighbouring provinces)	10.43	14.93
Sales to national market	37.61	36.58
Total exports	21.65	
Exports to foreign partner's market	9.53	23.12
Exports to Asian market	6.92	15.38
Exports to North America	1.78	8.35
Exports to other markets	3.41	10.75

Source: Survey of EU subsidiaries in China (1997).

Market orientation

EU subsidiaries are strongly oriented towards the Chinese market, as almost 80 per cent of their finished products find an outlet in the domestic market (Table 6.10). Further analysis shows that about 30 per cent of these products were sold in their immediate local market, that is, in the province and the city where the companies are located. The regional protectionism as well as underdeveloped transportation infrastructure and poor logistic services are probably the major causes for the high market concentration not only of foreign companies, but also Chinese firms.

The foreign companies with the highest proportion of local sales are in food (44 per cent), paper and wood (45 per cent) and automobiles and components (53 per cent). While the high local-market concentration, in the narrow sense, of firms in the food sector is evidently linked to the nature of these consumer

Table 6.11 Destination of sales of semi-finished products by surveyed EU
subsidiaries in China (in percentage) (1996)

	Mean (N = 68)	SD
Sales in China's market	71.66	
Chinese partner's companies in China	23.59	35.38
Foreign parent's companies in China	4.28	17.46
Other companies in China	43.79	41.90
Sales abroad	28.34	
Parent's companies in foreign markets	16.95	29.83
Other unrelated companies in foreign markets	9.67	22.56
Others	1.73	8.43

Source: Survey of EU subsidiaries in China (1997).

products, this reason can hardly explain the high local sales in the automotive
industry. The high geographical concentration of the producers of parts and components for the car assembly firms in clusters in the immediate neighbourhood is
responsible for this phenomenon. Especially, the automotive investments in
Hubei province are closely linked with the production of Citroën cars in Wuhan.

The companies that cover a wider market range, that is, a higher proportion
of sales in the Chinese regional and/or national market, are concentrated in supplying industries, such as electrical (55 per cent as compared to 48 per cent for
the average) and mechanical equipment (56 per cent) engineering and chemicals (52 per cent). The companies that have a higher export ratio, especially to
their European parent companies, are those operating in labour-intensive industries, such as leather (40 per cent as compared to 7 per cent on average) and
textiles (37 per cent).

The market orientation for semi-finished products is relatively different as
compared to that for finished products (Table 6.11). Among the surveyed EU
companies that manufacture semi-finished products (N = 68), one-fourth (in
sales value) sold them to their Chinese partners, 4 per cent to other subsidiaries
of the EU parent companies located in China and 44 per cent to other unrelated
local companies. This means that the EU companies play a relatively important
role in supplying inputs for their Chinese partners' companies. Yet, the linkages
between EU subsidiaries and their European parent companies are rather weak:
only 17 per cent of their products were exported to their parent companies for
further processing and assembly. This shows again that China is considered by
EU companies as a market, rather than an outsourcing basis.

Comparative analysis

First movers versus latecomers

When penetrating a newly opened market, the first movers may be facing
an unfamiliar environment with high investment risks that are related to the

general business environment and the changing regulations. Included in the country-specific risk factors are political risk, uncertainty about the economic and political conditions and government policies (Kobrin 1982; Simon 1982). These factors affect the growth and profitability of a foreign firm's operations in the host country and may even threaten its survival (Agarwal and Ramaswami 1992). Artificial barriers to protect the local industry and market are often reinforced by specific conditions for entering the targeted industry, such as the allowed degree of foreign ownership, the specific administration procedure extended to foreign investors and location requirements (Van Den Bulcke 1988; Contractor 1990; Dunning 1992a,b). For firms entering transition economies by setting up a production facility, the industry-specific risk is strongly associated with market and competitive uncertainties, such as the materials/labour supply (in terms of quality and quantity) and the possible rivalry from state-controlled firms that often benefit from a monopolistic position in the local market/industry or receive particular privileges from the host government.

About two-thirds of the surveyed EU firms were registered in China after 1992. These companies can be considered as latecomers as compared to the companies that entered China earlier, that is, during the 1980s and the early 1990s. Although this distinction may seem to be relatively arbitrary, it has to be recognised that China's investment environment substantially changed after 1992 (see Chapter 2) (Table 6.12).

In 1996 (year of reference), Europe's earliest investors had operated in China for on average about eight years, while the latecomers had less than two years of activity on their record. Although the one-way ANOVA test did not show significant differences between these two groups of enterprises with respect to their ownership, the latecomers registered a higher equity participation in their subsidiaries in China. This reflects not only the more liberal investment environment in China after 1992 but also the changing attitude of European MNEs themselves. The size of subsidiaries operated by early investors is much larger than for the latecomers in terms of assets, sales and employment. However, a large number of new establishments have not yet reached their full operational capacity. The market orientation of these two groups of investors is also significantly different. While the first movers exported 37 per cent of their production, the latecomers have a lower export-to-sales ratio. The widening of the domestic market to foreign companies and the liberalisation of foreign exchange control might have been the most determinant factors for this change (Table 6.13).

On the basis of the geographical orientation of EU subsidiaries within China, the surveyed companies can be split up into two principal locations, that is, either in the coastal or in the inland region. These two regions are quite dissimilar in terms of the level of development, the dominating economic system (i.e. market system and openness), the market size, the productivity and cost of labour. As already explained in Chapter 2, there is an impressive gap between the coastal and inland regions in China, mainly because of substantial differences in their factor endowments and the speed of the economic transition process. Although the inland provinces that are included in this study have

Table 6.12 European MNEs as first movers and latecomers in China: general characteristics (1996)

Characteristics	First movers			Latecomers			One-way ANOVA test	
	N	Mean	SD	N	Mean	SD	F-value	Significance
Length of operation (number of years)	85	7.64	3.60	159	1.84	1.10	351.7123	0.0000
Foreign equity share (%)	80	58.87	23.07	145	62.16	22.77	1.0637	0.3035
Assets (US$ million)	73	179.45	761.65	137	84.47	361.23	1.5015	0.2218
Sales (US$ million)	67	178.86	719.30	120	66.71	310.52	2.1929	0.1404
Number of employees	81	583.84	1,309.26	143	173.31	296.82	12.9284	0.0004
R&D expenditure as percentage of sales	61	6.08	9.26	91	3.59	4.31	4.9704	0.0273
Exports as percentage of sales	67	37.19	37.32	101	20.16	28.94	11.0478	0.0011

Source: Survey of EU subsidiaries in China (1997).

Table 6.13 European multinational subsidiaries as first movers and latecomers in China: specific characteristics (1996)

Characteristics	Number	First movers (%)	Latecomers (%)	Chi-square tests	
				Value	Significance
Location					
Coastal regions	174	77.01	63.69	4.6926	0.0303
Inland region	81	22.99	36.31		
Type of Chinese partner					
State-owned enterprises	162	74.71	57.74	10.8315	0.0285
Collective-owned enterprise	34	8.05	16.07		
Government institution	8	1.15	4.17		
Others	17	2.30	8.93		
No local partner	34	13.79	13.10		
Entry forms					
<24.9	4	3.61	0.66	30.2418	0.0000
25–48.9	65	28.92	26.97		
50	39	31.33	8.55		
51–94	90	20.48	48.03		
95–100	37	15.66	15.79		

Source: Survey of EU subsidiaries in China (1997).

a high level of industrialisation, the dominant share in their industrial output and employment is largely based on SOEs.

Of course, the entry barriers for newcomers are lower because of the initial limited presence of other foreign companies. Yet, the existence of large SOEs that occupy monopolistic positions in a number of supplier industries and some-times their relatively high technological level provide excellent opportunities for foreign MNEs for take-overs and to engage in collaborative strategies in the context of the reform programme of the SOEs. The survey shows that European late-comers are somewhat more geared towards the inland region than the first movers, as 36 per cent of their subsidiaries moved into the inland region as compared to 23 per cent for the former group.

There also are some significant differences between the European early investors and those who came in later with regard to entry form and partner selection. First, European firms that entered the Chinese market before 1992 relied rather heavily on equally owned JVs. About one-third of their subsidiaries established before 1992 were 50:50 JVs as compared to less than one-tenth for the late-comers. Second, the latecomers have a higher preference for majority control in their JVs as compared to the early investors. Nearly half of their subsidiaries in China are majority foreign-owned JVs, while this type of firms accounted for only one-fifth among subsidiaries established before 1992. Third, the early entrants of EU MNEs in China relied more on Chinese SOEs for creating JVs, while the latecomers more often have chosen non-SOEs as their local partners. Three-fourths of local partners of early established EU subsidiaries in China are

SOEs as compared to only about three-fifths (58 per cent) for the latecomers. To a large extent, the rising use of majority-owned JVs and non-state partners by the EU firms reflect the increasing liberalisation of FDI and the wider acceptance of higher foreign ownership in China as was already discussed in previous chapters.

Large versus small- and medium-sized MNEs

The EU parent companies of the surveyed subsidiaries can be divided into two major size groups. The first category includes all companies that are ranked among the top 500 EU companies and/or *Forbes International* top 500 in 1997 (*Forbes Magazine* 1997), while the second group covers the rest of the firms. This latter rest group is somewhat in an arbitrary way labelled as small- and medium-sized MNEs. This is the case at least in comparison with the former group.

The data show that large EU MNEs entered the Chinese market earlier than the SMEs. The former group has on average five years of operation in China, while the SMEs mainly established in the last three years before this survey was conducted. The one-way ANOVA test detected a difference between these two sets of enterprises at a significant level. The relatively abundant resources of large MNEs as well as their vast and rich experience allowed them not only to move rapidly into an uncertain market, but also to carry out high resource commitments in the overseas expansion immediately. The EU subsidiaries established by large EU MNEs are significantly larger than those set up by their small- and medium-sized counterparts.

The subsidiaries of the large MNEs employed on average 646 persons, realised US$ 176 million of sales and controlled US$ 207 million of assets in 1996, while the comparative figures for the group of the small- and medium-sized MNEs are, respectively, 199 persons, US$ 81 million and US$ 83 million (Table 6.14). The large MNEs also have higher equity participations in their subsidiaries as compared to the small and medium ones. This illustrates not only their ability to engage in a higher resource commitment, but also their stronger negotiating position with the Chinese government, which consequently might allow them more control over their operations, especially when investing in highly regulated sectors. The small- and medium-sized companies in general have less influence in such deals. With regard to the market orientation, large MNEs are – somewhat surprisingly – more local-market oriented, as their export-to-sales ratio reached only 22 per cent on average as compared to 29 per cent for the small- and medium-sized companies. The higher export ratio of the small- and medium-sized firms might be explained by a large number of small textile companies in its group, which were established in China mainly for export processing activities. A comparison between the R&D ratio (measured in R&D expenditures to total sales) for these two groups of MNEs did not show significant differences, although large companies have lower R&D expenditures to sales ratio.

Although the comparison of the location patterns between large and small MNEs did not illustrate a significant difference, large firms are likely to be more

Table 6.14 General differences between large and small EU MNEs with subsidiaries in China (1996)

Characteristics	Large MNEs			Small- and medium-sized MNEs			One-way ANOVA	
	N	Mean	SD	N	Mean	SD	F-statistic	P-value
Length of operation (in years)	64	5.00	4.45	181	3.44	3.15	9.2499	0.0026
Foreign equity share (in %)	65	65.42	21.52	166	59.53	23.13	3.1475	0.0774
Assets (US$ million)	55	207.46	575.08	160	83.16	510.96	2.2689	0.1335
Sales (US$ million)	48	176.20	567.09	142	81.26	467.05	1.3253	0.2511
Number of employees	60	646.33	1,484.61	169	199.24	343.07	13.4114	0.0003
R&D expenditures (% of sales)	40	4.02	5.20	115	4.72	7.26	0.3150	0.5755
Exports (% of sales)	45	22.14	26.39	126	28.58	35.40	1.2429	0.2665

Source: Survey of EU subsidiaries in China (1997).

Table 6.15 Some specific differences between large and small EU MNEs with subsidiaries in China (1996)

Characteristics	Number	Large MNEs (%)	Small- and medium-sized MNEs (%)	Chi-square tests	
				Value	Significance
Location					
Coastal region	177	74.29	65.45	1.8344	0.1756
Inland region	84	25.71	34.55		
Type of Chinese partner					
State-owned enterprises	168	77.14	59.69	10.3143	0.0355
Collective-owned enterprise	34	2.86	16.75		
Government institution	8	2.86	3.14		
Others	17	5.71	6.81		
No local partner	34	11.43	13.61		
Degree of ownership					
< 24.9	4	4.62	0.57	14.4396	0.0060
25–48.9	66	12.31	32.95		
50	39	21.54	14.20		
51–94	94	43.08	37.50		
95–100	38	18.46	14.77		

Source: Survey of EU subsidiaries in China (1997).

concentrated in the coastal region. This could be related to their entry patterns, that is, they moved into China during a period when the inland region was not yet receiving priority from the government and consequently did not get sufficient interest from foreign investors previously lured by the attractions in the coastal areas (Table 6.15).

As already mentioned, there is a substantial difference between large and small EU MNEs with regard to their ownership form and partner selection. Large MNEs have a higher propensity to use equally owned and majority-owned JVs, while small- and medium-sized EU MNEs are more involved in the establishment of minority-owned subsidiaries. This preference might be linked to differences in sectoral distribution. Large EU MNEs are more concentrated in the specialised-supplier and scale-intensive industries, in which high resource commitment and efficiency in production organisation are needed. Large MNEs therefore have the capability and strategic motivation to insist on higher ownership and subsequent control. However, because these industries are often highly regulated and controlled by SOEs, the negotiation might often have resulted in a 50:50 JV equilibrium.

The findings of this chapter confirm the impact of the timing factor on patterns and extent of EU subsidiaries in China that were analysed in Chapter 4. The comparative analysis showed significant differences between the European early entrants and latecomers with regard to their entry form, partner selection, location, industrial specialisation, and size of operation and other operating characters. The analysis also revealed the impact of factors that are related to the size and leading position of the European parent companies on the operations of their subsidiaries in China.

7 Managerial issues of EU manufacturing subsidiaries in China

In Chapter 6, operational aspects of EU subsidiaries in China on the basis of their business data were studied. This chapter analyses the managerial characteristics of EU subsidiaries from the point of view of the managers of these companies. The qualitative data that are used were also collected from the questionnaire survey of EU subsidiaries in China carried out in 1997. A number of questions concerning different aspects of management and strategies of MNEs were submitted to the managers of the surveyed companies. These questions specifically concern competition and R&D policy, decision-making authority as well as business confidence. The results reflect mainly the attitudes of the local managers, that is, the Chinese managers, as they were the ones who in the great majority of the responding firms in the sample provided the actual answers. Their opinions on issues such as the competitive position and performance of EU subsidiaries in China will allow for a confrontation with the views of European managers and should be useful for this latter group to evaluate their enterprises from a Chinese perspective.

Competitive position and competitiveness

The managers of the surveyed EU subsidiaries reported that the competition they encountered in China mainly came from their global competitors that are also established in the Chinese market. The competitive pressure from these companies has become much stronger and went from 3.1 to 3.6 on a five-point scale and was expected to intensify even more within the next five years (4.0) (Table 7.1). The cross-section analysis indicated that the large EU companies faced stronger competition from their global rivals than the smaller ones. However, no difference could be detected between the early entrants and the latecomers. As far as the industrial sectors were concerned, the competition from foreign established companies was the strongest for EU subsidiaries in resource-intensive and specialised-supplier industries, especially in food, transport equipment, non-metal minerals, electronics and chemicals.

Neither the Chinese SOEs nor the private enterprises (e.g. mostly TVEs) were regarded as major competitors by the managers of EU subsidiaries, even though the competitive position of these firms has somewhat improved over time. Yet,

Table 7.1 Major competitors of EU subsidiaries in China (1996)

Origin of competition	Experience at beginning of operations			Current assessment (1996)			Future expectation (2001)		
	N	Mean[a]	SD	N	Mean[a]	SD	N	Mean[a]	SD
Foreign competitors established in China	222	3.13	1.46	234	3.62	1.32	238	4.01	1.23
US exporters	178	2.68	1.36	185	2.95	1.39	192	3.14	1.38
EU exporters	180	2.69	1.45	190	2.91	1.37	194	3.16	1.41
Japanese exporters	177	2.65	1.36	186	2.90	1.35	193	3.13	1.38
Chinese SOEs	225	2.52	1.37	228	2.58	1.33	229	2.80	1.35
Private Chinese enterprises	212	2.07	1.30	213	2.43	1.36	216	2.61	1.46
Exporters from other countries	167	2.11	1.15	172	2.28	1.23	177	2.49	1.32

Source: Survey of EU subsidiaries in China (1997).

Note
a Scale from 1 (not at all important) to 5 (very important).

competition from Chinese SOEs and private enterprises was ranked highly by EU subsidiaries operating in labour-intensive and low-technological industries, such as paper, food and textiles. With the ongoing and gradual trade liberalisation in China, foreign exporters – especially those from the United States, European Union and Japan – are likely to become more serious rivals for EU subsidiaries with production activities in China. The competition from western exporters is particularly strong in capital-intensive and high-tech industries, such as electrical appliances, measurement equipment, chemicals, etc. The adhesion of China to the WTO is expected to intensify this type of competition even more. American exporters are likely to become stronger competitors of EU subsidiaries established in China, at least as compared to the Japanese ones.

A number of factors that are related to the quality and adaptability of products, economies of scale and technological level of local production, linkages with European parent company and support of the Chinese authorities were presented to the managers in order to help them with the evaluation of the sources/areas of their competitiveness. The importance of these factors was measured on a five-point scale. Managers of the surveyed subsidiaries considered that their competitive strengths were mainly backed by the quality of their products (4.4 on the five-point scale) and the brands and reputation of their European parent companies (4.1). The adaptability of their products to the local market was put forward as highly relevant (3.9) (Table 7.2). According to the managers, these factors would also affect the competitive position of EU subsidiaries in China in the coming years. On the other hand, factors such as integration in the production network of the parent companies and business information provided from headquarters, were not identified as strong determinants for the competitive advantage of EU subsidiaries in China. These results again confirm that most of the EU subsidiaries in China are strongly oriented to the domestic market and are often operating as stand-alone companies that are loosely integrated into the value-added networks of their European parent companies.

The survey also provided indications that factors related to the production and technology capabilities of the subsidiary – such as R&D capacity and production scale – have become increasingly important for the competitive position of EU enterprises in the Chinese market. The score for these two factors on the five-point scale went up, respectively, from 2.9 and 2.7 at the beginning of their activities in China to 3.1 and 3.2 in 1996 and 3.5 and 3.6, five years hence. The comparative analysis also indicated that economies of scale, local R&D capabilities and efficiency in distribution are of growing importance for the competitiveness of EU subsidiaries in China, at least according to the expectations of their managers. By contrast, factors – such as access to the foreign parent company's financial resources and support by the Chinese authorities – were not expected to have much influence on their competitive position in China in the coming years. These specific characteristics are linked to the Chinese investment environment that has become more and more market oriented. Consequently, factors related to the global competitiveness of firms – especially integrated production networks and technological and innovation capabilities – become

Table 7.2 Sources of competitiveness of EU subsidiaries in China (responses by Chinese managers) (1996)

Sources of competitiveness	Assessment at the beginning of operations			Current assessment (1996)			Future expectation (2001)		
	N	Mean[a]	SD	N	Mean[a]	SD	N	Mean[a]	SD
Related to the characteristics of products (combined)	213	3.95	0.90	220	4.17	0.71	228	4.41	0.66
Quality of products	232	4.21	0.99	240	4.40	0.80	244	4.65	0.65
Product adaptation to local market	214	3.69	1.09	222	3.92	0.92	231	4.15	0.90
Related to the linkages with the parent company (combined)	184	3.25	0.94	194	3.44	0.89	200	3.60	0.90
Brandname or foreign parent company's reputation	219	3.89	1.18	228	4.14	1.00	236	4.26	0.97
Continually updated technology from parent company	214	3.38	1.30	228	3.54	1.28	234	3.70	1.30
Access to foreign parent company's financial resources	216	3.25	1.43	228	3.34	1.35	233	3.36	1.34
Better business information from parent company	213	2.87	1.32	224	3.06	1.26	232	3.28	1.29
Integration of production within the foreign parent company's network	198	2.78	1.34	203	3.05	1.30	210	3.29	1.40
Related to the production capability of the subsidiary (combined)	190	3.08	0.94	193	3.40	0.83	203	3.75	0.85
Efficiency of distribution	206	3.33	1.23	210	3.60	1.10	219	3.92	1.05
High productivity	218	3.31	1.20	228	3.58	1.10	236	3.83	1.12
Economies of scale	219	2.73	1.21	225	3.21	1.13	230	3.64	1.12
Increasing R&D capacity	209	2.89	1.32	218	3.09	1.29	228	3.51	1.29
Support by the Chinese authorities	218	3.18	1.34	224	3.21	1.27	233	3.34	1.28

Source: Survey of EU subsidiaries in China (1997).

Note
a Scale from 1 (not at all important) to 5 (very important).

Table 7.3 Sources and characteristics of competitiveness of EU subsidiaries in China (1996)

Sources of competitiveness	Factors related to the characteristics of products, Mean[a]	Factors related to the linkages with the parent company, Mean[a]	Factors related to the production capability, Mean[a]	Factors related to the support of the Chinese authorities, Mean[a]
Size of the parent company				
Small	4.11[b]	3.36[b]	3.34	3.11[b]
Large	4.32[b]	3.61[b]	3.54	3.47[b]
Size of the subsidiary				
Small	4.10	3.46	3.29	3.11
Large	4.23	3.42	3.48	3.30
Degree of ownership				
Joint venture	4.19	3.39[b]	3.38	3.17
Wholly owned subsidiary	4.21	3.72[b]	3.41	3.21
Year of establishment				
Before 1994	4.12	3.31[b]	3.33	3.10
1994–1996	4.22	3.55[b]	3.46	3.31
Location				
Coastal region	4.16	3.42	3.40	3.19
Inland region	4.19	3.47	3.39	3.25
Industrial specialisation				
Resource-intensive industries	4.15	3.43	3.50	3.13

Labour-intensive industries	3.88	3.56	3.31	2.71
Specialised-supplier industries	4.21	3.49	3.51	3.34
Scale-intensive industries	4.15	3.29	3.27	3.13
R&D-based industries	4.41	3.41	3.19	3.48
Technological level				
Low technology	4.09	3.46	3.38	3.05
High technology	4.20	3.41	3.38	3.25
Intensity of factors				
Labour intensive	4.16	3.45	3.42	3.22
Capital intensive	4.18	3.38	3.33	3.15
Market orientation				
Local-market seekers	4.17	3.35	3.35	3.23
Export oriented	3.97	3.47	3.43	2.97

Source: Survey of EU subsidiaries in China (1997).

Notes
a Scale from 1 (not at all important) to 5 (very important).
b Difference was detected by one-way ANOVA test at 0.05 level.

increasingly relevant for EU subsidiaries. Factors that are related to government interventions (e.g. distribution, political support, etc.) rank rather low as determinants for successfully competing in the Chinese market, however.

It is likely that the competitive advantages of EU subsidiaries would be affected by the size of their European parent companies (Table 7.3). Subsidiaries established by large EU MNEs are apparently more confident about their competitive position in China as compared to those belonging to smaller EU parent companies, at least according to the opinion of their managers. The differences between these two groups of companies are detected by the one-way ANOVA test at the 0.05 level, with regard to factors such as characteristics of products, linkages with the European parent company and support from the Chinese authorities. Although differences between these two categories of EU subsidiaries were also found for their manufacturing capabilities and technological level of the local production units, these was not confirmed by the statistical tests as they were not significant.

The size of the subsidiary itself was not identified as a statistically significant factor affecting the competitive strength of EU subsidiaries in China. Yet, large EU subsidiaries attached more importance to factors such as economies of scale in production and quality of products, while the competitive position of smaller firms was more often backed by the technological and financial support from their parent companies.

The comparison between EU subsidiaries according to their degree of ownership, that is, wholly owned subsidiaries versus JVs, showed some differences in their sources of competitiveness. Linkages with the European parent companies, especially in terms of the integration with the production network of the parent company, the financial support and the continuation of the transfer of technology scored higher for wholly owned EU affiliates than the JVs. Similar differences were found between EU subsidiaries that started their operations in China in an early period and those that could be labelled late arrivals. EU firms that only entered the Chinese market in the mid-1990s attributed more relevance to the linkages with the parent company as a source of their competitiveness, than those subsidiaries that were established in China before 1994.

The comparison of EU subsidiaries operating in the inland region with those located in the coastal area did not reveal significant differences. Yet, the competitiveness of the former group was relatively more related to the support of the Chinese authorities, while the latter group relied more on the linkages with their European parent companies.

While firms operating in different industrial sectors seemed to evaluate their sources of competitiveness differently than others, these findings were not confirmed as significant by the statistical tests. For subsidiaries that were operating in labour-intensive and low-tech industries, such as food, paper, textiles and leather, the efficiency in distribution and the high productivity were considered to be the major sources of competitiveness. By contrast, the firms operating in capital-intensive and high-tech industries (e.g. chemicals), the regular transfer of updated technology from the parent companies are valued more highly. The integration with the production network of parent companies was ranked as very influential in specialised-supplier and R&D-based industries, such as machinery, pharmaceuticals and transport equipment. Yet, differences between companies operating in different industries were likely to be more industry than firm specific. Differences were also observed among subsidiaries with different levels of technology, but this variance was clearly related to the sectoral distribution itself.

The sources of competitiveness of EU subsidiaries in China were also different according to their market orientation. The local-market-oriented firms built up their competitiveness mainly on the basis of quality and local adaptability of their products and the support from the Chinese authorities, while export-oriented firms evidently relied more on the linkages with their parent companies and manufacturing capabilities of the local plants. Yet, statistical tests did not confirm that these differences were significant.

Local R&D activities

One hundred and fifty-one of the surveyed EU subsidiaries provided information about their R&D activities in China. About one-fifth of these companies did not engage in local R&D activities in 1996, while almost one-third (31 per cent) was at the start-up phase of such activities in China. Almost half (45 per cent) of the companies that were active in local R&D attributed less than 5 per cent of their sales revenue to the R&D budget, while more than one-fourth (28 per cent) of them spent between 5 and 10 per cent of their sales to R&D. Only 7 per cent of the surveyed companies used more than 10 per cent of their sales revenue for R&D purposes (Figure 7.1). Almost half (46 per cent) of the managers of these companies expected that their existing R&D expenditures would be maintained at the same level during the next five years, while a similar proportion (47 per cent) intended to increase the relative share of their research efforts. Only 7 per cent of the sampled companies were envisaging a reduction of the R&D expenditures as a percentage of sales.

Firms operating in resource-intensive industries spent on average 5.5 per cent of their sales on R&D activities in 1996. In processing industries such as food, R&D expenditures even reached a level of 7.7 per cent, while the average relative share for all sampled companies was only 4.6 per cent. R&D expenditures as a percentage of sales were only slightly higher in the specialised-supplier industries such as machinery and electrical equipment (5.3 per cent), but were especially high at the beginning of their activity in China (8.1 per cent). Companies operating in these industries typically carry out R&D activities that are necessary to adapt their products to the local market (discussed later). The R&D expenditures as a percentage of sales were relatively low in the scale-intensive and R&D-based industries (respectively, 4.6 and 3.4 per cent). The use of standardised products and process technologies on the one hand and the concentration of R&D in the home countries of the parent companies on the other hand are likely to be the main reasons for this rather paradoxical phenomenon.

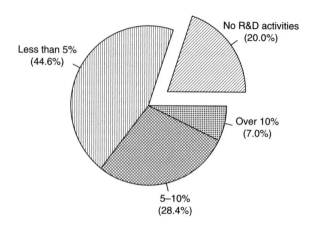

Figure 7.1 R&D expenditures of EU subsidiaries in China (as percentage of sales revenue) (*N* = 151) (1996).

Source: Survey of EU subsidiaries in China (1997).

Differences are observed between large and small companies as well as between early entrants and latemovers. Large firms spent a lower proportion of their sales on R&D as compared to smaller firms, while the early entrants attributed a higher share of their sales to R&D activities than latemovers. However, these differences might be related to the specific industrial patterns rather than the size and the timing of the entry into China of these companies themselves. Therefore, a more detailed and statistical analysis is needed before such a conclusion can be drawn.

The most important R&D activities of EU subsidiaries in China are concerned with the development of new products (4 on a five-point scale) and the adaptation of existing products (3.7) to the local market (Table 7.4). By contrast, the development of products for the worldwide market and basic research programmes received much less priority. While all the companies in the sample reported that the development of new products for the local market was their most important research concern, the other types of R&D have a different significance according to the industrial sector. For instance, the adaptation of existing products constituted a major form of R&D for firms manufacturing electrical appliances (4.1) and transportation equipment (4.2), but was of limited importance for export-processing industries, such as leather (1.0) and textiles (2.3).

The survey also confronted the managers of EU subsidiaries with a question about the key factors that have positively affected and/or will have positive effects on the decision-making of EU companies for establishing local R&D facilities in China (Table 7.5). To develop new products for the local market was mentioned by almost two-thirds of the surveyed managers as the main determinant to invest in local R&D. Other factors, such as the need to provide technical

Table 7.4 R&D activities of EU subsidiaries in China (1996)

	N	Mean[a]	SD
Development of new products for local market	113	4.04	1.04
Adaptation of existing products to local market	107	3.65	1.13
Customer technical service	101	2.96	1.46
Development of new products for worldwide market	105	2.67	1.46
Basic research	105	2.41	1.35

Source: Survey of EU subsidiaries in China (1997).

Note
a Scale from 1 (not at all important) to 5 (very important).

Table 7.5 Motivations of EU subsidiaries for establishing local R&D facilities in China (1996)

Motivations	Number of companies	% in the sample
To help develop new products for local market	147	63.64
Need to provide technical service to local production unit	115	49.78
To help modify/standardise products for local market	113	48.92
A large and growing local market where R&D is seen to be crucial	90	38.96
To match local R&D of competitors	87	37.66
To help develop new products for overseas markets	52	22.51
Low salaries for research personnel	44	19.13

Source: Survey of EU subsidiaries in China (1997).

services to local producers and to modify standardised products to the market conditions, were quoted by about half of the firms as motives for EU companies to set up local research centres or laboratories in China. The survey results also showed that the decision by EU subsidiaries to establish local R&D was neither influenced by the low salaries of the local research staff in China nor by the need to develop products for the worldwide market from China. Yet, the market size and the strategic reaction to the moves of their global rivals were considered by almost two-fifths of the sampled companies as having a positive influence on their decisions to establish local R&D facilities in China.

Autonomy of decision-making

The autonomy of decision-making in EU subsidiaries in China was analysed following the frequently used five-point Likert scale approach: (i) decision is taken by the parent company; (ii) decision taken by parent company after consultation with subsidiary; (iii) the parent company and the subsidiary decide together;

Table 7.6 Decision-making within EU subsidiaries in China (1996)

Decisions	At the beginning of operations			Current assessment (1996)			Future expectation (2001)		
	N	Mean	SD	N	Mean	SD	N	Mean	SD
Financial decisions (combined)	199	2.74	1.26	200	2.99	1.21	204	3.18	1.17
Royalty payments to parent company	216	2.66	1.28	219	2.80	1.30	225	2.92	1.28
Choice of capital investment projects	225	2.62	1.45	233	2.85	1.37	235	3.12	1.37
Target rate of return on investment	224	2.67	1.40	227	2.86	1.37	232	3.06	1.35
Dividend policy	212	2.75	1.33	214	2.87	1.32	222	3.03	1.29
Financing of investment projects	224	2.68	1.44	233	2.95	1.36	235	3.21	1.38
Setting financial targets	233	2.66	1.38	241	3.04	1.28	243	3.25	1.26
Preparation of yearly budget	232	2.84	1.39	241	3.17	1.26	242	3.35	1.28
Sale of fixed assets	224	2.99	1.53	230	3.21	1.44	234	3.38	1.42
Marketing decisions (combined)	173	3.35	1.39	229	3.51	1.26	228	3.79	1.21
Entering export markets	188	2.82	1.66	197	3.03	1.59	200	3.28	1.56
Setting prices for domestic market	193	3.20	1.60	203	3.37	1.51	207	3.68	1.42
Selection of suppliers	226	3.58	1.60	233	3.85	1.42	235	4.10	1.29
Selection of distribution networks in domestic market	221	3.91	1.51	225	4.11	1.34	228	4.27	1.23

	N	Mean	SD	N	Mean	SD	N	Mean	SD
Production decisions (combined)	223	3.27	1.41	179	3.59	1.22	184	3.88	1.15
Introduction of new products	224	3.12	1.52	231	3.39	1.40	232	3.66	1.34
Product range	228	3.24	1.55	235	3.44	1.46	236	3.71	1.40
Output volume	229	3.45	1.49	237	3.68	1.35	236	3.97	1.28
Employment decisions (combined)	224	3.66	1.29	232	3.88	1.13	235	4.06	1.07
Recruitment and remuneration of top management	227	3.29	1.47	235	3.51	1.36	236	3.70	1.33
Recruitment and remuneration of middle management	226	3.75	1.41	234	3.98	1.27	237	4.15	1.20
Recruitment and remuneration of employees	225	3.92	1.44	233	4.13	1.23	236	4.34	1.10
R&D and technology decisions (combined)	213	3.02	1.46	219	3.29	1.33	221	3.51	1.30
R&D planning	219	3.00	1.47	225	3.27	1.35	228	3.50	1.32
Choice of technology	217	3.02	1.55	222	3.28	1.43	223	3.49	1.39

Source: Survey of EU subsidiaries in China (1997).

Notes
The meaning of the five different points on the scale are (1) decision is taken by the parent company; (2) decision taken by parent company after consultation with subsidiary; (3) the parent company and the subsidiary decide together; (4) the subsidiary decides after having asked for the opinion of the parent company; and (5) the subsidiary decides.

(iv) the subsidiary decides after having asked for the opinion of the parent company; and (v) the subsidiary decides.

The major findings about decision-making are summarised in Table 7.6. First, as found in other studies on decision-making in MNEs, the most centralised decisions of EU subsidiaries in China are the financial ones, such as decisions about investment projects, royalty payments and dividend policy. The entry of the export markets of the parent company, R&D planning, budget preparation, pricing policy and choice of technology are also among the more centralised decisions, especially during the start-up stage of the operations of the subsidiary. The employment/personnel and marketing decisions, such as human resource issues (recruitment and remuneration), selection of local distribution channels and suppliers and determination of production volume, are mostly decentralised, as they score highest on the Likert scale. As far as production management is concerned, for example, the introduction of new products, the fixing of production volumes and widening of the product range, these decisions were mostly shared between the management of the subsidiary and the parent company.

Second, there are indications of a general trend in which EU subsidiaries in China are receiving more autonomy of decision-making over time with regard to practically all aspects of management. The domains in which the decision-making process became significantly more decentralised after the start-up of the activities of the subsidiary (i.e. until 1996) were: the setting of financial targets, the preparation of the annual budget and the introduction of new products. By contrast, the decisions about the dividend policy, royalty payments and pricing policy are thought to have become less decentralised during that same period. The surveyed managers reported that they were anticipating a more significant decentralisation in the coming years for setting prices, fixing production volumes and introducing new products. However, the financial decisions in terms of dividend and royalty payment, new investments and sale of existing assets would continue to be tightly controlled by the parent company.

Third, the autonomy of decision-making by EU subsidiaries in China seems to be more decentralised as compared to the results of earlier studies in developed countries (Young et al. 1985). This might be explained by the fact that – contrary to the situation in Europe itself – most EU subsidiaries in China are JVs and that their local partners hold specific assets and advantages with regard to market access, especially at the start-up of the production activities. Yet, other factors – such as the lack of local-market knowledge by the parent company, the unfamiliarity with the Chinese investment environment and the limited integration of the Chinese subsidiaries into the parent company's value-added network – are also at the origin of this more decentralised management system within EU subsidiaries in China.

The characteristics of both the parent company and the subsidiary, such as size, period of entry, ownership, location, industrial specialisation and technological level, generally influence the degree of autonomy in decision making by EU subsidiaries. Table 7.7 reports the differences in the autonomy of decision-making by EU subsidiaries in China according to these different criteria.

Table 7.7 Characteristics of EU subsidiaries in China and decision-making autonomy (1996)

Characteristics	Finance, Mean[a]	Production, Mean[a]	Marketing, Mean[a]	Employment, Mean[a]	R&D and technology, Mean[a]
Size of parent company					
Large	2.85	3.47	3.66	3.94	3.16
Small	3.05	3.53	3.56	3.86	3.34
Size of subsidiary					
Small	3.00	3.55	3.69	3.94	3.39
Large	2.99	3.47	3.50	3.83	3.20
Entry form					
Joint venture	3.09*	3.56*	3.66*	3.90	3.33
Wholly owned subsidiary	2.40*	3.15*	3.21*	3.77	2.99
Location					
Coastal region	2.96	3.48	3.58	4.00*	3.33
Inland region	3.06	3.58	3.60	3.64*	3.19
Year of establishment					
Before 1994	2.95	3.41	3.43	3.85	3.22
1994–1997	3.03	3.60	3.73	3.91	3.35
Industrial specialisation					
Resource-intensive industries	3.09	3.69	3.65	3.89	3.65
Labour-intensive industries	3.21	3.27	3.33	3.62	3.05
Specialised-supplier industries	3.11	3.60	3.74	4.01	3.38
Scale-intensive industries	2.87	3.48	3.63	3.88	3.12
R&D-based industries	2.76	3.36	3.30	3.95	3.17
Technological level					
Low technology	3.01	3.44	3.40	3.70*	3.31
High technology	2.99	3.56	3.70	3.99*	3.29
Intensity of factors					
Labour intensive	3.12	3.56	3.62	3.86	3.38
Capital intensive	2.85	3.47	3.57	3.95	3.18
Market orientation					
Local-market seekers	2.94	3.41	3.53	3.92	3.19
Export oriented	3.00	3.37	3.43	3.64	3.19

Source: Survey of EU subsidiaries in China (1997).

Notes
a Scale from 1 to 5.
* Significant at the 0.05 level.

The decisions in financial management, production and R&D and technology issues were more centralised within the subsidiaries that were established by large EU MNEs, while in the subsidiaries of smaller MNEs, the marketing and employment decisions were relatively more controlled. This particular finding might indicate that large MNEs rely more on financial and technological controls as compared to smaller MNEs to manage their subsidiaries in China. Yet, the statistical analysis did not confirm these differences in a significant degree. Neither does the absolute size of the subsidiary positively influence the degree of autonomy of decision-making within EU subsidiaries in China, although large subsidiaries were slightly more autonomous than the small ones, especially with respect to financial decisions.

The entry mode was identified as a major factor affecting the degree of autonomy in the decision-making process of the surveyed EU subsidiaries in China. Within the wholly owned subsidiaries, the decisions were more centralised as compared to the JVs in practically all management aspects. The differences between these two groups of enterprises were mainly found in the financial, production and marketing areas, as the statistical tests detected a significant difference at the 0.05 level.

As far as the entry period is concerned, the EU subsidiaries that only went into the Chinese market at a later stage – that is, after 1994 – received more autonomy in the decision-making process as compared with those that established in China before that period. An exception was registered for the financial management issues, however. Yet, the statistical test did not confirm that the differences between these two groups of companies were significant. The survey results also indicate that location did not significantly affect the autonomy of decision-making within EU subsidiaries in China. Although the decisions in financial, production and marketing management were more centralised in the firms located in the coastal region, this particular characteristic is supposed to be linked more with the industrial distribution of firms rather than the locational factors of the region as such.

The financial and R&D decisions in the EU subsidiaries operating in scale-intensive and R&D-based sectors were more centralised as compared to firms in other industries. These particular results might be explained by two considerations. First, as firms in scale-intensive industries, such as automobiles and chemicals, are likely to be relatively more integrated into the production network of the parent company, there is a need for more centralised decision-making, especially for managing product integration. Second, firms in R&D-based industries may be under pressure to grant less autonomy about R&D itself and transfer of technology issues, especially in an environment where intellectual propriety is not sufficiently protected and the dangers of the erosion of technological advantages are considered to be quite high.

Operational difficulties

A number of factors were presented to the managers of the surveyed companies in order to find out what they considered to be their major difficulties for operating in China. The issues investigated mainly concerned the business, legal and cultural environment as well as strategic ones, such as local logistics and business services, sourcing and distribution capabilities, patents and trademarks, dealings with the bureaucratic system and conflicts with joint venture partners, etc. As the answers were mostly provided by the Chinese managers who were in charge of the subsidiary, it is possible that certain aspects would have been evaluated somewhat differently by European managers working in China. Yet, the points of view of the Chinese managers should be of interest to anyone interested in FDI issues in China.

Table 7.8 presents the main categories of difficulties and their degree of 'seriousness' as interpreted by the surveyed managers. The most severe problem that EU subsidiaries encountered in China was the complexity of the Chinese bureaucratic system (2.83 on the five-point scale), followed by the underdeveloped stage of logistic systems and business services (2.51), the lack of reliable enterprises for local sourcing and distribution (2.44) and the absence of patent and trademark protection. By contrast, it was reported that disagreements between local partners and EU parent companies with regard to JV strategy were not a major problem. Difficulties arising from the complexity and lack of transparency of the Chinese bureaucratic system as well as from the business environment as a whole are likely to diminish over time. Actually, the survey results showed a decline in the assessment of the difficulties in the near future, that is, 2001.

The comparative analysis of the real and expected difficulties revealed some differences between EU subsidiaries according to their operational characteristics. Small EU subsidiaries complained more frequently about the limited availability and quality of local logistics and business services and the lack of reliable domestic enterprises for sourcing and distribution. More particularly, the unfamiliar business and cultural environment and business ethics were often regarded as problematic. By contrast, large EU subsidiaries were more concerned about the shortcomings of the patent and trademark protection system and the complexity of the Chinese bureaucracy.

With regard to the entry mode, European wholly owned subsidiaries in China were more concerned than EU JVs about problems related to the complexity of the Chinese bureaucracy and the unfamiliar nature of the business and cultural environment. The differences between these two groups of enterprises in their assessment of difficulties in the above-mentioned areas was significant at the 0.05 level. The surveyed managers of JVs only complained slightly more about the local logistics and services for sourcing and distribution, but were more worried about the protection of their technology and the strategic commitment of their local partners.

As a result of the gradual approach in China's regional development policy, the gap between the coastal and inland region has manifested itself not only in terms of the level of economic development, but also with regard to the investment environment. EU firms located in the inland region of China reportedly were more concerned about local sourcing, distribution and services. They also felt more uncertain with the business and socio-cultural environment in the inland provinces, as it had not yet opened up as much as in the coastal region at the time of the survey (Table 7.9).

The EU subsidiaries with long-standing operations in China were less affected by shortcomings in local logistics and services and complications with business and cultural environment as compared to those that were more recently established. The distinction between these two groups of subsidiaries is likely to be

Table 7.8 Major difficulties of EU subsidiaries operating in China (1996)

Difficulties	Beginning of operations			Assessment in 1996			Future expectation (2001)		
	N	Mean[a]	SD	N	Mean[a]	SD	N	Mean[a]	SD
Complexity of Chinese bureaucracy	219	2.87	1.27	225	2.83	1.25	230	2.79	1.30
Underdeveloped local logistics and business services	221	2.62	1.29	226	2.51	1.22	233	2.46	1.26
Lack of reliable local enterprises for sourcing and distribution	216	2.49	1.28	222	2.44	1.22	225	2.44	1.25
Lack of patent/trademark protection	218	2.27	1.37	224	2.29	1.31	228	2.33	1.41
Unfamiliar business environment	217	2.32	1.18	221	2.22	1.12	226	2.15	1.17
Unfamiliar cultural environment and ethics	219	2.26	1.19	222	2.19	1.17	228	2.12	1.17
Disagreement with local partner about joint venture's strategy	207	2.11	1.21	210	2.10	1.20	216	2.11	1.25

Source: Survey of EU subsidiaries in China (1997).

Note
a Scale from 1 (not at all important) to 5 (very important).

Table 7.9 Characteristics of EU subsidiaries and their major difficulties to do business in China (1996) – Mean[a]

	Underdeveloped local logistics and business services	Lack of reliable local enterprises for sourcing and distribution	Lack of patent/trademark protection	Disagreement with local partner about joint venture's strategy	Complexity of Chinese bureaucracy	Unfamiliar business environment	Unfamiliar cultural environment and ethics
Size of subsidiary							
Large	2.49	2.42	2.36	2.11	2.86	2.09	2.10*
Small	2.54	2.47	2.22	2.08	2.79	2.38	2.29*
Entry form							
Joint venture	2.42	2.39	2.27	2.16	2.79*	2.18*	2.16*
Wholly owned subsidiary	2.82	2.54	2.23	1.71	2.93*	2.44*	2.32*
Location							
Coastal regions	2.45	2.40	2.37	2.01	3.01	2.17*	2.11*
Inland region	2.64	2.53	2.14	2.27	2.42	2.33*	2.35*
Year of establishment							
Before 1994	2.44	2.44	2.44	2.19	2.73	2.08	2.04
1994–1997	2.58	2.44	2.16	2.01	2.91	2.35	2.32
Industrial specialisation							
Resource-intensive industries	2.32	2.29	2.11	1.94	2.65	1.92	2.05
Labour-intensive industries	2.10	2.36	2.09	1.64	2.59	1.86	1.76
Specialised-supplier industries	2.45	2.27	2.34	2.18	3.03	2.31	2.22
Scale-intensive industries	2.60	2.59	2.32	2.19	2.68	2.23	2.26
R&D-based industries	2.83	2.45	2.41	2.29	3.05	2.55	2.39

(Continued)

Table 7.9 (Continued)

	Underdeveloped local logistics and business services	Lack of reliable local enterprises for sourcing and distribution	Lack of patent/trademark protection	Disagreement with local partner about joint venture's strategy	Complexity of Chinese bureaucracy	Unfamiliar business environment	Unfamiliar cultural environment and ethics
Technological level							
Low technology	2.29	2.37	2.13	1.89	2.62	2.00*	2.02
High technology	2.56	2.42	2.34	2.18	2.89	2.28*	2.25
Intensity of factors							
Labour intensive	2.37	2.30	2.20	2.00	2.82	2.21	2.14
Capital intensive	2.63	2.54	2.38	2.22	2.78	2.18	2.22
Market orientation							
Local-market seekers	2.59*	2.46	2.46*	2.18*	2.89*	2.19*	2.14
Export oriented	2.03*	2.09	1.92*	1.54*	2.35*	1.83*	1.83

Source: Survey of EU subsidiaries in China (1997).

Notes
a Scale from 1 (not at all important) to 5 (very important).
* Difference was detected by one-way ANOVA test at 0.05 level.

related to the variation in their experience and acquired knowledge about operating in China. Yet, the longer established EU subsidiaries have more complaints about the strategic commitment of their local partners, maybe because they were expecting more involvement from them in the JV agreements.

European Union subsidiaries operating in different industries and with different levels of technology also varied in their concerns about the investment environment in China. Firms operating in scale-intensive and R&D-based sectors complained more about the quality and availability of sourcing, distribution and services provided by local firms. They were also worried more about patent and trademark protection and the complexity of the Chinese bureaucracy. These particular attitudes of EU high-tech enterprises might be linked to their local-market-oriented strategy for which more linkages with local enterprises and domestic market are needed. Compared to EU firms that were involved in export-processing activities in China, EU local-market-oriented subsidiaries in China ran into more problems, especially with regard to local logistics and services, protection of trademarks and patents, strategic agreements with their local partners and relations with the Chinese bureaucracy.

To conclude, the comparative analysis of the managerial dimensions in the EU subsidiaries operating in China provided a number of interesting results with regard to their competitive position, decision-making autonomy, local R&D policy and operating difficulties. The competitiveness of EU subsidiaries was identified as strongly determined by product quality, reputation of the European parent company and adaptability of product to the local market. The survey showed that the major competitors of EU subsidiaries in China were their global rivals who also established production facilities in China. However, with the growing liberalisation under the WTO membership of China, EU subsidiaries believed that the competition from foreign exporters, especially those from Western Europe and the United States, will become stronger in the coming years. Although EU subsidiaries were relatively more present in high-tech industries, their local R&D activities in China were rather limited. The motivations for EU subsidiaries to set up local R&D facilities were basically linked to the necessity for the development or adaptation of products to the local market. The study also demonstrated that significant differences exist across EU subsidiaries according to the type of industry. The EU subsidiaries that were specialised in scale-intensive and R&D-based activities showed less propensity to get involved in local R&D activities, while firms operating in specialized-supplier industries invested more in local engineering and product adaptation. This suggests that China was not yet considered by foreign MNEs as an attractive location for R&D activities, even though the salaries for qualified research personnel are relatively low.

With regard to the autonomy of decision-making within EU subsidiaries, the findings confirm previous studies in other countries suggesting that the most centralised decisions are about financial and strategic issues. The comparative analysis indicated that decision-making became more decentralised over time as a result of the growing knowledge and experience accumulated by local subsidiaries.

However, differences were found according to the ownership structures. JVs were given more autonomy in decision-making as compared to wholly owned subsidiaries, especially in the areas of finance, production and marketing.

The surveyed (Chinese) managers considered as major difficulties for EU subsidiaries to operate in China the complexity of the Chinese bureaucratic system and the limited availability and quality of local services. Yet, subsidiaries were affected in different ways by these problems because of varying degrees of integration with the local market and parent companies. Local-market-oriented firms were more concerned with local sourcing and distribution, while high-tech companies were relatively more dissatisfied by the insufficient protection of their patents and trademarks.

Although this chapter provided a number of useful insights about the management aspects of EU subsidiaries in China, some caveats should be noted. First, the low participation of expatriate managers in the survey did not allow to make a comparison between the views of Chinese and European managers working in the same companies or sectors. Because of differences in the educational and socio-cultural background, the opinions and approaches of these expatriate managers might have been somewhat different, especially for the qualitative questions. Second, this chapter did not carry out a multi-variable analysis that could have shown possible interactions between different operational factors and managerial practices. Despite its limitations, perhaps the most valuable insight of this chapter is the fact that the competitive position of EU subsidiaries in China as well as their operational preoccupations were strongly linked to the structure and performance of the Chinese industries. Given the local-market orientation of EU firms, the availability and quality of the local services for logistics, sourcing and distribution on the one hand and the improvement of the legal system for protecting technology on the other hand are likely to be the most important factors affecting the performance of EU subsidiaries in China.

8 Sourcing strategies of EU multinational subsidiaries in China

Sourcing in this chapter[1] is defined as the procurement[2] of all inputs of the production process or final assembly, that is, raw materials and semi-finished products. The questions that were submitted to the EU subsidiaries in the survey concerned the percentage of the inputs (in value) in their production process from different sources. The section on 'Analytical framework' provides a theoretical framework for assessing the interactions between location- and firm-specific factors and their impact on the sourcing decisions of EU MNEs. The specific characteristics of China as an economy in transition are examined in order to identify regional and sectoral differences in terms of the degree of market imperfections, government interferences and industrial structures. In the section on 'Data and methodology', sourcing patterns of inputs by European subsidiaries in China are analysed according to their operational characteristics, such as age, size, industrial specialisation, level of technology, ownership degree, market orientation and location. The concluding section discusses some theoretical and managerial implications of the empirical findings.

Analytical framework

The increasing liberalisation of markets and the growing importance of intra- and inter-firm collaboration agreements provide MNEs with increased opportunities to reorganise their value-added chain on a worldwide basis for reducing costs, increasing flexibility, sustaining a wider product portfolio and carrying out innovations and technical developments. Sourcing has become a key element in the global corporate strategy of MNEs and consists of a number of basic choices in the management of the flow of components in supplying their cross-border production activities. The sourcing decisions generally involve two fundamental questions, that is, *where* and *how* to source the major components for further processing or final assembly. The first question is related to the 'import or buy local' decision, that is, MNEs can procure components either locally (domestic sourcing) or from abroad (offshore sourcing). The second question is concerned with the choice between 'make or buy', for example, MNEs can either source components from the parent company or other subsidiaries of the group on an intrafirm basis or from independent suppliers on a contractual basis. The first type of

Geographical dimension

		Local	International
Contractual dimension	Intrafirm	S1. From parent and subsidiary companies of local partners (in case of joint venture) S2. From other subsidiary companies of MNE in the host country	S4. From parent and subsidiary companies of MNE in home and other countries
	Interfirm	S3. From local companies in the domestic market	S5. From other companies in the international market

Figure 8.1 Sourcing options of foreign subsidiary in host country.

sourcing is known as in-house sourcing, while the second one is commonly referred to as outsourcing (Swamidass and Kotabe 1992; Beamish *et al.* 1994). In the case of an international JV, the intra-firm sourcing can also include procurement from the parent or subsidiary companies of the local partner. The combination of the above-mentioned spatial and contractual parameters lead to the formulation of the different sourcing modes as presented in Figure 8.1.

Local versus offshore sourcing

The decisions about different locations and modes of supplying production are traditionally considered to be affected by two sets of factors, that is, the location-specific factors (LSFs) and the firm-specific factors (FSFs) (Cavusgil *et al.* 1993). LSFs pertain to the comparative attractiveness of particular locations, while FSFs refer to the competitive advantages of individual firms. The general objective of a global sourcing strategy for an MNE is to exploit both its own competitive advantages and the comparative location advantages of various countries in the global competitive environment (Kotabe 1996).

Firm-specific factors

The choice between local and offshore/import sourcing by MNEs is affected by characteristics such as product and technological orientation and specific inputs (Cavusgil *et al.* 1993). Firms operating in multi-domestic industries may favour an indigenous sourcing system to meet heterogeneous market demands (e.g. food industry), while in the more global industries sourcing may be managed in an integrated manner to take advantage of economies of scale (e.g. automobile industry). Moxon (1982) found that firms operating in labour-intensive industries with standardised manufacturing technology have a higher offshore sourcing intensity than those producing proprietary products with sophisticated technology.

The size of the subsidiary is also supposed to positively influence the outsourcing activities. Larger subsidiaries tend to be more vertically integrated than smaller ones (Halbach 1989). Since supplier relationships involve high-value inputs and operations, they carry a high risk (Earl 1996). As a matter of fact, supply and logistic management failures may lead to a deficient performance by the firm. A large company with a high degree of multinationalisation is supposed to be more inclined than small and domestic enterprises to use offshore sourcing. The period of time the foreign subsidiary has been located in the host country may also have an impact on the sourcing decision. Firms with a long tradition of operating in the host market tend to rely more on local sourcing than newcomers because they are better informed about the strengths and weaknesses of the local companies in terms of quality and timely delivery.

Location-specific factors/host government policy

Location factors are quite relevant for MNEs when they have to decide about where to source for their overseas production activities. Subsidiaries located in a region with less-developed transport infrastructure and communications will import less from abroad than firms located in a region with excellent linkages and communication networks with the rest of the world and have therefore more favourable alternatives for setting up sourcing activities. The proportion of subcontracting carried out by MNE affiliates is therefore likely to be related to both the level and the sophistication of the transport and trade infrastructure of the host country or a particular region in that country.

The extent to which subsidiaries source locally is an important indicator of their integration into the host economy. The host government's policy may be a key influence on the level and pace of local procurement by MNEs along with the size of the domestic market and the country's level of development (Lall 1980). In larger and more advanced developing economies, subsidiaries of MNEs may have forged substantial linkages, often as a result of the government's import restrictions and the imposition of local performance requirements (Dunning 1992a,b). The amount of 'local content' imposed by the host government on the value-creating activities of MNEs depends not only on the level of the indigenous technology and the skills of the local labour force (discussed later), but also on the industrial policy and development strategy of the host country.

Host governments that pursue export promotion rather than import-substituting policies usually impose no or fewer controls on the sourcing policies of the foreign affiliates established on their territory. These governments are aware of the fact that, unless such firms are free to acquire their intermediate products on the best possible terms, their ability to export will be adversely affected. Previous studies on the linkages established by foreign-owned firms in export-oriented manufacturing industries have shown that local sourcing by foreign subsidiaries in these latter sectors occurred generally less frequently than in the case of import-substituting affiliates (Reuber *et al.* 1973).

Import-substituting subsidiaries were found to generate considerably more inter-industry linkages than export-oriented ones at the local level. In some instances, local content as a percentage of the production value of foreign subsidiaries declined as companies moved from exclusive production for the local market to production for export markets (Urata 1995). However, affiliates that evolved from import-substituting ventures into international exporters were likely to establish more linkages with local subcontractors than those that were set up to service foreign markets shortly after their location in the host country.

The role of compulsory sourcing by MNEs imposed by the host government in the context of export-generating as well as import-substituting policies is strongly industry specific. For instance, in some of the most global industries, such as the automotive sector and telecommunications, the sourcing strategies of MNEs might be strongly conditioned by national regulations. In these specific sectors the market has become extremely global, meaning that technological progress has reduced the costs of international transactions; that cross-border flows of goods and money have expanded enormously and that national markets became more strongly integrated with the world economy. Yet, these particular markets remain primarily ruled by national measures: that is, the so-called 'localisation' of 'global' firms. The sourcing patterns of MNEs operating in these sectors are not only based on their global reach, but also depend on the explicit or implicit constraints of both home country and host country regulations and their interaction. In an emerging transitional economy such as China these influences may be very strong.

In-house sourcing versus outsourcing

The internalisation theory of FDI offers a substantial explanation for intra-firm sourcing by MNEs (Buckley and Casson 1976, 1985). The 'internalisation' of component procurement is considered as one important 'raison d'être' of international production. The sourcing by subsidiaries belonging to worldwide MNEs reduces production and transaction costs and assures price stability and high-quality procurement. Certain studies found that the intra-firm sourcing from overseas subsidiaries was strongly associated with the global market performance of American and Japanese MNEs (Swamidass 1993; Nishiguchi 1994) and their competitive position in particular industries and regions (Borrus 1996).

Firm-specific factors

Whether and to what extent a firm should outsource its components is usually a function of two key determinants: that is, the nature of the technology and the product/process specification requirements of the product in question (Alexander and Young 1996). Emerging technologies that have a promising future should be nurtured in-house. In general, labour-intensive, low-technology components are routinely outsourced to external suppliers, while patented, high-technology production inputs are mostly produced internally. A company's sourcing strategy is highly related with technological and cost issues. The outsourcing of non-core activities, that is, standardised production and low-value-added activities, may allow a company to focus more on the development of its competitive advantages and become a driving force for growth and renewal (Cronk and Sharp 1995). However, outsourcing also carries the risk that internal skills and tacit knowledge available within the firm may be lost and the company will gradually become extremely dependent on its suppliers.

Initially, the intra-firm sourcing, that is, the vertical integration, was often a response to the lack of appropriate local supply channels. As a result the subsidiary relied upon the parent company or other subsidiaries of the group to source value-creating activities. The benefits of such a sourcing strategy include: cost reduction through economies of scale, lower transaction costs, better control over price and quality of the supplies, protection of knowledge, etc. (Jennings 1996). However, in-house arrangements may reduce flexibility by eliminating opportunities to tap different suppliers. Also, it may be difficult to reach the minimum volume required to exploit potential economies of scale, especially for small MNEs that are at the 'stand-alone' stage of their internationalisation. On the other hand, the foreign investments carried out by small- and medium-sized companies are less likely to be driven by the desire to exploit their ownership-specific advantages through internalisation of sourcing than by LSAs such as low labour costs and abundant resources.

Empirical studies have also indicated that to build up in-house sourcing facilities requires large investments, and that especially firms with strong market positions tend to prefer vertical integration (Buzzell 1983). Intra-firm sourcing can also be used by MNEs for strategic and financial purposes. Some intermediate products will be acquired either on the open market at world prices or bought from external subcontractors at negotiated prices. Other products or components may be supplied or procured by the parent company or one of its affiliates. Such purchases are particularly likely to occur in the case of idiosyncratic inputs, where: foreign suppliers have a unique competitive advantage; the parent company can monitor quality and prices; marginal costs are less than average costs; economies for bulk purchases are available; and a parent company may want to use its intra-group transactions to engage in transfer pricing transactions.

Location-specific factors/host government policy

For the 'make or buy' decision, the location factor plays a central role. As already indicated, firms located in an area with insufficiently developed supplier capabilities will buy less from outside, while firms located in a region with excellent support and infrastructural facilities will rely more on outsourcing. Subcontracting as a percentage of the total activity of MNE subsidiaries is positively related both to the sophistication of the industrial infrastructure of the host country and the length of time they have been active in that market.

The 'local content' requirement by the host government is not necessarily beneficial to the domestically owned firms themselves but might favour other foreign subsidiaries located in the host economy. In other words, over time, MNEs may tend to replicate their long-standing networks of suppliers from the home economy in the host country. The follow-up investment by suppliers of MNEs in the host economy may also have a greater potential positive effect on the development of local entrepreneurs. These former enterprises occupy relatively low-technology niches in which local enterprises might be more easily integrated into (Ravenhill 1996).

Data and methodology

The sample with data about input sourcing covers 245 enterprises originating from Germany (73), France (46), the United Kingdom (34), the Netherlands (15), Italy (12) and other EU countries (65). These subsidiaries produce mainly chemicals and allied products (24 per cent), electric and electronic equipment (18 per cent), machinery and fabricated metals (13 per cent), food and kindred products (10 per cent) and transportation equipment (10 per cent).

Following the geographical and contractual dimensions presented in Figure 8.1, procurement sources are divided into local (S1 + S2 + S3) and international offshore (S4 + S5) sourcing on the one hand, and in-house (S1 + S2 + S4) and outsourcing (S3 + S5) on the other hand. The different sourcing configurations in the matrix of Figure 8.1 include the local market (S3), the international market (S5), the parent companies and subsidiaries of both the foreign investor (S2 + S4) and in the case of JVs those of the local partner (S1). All these dependent variables and their combinations are measured in percentages of the total sourcing value.

Based on the findings of previous studies and the specific characteristics of the Chinese economy, several independent variables that might be relevant to the sourcing strategy of European subsidiaries in China are proposed. The FSFs that are taken into account are the size of the firm (measured by the number of employees), the number of years the subsidiary has been in operation, the industrial specialisation, the ownership degree, the type of local partner, the export orientation (measured by the ratio of exports to total sales) and the technological level. A more detailed explanation of a number of these variables is given below, even though some have already been explained in previous chapters.

The foreign share in the total equity capital is used to measure the ownership control by MNEs in their subsidiaries and to classify them into minority-owned JVs (25–49 per cent), equally owned JVs (50 per cent), majority-owned JVs (51–94 per cent) and WOFEs (95–100 per cent). The study also introduces the ownership nature of the Chinese partner as an independent variable. The major types of corporate ownership in China include SOEs, collective enterprises (including the recently emerged private businesses), government institutions with foreign-business-related activities, and other new corporate forms such as shareholding companies. Within the specific economic and business environment in China, these companies have followed varying development paths and have acquired different characteristics with regard to their FSAs, such as their intra- and inter-firm relations for the supply, production and distribution, their market position and their relationship with the national and local government (Boisot and Child 1996; Zhang and Van Den Bulcke 1996). As SOEs and non-SOEs are quite dissimilar in terms of organisation and operation, the ownership nature of local partner enterprises is supposed to affect the sourcing patterns of their JVs with foreign companies.

The industrial specialisation and the technological level of European manufacturing companies in China are also classified into five groups on the basis of the method developed by OECD. Resource-intensive industries include: food, beverages and tobacco; wood products; petroleum refining; non-metallic mineral products and non-ferrous metals. The labour-intensive industries cover textiles, apparel and leather; fabrication of metal products and other manufacturing. The specialised-supplier industries consist of non-electrical machinery, electrical machinery and communication equipment and semiconductors. The scale-intensive industries include paper and printing, chemicals (excl. drugs, rubber and plastics), iron and steel, shipbuilding, motor vehicles and other transportation, while the R&D-based industries are composed of aerospace, computers, pharmaceuticals and scientific instruments. In order to measure the technological level of the product/process, a four-digit SIC classification is used to put the surveyed companies into four groups on the basis of the intensity of the respective production factors (Dunning 1979; Lee 1983; Schroath *et al.* 1993).

The surveyed companies are divided into two groups according to their location, that is, either in the coastal or in the inland region. The difference between these two regions will be assessed in terms of the level of development, the dominating economic system (i.e. market system and openness), the local-market size, the productivity and cost of labour.

The results of the survey are presented in two parts. First, a statistical description of the sourcing patterns of EU subsidiaries in China is given. Firm and location factors, which might be relevant for the different sourcing strategies, that is, local versus offshore procurement as well as in-house versus outsourcing, are discussed. A one-way ANOVA test is used to check for differences among firms in their procurement policies. Second, a regression analysis is carried out to identify and measure the importance of the different factors that might determine the sourcing patterns of European manufacturing subsidiaries in China.

Descriptive analysis

Local versus offshore sourcing

Table 8.1 illustrates the importance of local and offshore sourcing in the supply chain of European invested enterprises in China. On average, the locally

Table 8.1 Local versus offshore sourcing (percentage of inputs) (1996)

Firm characteristics	No. of companies	Local sourcing						Offshore sourcing					
		Total (S1 + S2 + S3)		In-house (S1 + S2)		Market (S3)		Total (S4 + S5)		In-house (S4)		Market (S5)	
		Mean	SD	Mean	SD	Mean	SD	Mean	SD	Mean	SD	Mean	SD
Period of starting operation													
1980–1993	86	59.30	38.59	18.60	30.18	40.70	38.68	39.49	38.42	24.07	34.83	15.41	27.72
1994–1997	148	60.91	36.30	20.82	32.09	40.09	39.17	37.02	36.41	28.29	35.66	8.73	18.02
F-statistic (p-value)		0.10	(0.75)	0.27	(0.60)	0.01	(0.91)	0.24	(0.63)	0.77	(0.38)	4.98	(0.03)*
Size (number of employees)													
<50	69	65.22	38.13	21.12	33.27	44.10	40.04	32.80	38.35	27.86	37.55	4.94	12.82
50–99	49	54.65	34.31	20.76	32.45	33.90	35.83	41.88	35.72	30.03	36.92	11.85	22.18
100–499	71	65.42	36.28	19.11	31.41	46.31	38.82	33.41	35.69	19.99	30.11	13.41	25.25
500 and over	31	52.34	32.66	20.46	26.54	31.88	33.77	47.34	32.17	23.24	29.35	24.10	30.64
F-statistic (p-value)		1.78	(0.15)	0.05	(0.98)	1.79	(0.15)	1.69	(0.17)	1.06	(0.37)	5.43	(0.00)***
Industrial specialisation													
Resource-intensive industries	43	77.33	27.41	24.00	35.80	53.33	39.43	21.84	26.88	8.95	17.00	12.89	24.71
Labour-intensive industries	26	55.50	42.74	11.96	27.20	43.54	41.62	42.96	43.62	28.62	41.40	14.35	29.30
Specialised-supplier industries	68	53.57	36.35	21.53	29.31	32.04	36.06	43.22	37.17	31.51	35.11	11.71	24.76
Scale-intensive industries	76	63.39	35.19	21.32	32.91	42.07	38.88	35.24	34.75	24.76	33.74	10.48	19.71
R&D-based industries	28	59.27	42.53	23.12	36.74	36.15	38.40	39.66	42.67	33.19	42.14	6.47	10.84
F-statistic (p-value)		3.14	(0.02)**	0.63	(0.64)	2.18	(0.07)*	2.62	(0.04)**	3.52	(0.01)**	0.52	(0.72)
Technological level													
Labour intensive and low technology (LI-LT)	64	66.97	37.20	20.11	33.00	46.86	40.90	31.33	36.59	19.48	32.54	11.84	23.62
Labour intensive and high technology (LI-HT)	73	53.88	36.19	21.70	28.94	32.18	35.95	42.73	37.03	31.41	35.32	11.32	24.02
Capital intensive and low technology (KI-LT)	14	65.14	33.62	9.00	24.65	56.14	36.52	31.16	34.83	16.21	30.69	14.95	24.04

Capital intensive and high technology (KI-HT)	90	63.97	36.84	23.09	35.30	40.88	38.94	35.82	36.74	25.74	35.51	10.08	20.39
F-statistic (p-value)		1.71	(0.17)	0.80	(0.50)	2.49	(0.06)*	1.23	(0.30)	1.70	(0.17)	0.22	(0.88)
Ownership degree													
25–49	49	70.61	32.12	26.39	32.95	44.22	39.18	29.39	32.12	20.63	29.86	8.76	15.46
50	32	63.39	37.15	27.36	31.46	36.03	36.40	36.52	37.22	28.28	35.99	8.23	22.93
51–94	95	59.89	36.00	20.54	33.57	39.35	37.90	37.87	36.18	24.76	33.97	13.11	23.28
95–100	41	53.95	38.17	11.10	24.89	42.85	40.14	43.12	38.91	29.63	38.02	13.49	25.09
F-statistic (p-value)		1.76	(0.16)	2.25	(0.08)*	0.38	(0.77)	1.14	(0.33)	0.61	(0.61)	0.76	(0.52)
Type of local partner													
State-owned enterprises	157	63.20	35.89	23.54	32.80	39.66	37.75	35.03	35.93	23.75	32.94	11.27	23.03
Collective-owned enterprises	36	71.50	33.81	22.47	36.18	49.03	41.60	28.50	33.81	22.33	33.83	6.17	13.38
Government institution	9	32.11	35.07	17.11	35.14	15.00	23.72	67.89	35.07	51.67	40.16	16.22	20.21
Others	22	48.00	36.97	13.91	22.92	34.09	38.87	45.64	39.02	33.82	38.96	11.82	23.28
F-statistic (p-value)		4.15	(0.01)**	0.63	(0.59)	2.14	(0.10)	3.45	(0.02)**	2.46	(0.06)*	0.77	(0.51)
Location													
Coastal region	160	58.02	36.41	14.06	26.15	43.96	38.58	40.43	36.33	25.69	33.77	14.74	25.73
Inland region	85	67.01	37.16	33.65	38.06	33.37	38.14	30.88	37.34	26.44	37.23	4.45	11.35
F-statistic (p-value)		3.34	(0.07)*	22.45	(0.00)***	4.22	(0.04)**	3.76	(0.05)*	0.03	(0.87)	12.30	(0.00)***
Export ratio (as percentage of sales)													
No exports	55	57.23	36.37	18.26	28.00	38.96	38.25	40.06	36.98	31.81	36.70	8.25	18.83
1–29%	50	66.51	30.25	20.27	29.06	46.24	37.46	32.89	30.22	23.91	29.50	8.98	11.47
30–49%	25	68.04	27.95	21.84	31.89	46.20	29.31	29.36	28.14	13.92	23.69	15.44	22.84
50% and more	39	52.23	40.42	18.33	28.22	33.90	39.03	47.65	40.53	29.26	37.37	18.39	33.53
F-statistic (p-value)		1.81	(0.15)	0.12	(0.95)	1.03	(0.38)	1.93	(0.13)	1.85	(0.14)	2.12	(0.10)

Source: Survey of EU subsidiaries in China (1997).

Note
*$p < 0.10$; **$p < 0.05$; ***$p < 0.01$.

procured inputs (S1 + S2 + S3) accounted for 61 per cent of the total sourcing of these companies in 1996, while the offshore procurement (S4 + S5) had a share of about 37 per cent.[3] The factor analysis provides several interesting insights into the spatial configuration of the sourcing activities of European subsidiaries in China.

First, contrary to the findings of some previous studies, the number of years the subsidiary has been active in China, that is, the length of operation, does not have a significant positive impact on the local sourcing activities of the surveyed companies. The subsidiaries with a longer production experience in China sourced nearly the same proportion (59 per cent) of their inputs locally than the latecomers. However, this specific finding may be partly explained by the fact that most of the European subsidiaries (61 per cent) in the survey started their operation more or less within the same timespan, as the length of their manufacturing presence in China averaged less than four years. During such a short period of time, companies may neither have been able nor been willing to build up a local sourcing channel/network either by outsourcing from local firms or by developing in-house sourcing facilities, especially in a new and unfamiliar business environment such as China. However, the companies with a longer production record in China apparently rely more on offshore sourcing, especially from non-affiliated foreign companies (S5). The statistical test (one-way ANOVA) found differences at the 0.05 level of significance. The higher percentage for offshore procurements by companies with a longer operation in China may be related to their stronger presence in the coastal region (71 per cent as compared to 62 per cent for the second group). The LSFs of the coastal region, especially with regard to their more open economic structure, better transport facilities and infrastructure and more advanced market economic system are likely to have affected the sourcing strategies of the EU subsidiaries in China in a positive way.

Second, as far as firm size is concerned, the larger subsidiaries show a higher propensity to source from abroad (S4 + S5) than the smaller ones. Those with more than 500 employees procure 47 per cent of their components from offshore operations, while the relative proportion for firms with less than 50 employees was only 32 per cent. The difference between large and small subsidiaries in offshore sourcing is particularly significant with regard to their procurement from unaffiliated companies (S5). The larger companies more frequently opted for global sourcing than the smaller ones for their production activity in China. Yet, although the size of the company was positively related to the percentage of offshore sourcing, other factors – such as the location of the production site and the industrial specialisation of the firm – could also have important effects on the sourcing policy.

Third, firms operating in the so-called resource-intensive industries, for example, food, beverages and tobacco, wood, non-metallic minerals and non-ferrous metals, strongly relied on local sourcing (77 per cent). Subsidiaries in the specialised-supplier industries (such as non-electrical and electrical machinery, communication equipment and semiconductors) and labour-intensive processing manufacturing (such as textiles, apparel and leather, metal products) sourced relatively more from abroad (about 43 per cent as compared to 22 per cent in the resource-intensive industries). The high percentage of offshore sourcing by this latter group is due to the high intra-firm flows of inputs from MNE groups (S4) to their subsidiaries in China (discussed later).

The analysis shows that firms with a lower level of technology achieve a higher procurement from the local market (S3) (respectively, 47 and 56 per cent), while the high-tech companies rely more on their foreign parent companies (S4) to source components and semi-finished products (31 and 26 per cent). Yet, the statistical evidence of this particular feature is not significant given the statistical tests in Table 8.2. Normally, MNEs are more hesitant to outsource high-tech products because of the risk of loss of proprietary know-how and competitiveness (discussed later). At the same time, these companies experience more difficulties to find suitable inputs to supply their production from the local market because of the lower production quality of the local supplying firms (De Bruijn and Jia 1993, 1994). Certain strategic and financial reasons might also explain the higher percentage of international procurement by high-tech enterprises. For instance, high intra-firm sourcing by certain pharmaceutical MNEs in China allows these companies to apply favourable transfer prices in order to compensate for the erosion of their technology and to avoid difficulties with the repatriation of profits (Van Den Bulcke, Zhang and Li 1999).

Fourth, the ownership degree of MNEs in their subsidiaries is negatively related to the proportion of local procurement. Although the statistical test is not significant, it is worth mentioning that firms with relatively low foreign equity participations, for example, minority JVs, rely more on local sourcing (71 per cent) than majority or wholly owned subsidiaries (respectively, 60 and 50 per cent). Apparently, the ownership status of the Chinese partners also to some extent affects the sourcing policy of European subsidiaries in China. JVs with non-SOEs, that is, collective ones, rely more on local sourcing (71 per cent), while the JVs with government institutions (mostly foreign-business-related offices) procure a high percentage of inputs from abroad (68 per cent). The high local procurement, especially from domestic companies (S3), by JVs of European firms with non-SOEs might be linked to their concentration in the smaller-sized categories, meaning that as small firms they have less possibilities to source from abroad. Also, the limitations of the operating scale and scope of their Chinese partners does not always allow them to procure locally from in-house sources, as most of their Chinese partners are stand-alone companies. For these companies, the access to state controlled raw materials and scarce resources may be quite restricted. As far as JVs with government institutions are concerned, a more detailed analysis indicates that they are mostly active in specialised-supply industries (44 per cent as compared to the average of 29 per cent). MNEs establishing JVs with Chinese government institutions seem to be strongly motivated by their export-led investment strategy, that is, they invested in China to promote the sales of products from the parent company into China. Because the procurement from the parent companies and/or other subsidiaries in these industries is

Table 8.2 In-house sourcing versus outsourcing (percentage of inputs) (1996)

Firm characteristics	No. of companies	In-house sourcing				Outsourcing			
		Total (S1 + S2 + S4)		Chinese partner (S1)		Foreign partner (S2 + S4)		Total (S3 + S5)	
		Mean	SD	Mean	SD	Mean	SD	Mean	SD
Period of starting operation									
1980–1993	86	42.67	41.56	14.11	26.39	28.56	36.41	56.11	41.32
1994–1997	148	49.11	41.26	16.68	28.50	32.44	35.90	48.82	41.50
F-statistic (*p*-value)		1.32	(0.25)	0.47	(0.50)	0.63	(0.43)	1.68	(0.20)
Size (number of employees)									
<50	69	48.97	41.26	16.42	29.50	32.55	38.39	49.04	40.86
50–99	49	50.79	41.78	18.41	30.68	32.38	35.93	45.74	42.09
100–499	71	39.10	39.61	14.15	26.26	24.94	31.83	59.72	39.62
500 and over	31	43.70	39.97	13.08	22.55	30.62	33.78	55.98	40.36
F-statistic (*p*-value)		1.05	(0.37)	0.33	(0.80)	0.68	(0.56)	1.44	(0.23)
Industrial specialisation									
Resource-intensive industries	43	32.95	39.64	20.98	32.41	11.98	18.25	66.22	39.72
Labour-intensive industries	26	40.58	44.88	10.42	26.48	30.15	42.73	57.88	44.12
Specialised-supplier industries	68	53.04	40.16	16.51	25.81	36.53	35.68	43.75	40.63
Scale-intensive industries	76	46.09	41.22	16.26	28.42	29.82	34.89	52.55	41.34
R&D-based industries	28	56.31	40.50	13.16	27.88	43.15	41.76	42.62	40.18
F-statistic (*p*-value)		2.15	(0.08)*	0.66	(0.62)	4.52	(0.00)***	2.48	(0.04)**
Technological level									
Labour intensive and low technology (LL-LT)	64	39.59	41.65	18.08	31.15	21.52	33.18	58.70	41.88
Labour intensive and high technology (LL-HT)	73	53.11	39.86	16.89	25.73	36.22	35.80	43.49	40.18

Capital intensive and low technology (KI-LT)	14	25.21	38.70	6.14	16.43	19.07	31.12	71.09	37.73
Capital intensive and high technology (KI-HT)	90	48.82	41.65	15.83	29.22	33.00	36.85	50.96	41.78
F-statistic (p-value)		2.60	(0.05)*	0.71	(0.55)	2.65	(0.05)*	2.63	(0.05)*
Ownership degree									
25–49	49	47.02	40.39	22.00	28.88	25.02	29.46	52.98	40.39
50	32	55.64	40.76	24.16	29.44	31.48	36.77	44.27	40.76
51–94	95	45.30	40.66	14.47	28.33	30.83	35.86	52.46	41.36
95–100	41	40.73	43.15	7.07	21.24	33.66	38.65	56.34	42.62
F-statistic (p-value)		0.83	(0.48)	3.26	(0.02)**	0.51	(0.68)	0.54	(0.66)
Type of local partner									
State-owned enterprises	157	47.29	40.08	18.27	29.36	29.02	34.64	50.94	40.08
Collective-owned enterprises	36	44.81	43.75	16.83	29.00	27.97	35.11	55.19	43.75
Government institution	9	68.78	39.54	12.22	24.38	56.56	36.05	31.22	39.54
Others	22	47.73	42.61	8.68	19.03	39.05	37.97	45.91	43.14
F-statistic (p-value)		0.86	(0.46)	0.82	(0.48)	2.23	(0.09)*	0.92	(0.43)
Location									
Coastal region	160	39.75	40.24	9.41	20.80	30.34	35.62	58.69	40.46
Inland region	85	60.08	40.12	28.40	34.83	31.68	36.58	37.81	39.96
F-statistic (p-value)		14.21	(0.00)***	28.50	(0.00)***	0.08	(0.78)	14.91	(0.00)***
Export ratio (as per cent of sales)									
No exports	55	50.07	41.28	12.47	20.85	37.60	38.62	47.22	41.21
1–29%	50	44.17	37.23	16.05	25.22	28.13	28.83	55.23	37.24
30–49%	25	35.76	35.70	14.44	26.96	21.32	28.45	61.64	35.99
50%	39	47.59	43.82	16.79	27.99	30.79	38.45	52.29	43.83
F-statistic (p-value)		0.79	(0.50)	0.29	(0.83)	1.44	(0.23)	0.83	(0.48)

Source: Survey of EU subsidiaries in China (1997).

Note
*p < 0.10; **p < 0.05; ***p < 0.01.

a crucial objective for these subsidiaries, their purchases from foreign affiliated companies accounted for 52 per cent of their total sourcing, while the average for the total sample was only half as high (26 per cent).

Fifth, the location of European manufacturing subsidiaries in China apparently has a significant impact on their sourcing patterns. Not surprisingly, firms located in the inland region have a higher percentage of local inputs (67 per cent) (S1 + S2 + S3) than those based in the coastal region (58 per cent). Although, at a low level, the latter group of firms relied more strongly on foreign sources (15 per cent) for supplying their production activities in China as compared to the former group (only 4 per cent). The differences between firms that operated in the inland region and the coastal provinces is related to LSFs (Table 8.2). Firms located in the inland areas of the country are undoubtedly confronted with more physical and other constraints to source from abroad. As a result, they may turn to their Chinese partners (mostly SOEs) to supply components or semi-finished products. This is illustrated by the high percentage of the inland subsidiaries with in-house sourcing of 34 per cent (S1 + S2) as compared to 14 per cent in the 'coastal companies'. The higher overhead costs, linked with inefficient communication systems, the inappropriate transport infrastructure and less-effective public services in the inland region as compared to the coastal area, mean that these enterprises might have dropped the offshore sourcing option. Subsidiaries located in the coastal region clearly benefit from a more open economic and better trade system and transport infrastructure which makes them more intensely integrated into the international sourcing systems of MNEs.

Sixth, although export-oriented enterprises in the survey (i.e. with an export ratio of 50 per cent or more) seemed to prefer offshore sourcing (48 per cent) more than local-market seekers (i.e. with no exports or a low export ratio), the strong links that were found in most of the previous studies on sourcing were confirmed (Reuber *et al.* 1973; Urata 1995). The absence of a significant statistical link between the export ratio and the proportion of outsourcing activities may be explained by the fact that 30 per cent of the sampled companies have a high percentage of overseas procurement without any export activities. These so-called export-led market seekers achieved a high sourcing of inputs from abroad, but were rarely involved into export activities.

In-house sourcing versus outsourcing

On average in-house sourcing (S1 + S2 + S4) accounted for almost half (47 per cent) of the total component and semi-finished products procurement of European manufacturing subsidiaries in China in 1996. Thirty-one per cent of this intra-firm sourcing originated from the European parent companies or from their subsidiaries abroad (26 per cent) (S4) and/or those located in China (5 per cent) (S2), while the rest (16 per cent) was acquired from the parent and subsidiary companies of their Chinese partners (S1). Outsourcing as an alternative to in-house purchases represented on average 52 per cent of the total sourcing of the surveyed companies, of which 40 per cent was locally procured. Table 8.2 provides some statistical tests of the in-house procurement and outsourcing of European manufacturing subsidiaries in China.

The in-house procurement was slightly higher for newly established companies (49 per cent) than for those with several years of activity in China (43 per cent). The lower level of in-house sourcing from both the foreign and Chinese group, resulted from (or lead to) a rise of outsourcing, especially from the international market. This tendency might again be related to location factors, as early movers (i.e. companies with a longer tradition in China) were mostly located in the coastal region, which offers easier access to international suppliers.

Although the size of the firm had no significant impact on the in-house sourcing pattern of European subsidiaries in China, the analysis on the basis of industrial specialisation provided some interesting results. First, the companies specialised in R&D-based industries, such as aerospace, pharmaceuticals and scientific instruments, registered a high percentage of intra-firm sourcing of inputs (56 per cent), of which a dominant part was procured by their European parent companies (43 per cent). The intra-firm sourcing linkage was also strongly significant in the so-called specialised-supplier industries as the European parent companies in these sectors sourced on average 37 per cent of the inputs from their Chinese subsidiaries in-house, while the relative percentage for all companies of the survey reached only 26 per cent. Second, the intra-firm sourcing from the Chinese parent companies was relatively higher in the firms operating in resource-intensive industries, which might be related to the monopolistic position of many SOEs and their privileged access to natural resources.

With respect to the level of technology, high-tech firms (intensive in labour as well as in capital) tended to use internal sourcing relatively more (53 and 49 per cent), especially from the European parent companies. Firms with a low level of technology sourced out inputs (respectively, 59 and 71 per cent) in both labour- and capital-intensive industries. The statistical test found a difference at the 0.05 level of significance. The more advanced the subsidiary's product or technology, the higher the company's import content.

As mentioned earlier, the ownership by European MNEs of their subsidiaries in China was negatively linked to the relative importance of local procurement. The high local procurement by minority JVs was strongly related to the in-house sourcing from the Chinese partners. However, this specific feature might be due to the high concentration of these enterprises in the inland region (32 per cent as compared to 18 per cent in the coastal region), where other sources of inputs were less readily available.

In fact, the location characteristics of the Chinese inland and coastal region clearly demonstrate their impact on the sourcing strategies of European MNEs in China. The in-house sourcing from the Chinese partners' affiliated companies (S2) was three times higher in the inland region than in the coastal provinces (28 versus 9 per cent). Again, this was likely due to market imperfections and the lack of suitable transport and distribution facilities in this latter region. Firms located in the coastal region rely more on the international market (S5) for sourcing (15 per cent) as compared to 5 per cent for the inland provinces.

Regression analysis

Table 8.3 provides the results of the regression analysis about the influence of firm and location factors on sourcing strategies of European subsidiaries in China in order to present a multivariate approach of the descriptive statistics discussed earlier.

The in-house sourcing from the Chinese partners' parents and affiliated companies (S1) is significantly linked with the ownership degree and location of European subsidiaries. Firms with low foreign ownership and located in the inland region tended to source more from their local partners for their inputs. It is also observed that the in-house sourcing from subsidiaries established by European investors in the local market (S2) was more often used by firms with a higher foreign equity participation. These findings demonstrate that ownership has a most pervasive influence on intra-firm vertical integration. The higher the level of ownership, the more likely the investors – that is, the Chinese local partners as well as the European MNEs – set up intra-firm vertical industrial linkages.

The procurement by European manufacturing subsidiaries in the Chinese market (S3) was significantly influenced by their industrial specialisation, technology level and location. Firms operating in the inland region and specialised in labour-intensive industries (e.g. textiles and electronics) rely less on local markets to source their components. The significance of these factors provides useful information about the sourcing patterns of European manufacturing subsidiaries in China. For instance, firms operating in labour-intensive industries are likely to concentrate on processing activities on behalf of their parent companies. The sourcing from the foreign parent companies and their subsidiaries elsewhere (S4) is relatively high in these latter sectors.

The inverse relationship between sourcing from the foreign parent and the technology level in high-tech subsidiaries contrasts with previous studies, which found a strong positive relationship between these two factors (Kotabe and Omura 1989; Cavusgil *et al.* 1993). This result probably demonstrates the impact of an effective 'local content' policy by the host government on sourcing policy of MNEs, such as the Chinese 'localisation' policy in the automotive industry (Zhang and Van Den Bulcke 2000). The differences between firms in their intensity to outsource from the international markets (S5) is likely to be related to size. The higher percentage of outsourcing from abroad by the large firms – as compared to the small and medium ones – may be explained by their better connections and more intensive links to the international component and semi-finished goods producers on the one hand and their more global sourcing strategy on the other hand.

Table 8.3 Multiple regression analysis of sourcing strategies of European manufacturing subsidiaries in China (1996)

Regression coefficients

	S1		S2		S3		S4		S5	
	t	Sig.	t	Sig.	t	Sig.	t	Sig.	t	Sig.
(Constant)	2.28	0.03	-2.05	0.04	2.35	0.02	0.10	0.92	-1.91	0.06
Age +	0.16	0.87	0.20	0.85	1.32	0.19	-0.96	0.34	-1.34	0.18
No. of employees +	-0.39	0.70	0.19	0.85	0.36	0.72	-1.42	0.16	1.68	0.10*
Equity share +	-1.89	0.06*	2.06	0.04**	-1.45	0.15	1.19	0.24	1.58	0.12
Export ratio +	0.57	0.57	0.21	0.84	-0.93	0.35	-0.57	0.57	1.56	0.12
Industry 1	0.69	0.49	-0.32	0.75	-1.44	0.15	1.23	0.22	-0.25	0.81
Industry 2	0.33	0.74	-0.36	0.72	-1.91	0.06*	1.91	0.06*	-0.07	0.95
Industry 4	-0.09	0.93	-0.48	0.63	-0.50	0.62	1.15	0.26	-0.81	0.42
Industry 5	-0.38	0.70	0.39	0.70	-0.57	0.57	0.97	0.34	-0.77	0.44
Partner 1	-0.33	0.74	1.22	0.23	-1.03	0.31	0.08	0.93	1.07	0.29
Partner 3	-0.88	0.38	-0.43	0.67	-1.04	0.30	1.22	0.22	1.30	0.20
Partner 4	-0.06	0.95	0.74	0.46	-0.42	0.68	0.59	0.56	-0.19	0.85
Inland region	1.93	0.06*	0.21	0.83	-1.68	0.10*	1.30	0.20	-1.34	0.19
KI-HT	-0.04	0.97	0.58	0.57	1.29	0.20	-1.77	0.08*	0.66	0.51
KI-LT	-1.01	0.32	-0.09	0.93	2.19	0.03**	-1.81	0.07*	0.26	0.79
LI-LT	-0.64	0.53	0.27	0.78	2.18	0.03**	-2.06	0.04**	0.23	0.82
R2	0.17		0.12		0.18		0.18		0.21	

Source: Survey of EU subsidiaries in China (1997).

Note
Variables with + are transformed in logarithmic value, while others are dummy variables. *$p < 0.10$; **$p < 0.05$; ***$p < 0.01$.

Conclusion and policy implications

This chapter revealed several specific characteristics of sourcing strategies of European subsidiaries in China. First, the FSFs that have been found in previous studies (Reuber *et al.* 1973) as the most important ones in affecting the sourcing patterns of MNEs, such as the export ratio and the length of operation, are not significantly linked with the sourcing patterns of European subsidiaries in China. By contrast, factors that are related to the degree of ownership and the type of local partners were found to be important factors affecting sourcing decisions. The subsidiaries with a high equity participation by local partners rely more on local in-house sourcing, especially when the local partners are SOEs. This feature can be attributed to the specific operating environment of China, where SOEs still play a dominant role in production and distribution activities, especially in the inland region where institutional factors have a determining influence. The high proportion of in-house procurement by European subsidiaries from their Chinese partners might also be explained by the highly regulatory nature of the Chinese FDI policy that increasingly focuses on the integration of SOEs with foreign production systems and markets, in order to improve the performance of Chinese industry.

Second, the sourcing patterns of European subsidiaries in China are strongly linked with the location of their plants. The comparative location factors, such as, for example, the functioning of the market mechanism, the industrial and distribution infrastructure, are still highly different between the coastal and inland region. This is a result of the Chinese government's gradual regional development and liberalisation policy. The firms based in the inland region have a higher percentage of local in-house sourcing – mostly from their Chinese state-owned partner companies – and lower outsourcing from the local and international market. The limited access of the companies in the inland region to the foreign market, because of transportation and distribution constraints on the one hand, and the more frequent imperfections of the market economy on the other hand, oblige the European subsidiaries located in the inland region to rely more heavily on their local partners for sourcing purposes.

Third, the relationship between the level of technology and the sourcing patterns of European subsidiaries in China is rather contrary to previous findings in other countries (Halbach 1989). This particular result can be attributed to the highly regulatory character of Chinese FDI policy that is integrated into the country's sectorial development programme. A similar result was found in the Indian case (Lall 1980).[4] Although firms operating in capital- and technology-intensive industries are generally encouraged by the Chinese government's import substitution policy, the 'localisation' programme imposed by the Chinese government has in some global industries obliged MNEs to source locally by using the network of their local partners. A number of European subsidiaries tended also to establish local vertical integration links by investing in upstream activities or by convincing their suppliers of the need to invest locally (Zhang and Van Den Bulcke 1996). In labour-intensive industries, European firms import from the foreign parent/subsidiary company rather than buy locally. Most of this latter group of subsidiaries act as resource seekers (e.g. for low-cost labour) and use their Chinese subsidiaries to carry out processing or final assembly operations in order to export to the home market of the foreign parent company or to third markets.

The options considered in this study on sourcing pattern of MNEs are more numerous and complex than the dualistic approach (i.e. only local versus off-shore sourcing) that was mostly used in the literature until now. The previous studies on sourcing strategy have strongly focused on the dominant role of the parent company in resource-creating activities and their allocation. In most cases, the foreign subsidiaries that belong to the group as well as the role of the local partner and the host government have not been sufficiently taken into account. The traditional 'ethnocentric' approach to sourcing has many limitations and ignores aspects of the recent developments in the globalising economy.

First, the growing structural decentralisation and deconcentration within the MNEs themselves have resulted in an increasing independence of subsidiaries or production units vis-à-vis their parent companies or/and other subsidiaries (Hedlund 1986; Bartlett and Ghoshal 1989; Plasschaert and Van Den Bulcke 1992; Nohria and Ghoshal 1994). These structural changes might lead MNEs to use a more decentralised approach for the sourcing strategy of their subsidiaries. Such a strategy could positively affect not only the performance of the subsidiary, but also the overall competitiveness of the group. It is therefore necessary to study the specific aspects of the sourcing options of subsidiaries and to link these options with the global strategy of the parent company.

Second, the spatial widening of economic activities (i.e. globalisation) has increased the pressure on nations and localities to reassert their distinctive clusters (Dunning 1997). There is an increasing need to assess the interactions between the affiliates of MNEs, the local partners and the host and home governments. Given the importance of the above-mentioned changes, future studies about sourcing strategies of MNEs should focus more on the interactions among different actors, especially with regard to the specific role of the local partner and the host government in the sourcing strategies of MNEs. These propositions are not only relevant for emerging economies where the role of the government is still quite high, but also for developed countries where policies are changing from macro-economic policies to more macro-organisational measures (Dunning 1997).

Although the extent to which foreign subsidiaries source locally is an important indicator of their integration into the host country and what their real impact is on the economy, the rising tendency to integrate sourcing activities of foreign subsidiaries into the global market also has a very strong influence on the globalisation of the host economy. To help domestic companies to benefit from the sourcing strategy in the long term and to engage in a more global positioning of MNEs, the Chinese government has to ensure a higher market efficiency and better locational conditions. On the one hand, the government has to upgrade the FDI investment climate by the development of created assets with more human-capital-intensive infrastructure in order to allow MNEs to engage into local-market-oriented operations and to stimulate them to set-up linkages with local firms. On the other hand, the government has to adopt a more global FDI policy, because the future development of FDI in China depends not only on the specific measures to 'guide' MNEs into local economic linkages, but more on the integration of local economies into the global trade and investment system of multinational enterprises. The integration of domestic enterprises into the global economy will lead MNEs to create more linkages with the local economy. Besides, the integration of China into the world trading system and the WTO will oblige China to change its 'localisation' policy and make it more market oriented (UN/UNCTAD 2001).

9   Concluding comments

This study focused on three major aspects of EUDI in China. First, it examined the evolution of the Chinese FDI policy during the last two decades and discussed its impact on FDI in China in general and EUDI in particular. The upgrading of locational factors and changing FDI policy of the Chinese government were analysed in the context of the transition of the Chinese economy towards the market system. Second, the extent and characteristics of EU subsidiaries in China were studied on the basis of a statistical analysis and questionnaire surveys. Also, their salient characteristics were compared with those of other developed economies such as the United States and Japan and Asian NIEs. Third, the report dealt with certain operational and managerial issues of EU subsidiaries in China, such as their industrial concentration, level of technology, R&D, sourcing, competitive position, autonomy of decision-making and the major difficulties experienced in their daily operations in China. Fourth, special attention was devoted to the sourcing policies of EU MNEs in China, a topic of great concern to Chinese policymakers.

This concluding chapter does not intend to summarize all of the above-mentioned aspects. Instead, it concentrates on some key features of EUDI in China and its evolution in the context of China's changing environment. Most importantly, these final comments try to analyse the political and business implications of some central findings of this study, especially from the perspective of Chinese FDI policy. The new development of the Chinese economy – especially its entry into the WTO and WDS ('Go West') – and its likely impact on the possible future moves of EU MNEs are also emphasised.

Key characteristics of EUDI in China

On the basis of both official statistics and special surveys, this study reviewed the trends and patterns of the EUDI in China and examined the specific characteristics of EU subsidiaries operating in this continuously evolving and changing market. China's LSFs and its FDI policy as determinants of the EUDI in China and the changing strategic options and operating characteristics of EU MNEs were also analysed.

Importance and motivations

During the last two decades of the previous century, China developed into the largest host developing country of FDI and achieved extremely rapid growth in industrial production and exports of manufactured products. The growth of inward FDI became intertwined with the transition and globalisation processes of the Chinese economy. This rapidly changing environment not only provides unique opportunities, but also presents enormous challenges and numerous difficulties for foreign investors.

One of the key findings of the statistical analysis of Chinese inward FDI indicates that enterprises from the European Union, especially the small- and medium-sized ones, lag behind their Japanese and United States counterparts in investing in China. As compared to its major rivals, the European Union clearly occupied a weak investment position until 1996, as it accounted for less than 4 per cent of total Chinese inward FDI. Although EU firms have been catching up rapidly and increased their share to about 7 per cent in 1999, on aggregate the volume of EU FDI in China is still being surpassed by its principal competitors, meaning that it is underrepresented in the most important and dynamic emerging market of the world.

There are substantial differences among EU member countries, industries and firms with regard to their FDI operations in China, however. Germany, the United Kingdom and France as well as some small open economies, such as the Netherlands, Belgium and Sweden, achieved a relatively higher penetration than other EU member countries. With regard to the sectoral distribution, EU firms acquired a strong competitive position in R&D-based and scale-intensive industries in China, especially in the automotive industry, telecommunications, pharmaceuticals and basic chemicals, while their presence in consumer markets and outsourcing operations is relatively limited. The analysis at the firm level showed that the EU firms with a high involvement in FDI operations in China are mostly large and leading MNEs, while EU SMEs are still relatively absent from the Chinese market.

The investment decisions by EU MNEs in the Chinese manufacturing industry were mainly based on strategic and market-seeking motivations, while the reasons for cost/supply and efficiency considerations figure less prominently. The study has clearly shown that most EU MNEs considered their investment in China as a way to gain a foothold in a growing market. The moves by global competitors into the Chinese market triggered investment decisions by EU MNEs to carry out follow-up investments to counter such global competition. The strong market-oriented operations by EU MNEs in China determined their relations with Chinese industry on the one hand and the investment environment and business climate on the other hand.

patterns

)ach followed by the Chinese government in combining regional devel-
id the liberalisation of FDI has substantially influenced the geographical

pattern of FDI in China. While the setting up of SEZs at the beginning of the 1980s offered only a limited attraction to EU MNEs, the opening up of the large coastal cities – especially Pudong in 1992 – with a more sophisticated industrial and trade infrastructure was crucial for many European firms to move into China. As a result, most of the EU MNEs concentrated their production and service activities in large urban centres, that is, especially in Shanghai, Tianjin, Guangzhou and their neighbouring regions. The existing industrial basis and large local market of these cities and their hinterland convinced market-seeking investors in general and EU MNEs in particular that it made sense to set up local production and distribution facilities in China and to rely on local firms for sourcing and distribution. The presence of certain industrial clusters – for instance, the automotive industries in Shanghai, Hubei and Changchung – has attracted leading MNEs wanting to tap into related sectors for building up production networks. The moves of European firms into such zones or centres are still limited, however.

The opening up of the inland region, especially those with a concentration of resource-intensive and defence industries (e.g. the provinces of Hubei, Sichuan and Shaanxi) constituted a new step in the regional development policy of the Chinese government, although its significance has only been slowly recognised by the potential European investors. A number of large SOEs in the specialised-supply industries and the resource-intensive sectors, such as machinery engineering and electronics and energy, are quite competitive, while their production scale and manufacturing technology are compatible with those of European firms. The collaboration agreements and specific alliances with such Chinese firms carried out in the context of the corporate restructuring of SOEs might allow European companies to extend further into the Chinese inland regions and to establish a strong position in related industries. Although not many European firms had already taken such steps, a number of the larger ones, for example, Siemens, Rolls-Royce and Volvo, have carried out such strategic decisions.

Industrial orientation

As compared to Asian and other investors, European firms in China are relatively more concentrated in the manufacturing sector. The industries in China in which they have established a strong position are mostly scale intensive, R&D based and specialised suppliers, such as chemicals, machine construction, telecommunications, transport equipment and pharmaceuticals. The high technological capability and strong competitive position of European firms in these global industries allowed them not only to acquire a large market share in Chinese industries, but also to become leaders in setting norms and standards for further industrial development. However, because of the rising globalisation of the Chinese market and industry and the entry of other global companies, the competition in these Chinese industries has become quite intensive. As a result, a number of European firms have been facing competitive threats from their foreign counterparts and even lost out in competitiveness in these sectors.

The decline in the rate of protection as a result of the gradual opening up of China to the world trade system (e.g. entry of China into the WTO) means that also established foreign-invested companies in China will certainly face intensified competitive pressure from imports.

Two factors are likely to affect the competitive position of European firms in the Chinese supplying industries and the scale-intensive sectors. First, the reduction of production costs by increasing local-sourcing capability (through upstream and downstream investment) and/or by integrating global suppliers in their local production activities will be crucial moves for these companies in order to remain competitive in China. Such moves can already be observed in the automotive sector, where European producers (e.g. Volkswagen and Citroën) convinced certain global suppliers to establish a plant in China. Yet, the upstream integration by European pharmaceutical firms in China is still very limited, which could negatively affect their future market position. Second, the extension of the economies of scale and scope in China will be essential for establishing dominant market positions and consolidating technological advances. A number of European firms as well as American and Japanese companies increased their 'visibility' in China by extending their value-added chain to the Chinese market, by setting up co-ordination structures for managing their financial and marketing activities within multiple operating units and by using China as a regional headquarter.

Ownership control and entry mode

European firms used EJVs more frequently as a form of entry for their operations in China than Asian and other investors from developed countries. The strong presence of EU companies in the EJVs established in China, especially the majority-owned ones, has to some extent been determined by their market-seeking motivations and the high technological level of their subsidiaries. Several characteristics were identified in this study about the ownership structure and the entry form of EU subsidiaries in China. First, because most of the EU MNEs invested in China for market-seeking motives, they were especially concerned with the accessibility of the domestic market (distribution network and market information) and the relationship with the host government. Therefore, they needed local partners to develop political connections and efficient links with the bureaucracy to fully benefit from the existing administrative facilities and incentives. For these reasons, EU market-seeking MNEs preferred JVs to wholly owned subsidiaries, especially in the early years when their concern with the culturally different and complex institutional and bureaucratic environment in China was extremely high.

Second, European MNEs demonstrated a strong preference for majority-owned EJVs and a tendency to increase their equity participation or even to buy out their local partners after a few years of operations. The preference for high equity stakes by European MNEs in their JVs is likely to be related to the technological character of many of their subsidiaries. The wholly or majority-owned subsidiaries provide more certainty for the appropriation of the economic rents and better protection against technological erosion. The transfer of technology by European MNEs to their subsidiaries in China undoubtedly was a vital bargaining item in the negotiation process about the establishment decision. Although the MNEs' strengths in technology are counterbalanced by their need for a local partner with strong political links and good local-market connections, many successful Western firms have considered their JVs as a stepping stone towards wholly owned operations. These companies realised that they have to take total control of their supply and distribution chain activities in order to build up an efficient national sales and distribution system.

Third, the moves of European MNEs towards a more frequent use of wholly and majority-owned subsidiaries reflect the changes that have occurred in the firm- and location-related factors. For instance, the improved performance of the Chinese market mechanism allowed foreign MNEs to decrease their dependence on the Chinese government for marketing support. On the other hand, acquired experience and the entrenched position by the foreign investors in China tended to result in a diminishing need for the reliance on Chinese partners. Also, the control of foreign ownership exercised by the Chinese government has been significantly relaxed in the 1990s.

China has started to experience with new collaborative forms with leading MNEs, such as alliances with one particular global firm at the whole sector/subsector level and privatisation of SOEs through M&As and B shares in the stock market. The multiple take-overs by Kodak of companies in the Chinese photosensitive industry and the JV agreements of Bosch with several Chinese manufacturers for producing automotive electronic systems are illustrations of such developments.

Operations and management

Half of the EU parent companies reported that they failed to reach their profitability expectations and anticipated cost reductions, while more than two-thirds stated that they attained and even exceeded their strategic targets with regard to the accumulation of local knowledge and the acquisition of a sizable market share. Therefore, these results show that EU MNEs were generally satisfied with their operations in China at the time of the survey, even though profitability was not achieved.

The competitive advantages of EU subsidiaries in China were identified as being strongly influenced by product quality, reputation of the European parent company and adaptability of the product to the local market. These findings strongly suggest that a large number of EU subsidiaries, especially those located in the coastal region, depend upon a number of internal factors, such as economies of scale, high productivity and continued transfer of technology from the parent company, to uphold and strengthen their competitive position in China.

Although EU subsidiaries were highly concentrated in high-tech industries, their local R&D activities in China were quite limited at the time of the survey.

The low involvement of EU subsidiaries in local R&D activities, especially those operating in scale-intensive and R&D-based industries, might negatively affect their long-term competitive position and strategy. Also, the setting up of production facilities in downstream activities will be a crucial step in strengthening the competitive position in related industries. These findings suggest that the competitive position of EU subsidiaries in China as well as their operational concerns were strongly linked to the structure and performance of the Chinese industries.

With regard to the autonomy of decision-making within EU subsidiaries, the findings of this study show that it became more decentralised over time as a result of the increasing knowledge and experience accumulated by local subsidiaries. Yet, the 'localisation' of management had to be envisaged not only for cost-cutting reasons, but also as an opportunity to enhance the integration into the local business and cultural environment.

A number of factors were listed by the surveyed managers as major difficulties for EU subsidiaries to successfully operate in China. These constraints were mainly linked with the complexity of the Chinese bureaucratic system and the low availability and quality of local services. Yet, firms were concerned with these problems in different ways as their degree of integration with local markets and industries varied. Local-market-oriented firms were more concerned with local sourcing and distribution, while high-tech companies complained more about the lack of protection of their patents and trademarks.

Given all the above-mentioned characteristics of EUDI in China, a number of political and business implications need to be emphasised with regard to the Chinese central and local governments.

Some policy implications

This study did not specifically examine the measures that might be taken by the Chinese governments to attract FDI from the EU countries. Yet, the questionnaire survey demonstrated a number of obstacles and difficulties that European firms encountered in their operations in China. The major concerns of EU companies about China were related to the complexity of the Chinese bureaucracy, the underdeveloped local logistics and services and the low capability and quality of local firms for sourcing and distribution. Consequently, the improvement of these factors should not only contribute to the further liberalisation of FDI in service sectors, but can also assist in the acceleration of the market transition through ownership reform and the restructuring of SOEs.

Most of the Asian countries that seriously suffered from the financial crisis of 1997–1998, such as South Korea, Thailand and Malaysia, carried out a number of liberalisation measures and incentives for attracting FDI and restructuring their economy. The number of M&As has increased rapidly in those countries in the two years after the crisis as a result of changes in their legal framework and FDI policy. In addition to this new wave of competition among Asian countries for attracting FDI, the Chinese government faces a number of policy choices relating to its FDI policy framework (Henley *et al.* 1999), especially with regard to regional development, sectoral liberalisation and corporate restructuring.

Regional reconfiguration

As suggested by the survey results, EU MNEs were lured to China because of the size of the Chinese market and its growth prospects, rather than for its low labour costs and its special investment incentives. Although tax advantages and low production costs might to some extent have been attractive for foreign investors operating in export-processing activities in the coastal region, particularly those from Asian economies, they had only a limited effect on EU enterprises involved in local-market-seeking investment. For those latter investors, the infrastructure, the availability and quality of local services and the accessibility of the market and the administration were key factors in their investment decisions. For these reasons, the Chinese central government as well as the local authorities should recognise that the deregulation of state monopolies in the infrastructure and the energy sector and the introduction of transparency and effectiveness in the administration – rather than tax incentives as such – affect location decisions of foreign investors in general and EU MNEs in particular. Also, the increase of FDI in China's inland region will depend on the central government's ability to implement its overall regional development policy to create linkages between the coastal and inland provinces as economic co-operation between these two parts of the country has often been impeded by regional protectionism. The lack of cross-regional co-operation between domestic firms/industries on the one hand and the presence of trade barriers among regional Chinese markets on the other hand are two major issues that have to be dealt with in China's regional policy towards FDI.

Sectoral liberalisation

The complaints of EU subsidiaries about the limited availability and low quality of logistics and business services in China and the lack of local enterprises for sourcing and distribution purposes suggests that it is necessary for the Chinese government – as it has accepted in the WTO agreement – to continue to open up the domestic industries and markets to FDI, including the financial, legal, consulting and other business-related services. Changes in this direction might ensure more competition in these supporting sectors and stimulate the development of local entrepreneurship.

Three factors are to be carefully considered, however. First, a long-term sectoral policy has to be carried out in order to avoid frequent short-term changes and 'special deals'. The implementation of a long-term and constant sectoral policy should improve the quality of inward investment and would be helpful for the industrial restructuring process and the updating of the innovation capabilities of local firms.

Second, within the context of joining WTO, foreign affiliates initially established as a means of accessing the Chinese market will be shifted towards a more export-oriented role in the future as trade will become more open with China. The competition from foreign exporters might push foreign subsidiaries to move from local-market-oriented to internationally integrated operations. Such a change needs a more appropriate sectoral policy combined with internationally standardised foreign trade policy, such as antidumping regulations.

Third, incentives are to be introduced in order to create a favourable environment for both domestic and foreign enterprises to engage in R&D activities and to favour partnerships between universities, research institutions and enterprises. China needs to keep foreign investors interested to sustain robust growth, speed up the adoption of technology and to raise efficiency in its industrial system. As Western companies invest more strongly in sourcing activities, the Chinese government should provide the necessary support for attracting further investments and transfer of technology into downstream activities. In this context, the improvement of the legal framework to protect intellectual propriety is indeed essential.

Creating linkages with domestic industries

The findings about sourcing strategies of EU subsidiaries in China suggest that the Chinese government needs to promote backward linkages between foreign subsidiaries and domestic supplier firms. As such a 'linkage promotion programme' has become a inherent part of FDI policy for many host countries, UNCTAD recommended a number of policy measures in its newly published World Investment Report (UN/UNCTAD 2001). The implication of these measures for China is vital as it could help to increase domestic sourcing capability by attracting FDI from small- and medium-sized foreign supplier firms and to deepen and upgrade existing linkages between Chinese firms and foreign producers. China urgently needs such a programme, as its industries as well as FDI are under a heavy restructuring process, in which creating backward linkages between domestic and foreign firms on the one hand and establishing alliances between coastal and inland regions on the other hand are key factors for the next move forward of the Chinese economy. Especially, the linkages promotion programme should favour initiatives of SMEs and allow them to be integrated into the sourcing and distribution activities of MNEs.

Notes

1 Introduction

1 The terms and classification of statistics of Chinese inward FDI are defined on the basis of 'The Statistical Regulation on Using Foreign Capital'. The project numbers refer to the approved enterprises with foreign investment. The contracted (or approved) amount refers to the investment that is to be supplied by foreign investors on the basis of the approved or signed contracts, while the utilised (or current) amount is the investment that has been actually used, including cash, equipment and intangible capital, such as services and technology. In this study, the amount of foreign capital will normally be expressed in current value; otherwise, it will be explicitly mentioned that contracted or approved value is meant.

2 MOFTEC stopped the publication of this type of information in its statistical yearbook as of 1998.

3 Amadeus is a Pan-European company level financial database that includes approximately 170,000 European companies having a turnover of more than US$ 13 million, assets of more than US$ 26 million or an employment of more than 150 people. It covers the top companies of the fifteen countries of the EU plus Switzerland and Austria.

2 Determinants of foreign direct investment and the changing Chinese business environment

1 Although this taxonomy or typology of FDI has been largely used in the literature, the definition of as well as distinction among different forms of FDI are not always interpreted in the same way. Certain authors see them rather as a historical sequence from resource-based FDI, to local-market-oriented FDI, to internationally integrated FDI (within which affiliates become a source of competence or know-how).

2 The authors of these surveys are not directly referred to. See UNCTC (1992) and Dunning (1992a) for more detailed references on this subject.

3 The investment risk factors not only consist of political risk, for example, uncertainty about the economic and political conditions and the government policies, but also industry-specific risks. These latter risks are strongly associated with competition and transaction uncertainties. The competition uncertainties are closely related to industrial restructuring, increasing rivalry among established firms and entrance of new firms, while the transaction uncertainties are more limited to the technology transfer.

4 These measures intended to balance the revenues and expenditures of foreign exchange by engaging into import substituting activities, purchasing Chinese commodities for subsequent exporting, reinvesting profits in Renminbi in Chinese enterprises and globalising foreign exchange earnings from multiple ventures and trading in the SWAP markets (Plasschaert 1989).

5 Until 1997, less than ten foreign funded enterprises were registered in the form of a joint stock company in China. As compared to the equity joint venture, contractual joint

venture, wholly foreign owned company and holding company, the joint stock company is quite a complicated form. It is a legal entity of which the capital stock is made up of equal value shares contributed by both domestic and foreign shareholders. The registered capital of this type of company shall be at least RMB 30 million. Total value of the shares purchased and held by the foreign shareholders should be no less than 25 per cent of the company's total registered capital (EU 1997).

3 Overview of inward foreign direct investment in China

1 The 'reverse' investment refers to domestic investment made under the guise of foreign investment, and is aimed at taking advantage of fiscal and other benefits available in a given country to foreign investors. The capital that originates from China to be invested in Hong Kong and then re-enters China as foreign investment answers to this type of definition.

4 Salient and evolving features of EU direct investment in China

1 The section on 'Comparative analysis' of this chapter is based on a paper that was presented at the conference 'Major challenges for European corporations in the Asian globalising economy' held in Macau in April 1998.
2 During the 1980s, almost all Japanese investment was directed towards South-East Asia. Europe and North America come into the picture mainly during the 1990s. Especially in the 1980s, few Japanese enterprises considered China as a priority location for overseas expansion.
3 The industrial classification of manufacturing companies was carried out on the basis of an OECD method. Resource-intensive industries include food beverages and tabacco, wood products, petroleum refining, non-metallic mineral products and non-ferrous metals. The labour-intensive industries cover textiles, apparel and leather, fabrication of metal products and other manufacturing. Specialized-supplier industries are non-electrical machinery, electrical machinery and communication equipment and semiconductors. Scale-intensive industries consist of paper and printing, chemicals excl. drugs, rubber and plastics, iron and steel, shipbuilding, motor vehicles and other transport, while R&D-based industries are aerospace, computers, pharmaceuticals and scientific instruments.
4 The technological level of the surveyed companies is measured on the basis of the intensity of the production factors, that is, labour intensive with low technology (LI–LT), labour intensive with high technology (LI–HT), capital intensive with low technology (KI–LT) and capital intensive with high technology (KI–HT) (Dunning 1979; Lee 1983; Schroath *et al.* 1993). The classification is carried out by using four-digit SIC. LI–LT includes companies operating in flowers and plants, food and kindred products, tobacco, textiles, apparel products, lumber, wood products, paper industries, rubber and plastics, leather products, etc. LI–HT covers non-electric machinery, electrical and electronic products and measuring equipment. KI–LT consists of non-metal mineral products and primary metal industries, while KI–HT includes chemicals, petroleum, transportation equipment, etc.
5 The residuals give the difference between the observed and expected values. The standardised residual is expressed in standard deviation units above or below the means.

5 Operational and strategic characteristics of EU parent companies with investment operations in China

1 After two successive mergers with Petrofina in 1999 and Elf Aquitaine in 2000, Total became TotalFinaElf.

6 Characteristics of EU subsidiaries in the Chinese manufacturing sector

1 A preliminary version of this chapter was presented as a paper at the International Conference 'China and Zhuhai in the Globalisation of the World Economy', 6–7 December 1998, Zhuhai, China.
2 According to the third survey of Chinese manufacturing companies in the machinery sector, the sales of Chinese companies averaged to US$ 6 million, while their assets reached only US$ 8.8 million in 1995 (Ministry of Machinery 1996).

8 Sourcing strategies of EU multinational subsidiaries in China

1 An earlier version of this chapter was presented at the 24th Annual Conference of the European International Business Academy (EIBA) in Jerusalem, Israel, in December 1998.
2 The terms 'sourcing' and 'procurement' are used interchangeable.
3 The total of local and international sourcing does not reach 100 per cent because a small percentage of inputs is procured from other sources about which the responding companies did not give sufficient specifications.
4 Lall's study (1980) on the sourcing strategy of foreign affiliates in the auto industry in India, Peru and Morocco showed that the local content in India reached 94 per cent, while it was only 35 per cent in Peru and 15 per cent in Morocco. The author argued that the Indian government's policy was the key variable in affecting the sourcing strategy of foreign subsidiaries, along with the size of the domestic market and the level of industrial development (Dunning 1992a).

Bibliography

Agarwal, S. and S. N. Ramaswami (1992) 'Choice of Foreign Direct Market Entry Mode, Impact of Ownership, Location and Internationalisation Factors'. *Journal of International Business Studies*, 23: 1–28.

Alexander, M. and D. Young (1996) 'Strategic Outsourcing'. *Long Range Planning*, 29(2): 116–119.

Ash, R. F. and Y. Y. Kueh (1993) 'Economic Integration within Greater China: Trade and Investment Flows between China, Hong Kong and Taiwan'. *The China Quarterly*, 136: 711–745.

Bartlett, C. and S. Ghoshal (1989) *Managing Across Borders: The Transnational Solution*. Boston: HBS Press.

Beamish, P. W. (1988) *Multinational Joint Ventures in Developing Countries*. London and New York: Routledge.

Beamish, P. W., J. P. Killing, D. L. Lecraw and A. J. Morrison (1994) *International Management*. Irwin: Burt Ridge, Ill.

Blodgett, L. L. (1991) 'Partner Contribution as Predictors of Equity Share in International Joint Ventures'. *Journal of International Business Studies*, 22(1): 63–78.

Boisot, M. and J. Child (1996) 'The Institutional Nature of China's Emerging Economic Order', in: Brown, B. and R. Porter (eds), *Management Issues in China*, Volume 1. London: Routledge.

Borrus, M. (1996) 'Left for Dead: Asian Production Networks and the Revival of US Electronics'. *BRIE Working Papers*, No. 100, University of California, Berkeley.

Bruche, G. (1996) 'Entry Strategies of Multinational Companies in China's Pharma-Market: A Case in Competitive Positioning', in: Antonio, N. and H. Steele (eds), *Managing International Business in the Twenty First Century. The Second South China International Business Symposium*, University of Macau.

Buckley, P. J. and M. Casson (1976) *The Future of the Multinational Enterprise*. London: Macmillan.

Buckley, P. J. and M. Casson (1981) 'The Optimal Timing of a Foreign Direct Investment'. *Economic Journal*, 91: 75–87.

Buckley, P. J. and M. Casson (1985) *The Economic Theory of the Multinational Enterprise*. London: Macmillan.

Buzzell, R. D. (1983) 'Is Vertical Integration Profitable?'. *Harvard Business Review*, 61: 92–102.

Buzzell, R. D. (1988) 'The World Pharmaceutical Industry: Prospects for the 1980s', in: Buzzell, R. D. and J. A. Quelch (eds), *Multinational Marketing Management: Cases and Readings*. Massachusetts: Addison-Wesley.

thesis of Foreign Direct Investment Theories and Theories of ...al of International Business Studies, Spring/Summer: 43–59.
...ic Guide to Equity Joint Ventures in China. Oxford: Pergamon

...gical Innovation and Multinational Corporation. Oxford: Basil

...hnological Competence Theory of International Production
...: Mcfetridge, D. (ed.), Foreign Investment, Technology and
.... Toronto: University of Toronto Press.

Cao, J. W. (1991) Modern China and the Making Use of Foreign Capital. Shanghai: Shanghai Academy of Social Sciences Press (in Chinese).

Capener, C. R. (1998) 'M&A in China Comes of Age'. The China Business Review, 25(4): 14–21.

Caves, R. E. and S. K. Mehra (1986) 'Entry of Foreign Multinationals into US Manufacturing Industries', in: Porter, M. (ed.), Competition in Global Industries. Boston: Harvard Press.

Caves, R. and M. Porter (1977) 'From Entry Barriers to Mobility Barriers'. Quarterly Journal of Economics, 91: 241–261.

Cavusgil, S. T., A. Yaprak and P. L. Yeoh (1993) 'A Decision-Making Framework for Global Sourcing'. International Business Review, 2(2): 143–156.

Chaudhry, P. E. and M. G. Walsh (1995) 'Intellectual Property Rights: Changing Levels of Protection Under GATT, NAFTA and the EU'. The Columbia Journal of World Business, Summer: 81–92.

CITIC (1984–1986) The China Investment Guide. Hong Kong: Longman.

CNAIC (1996) Directory of Parts Suppliers for Chinese Introduced Vehicle. Beijing: Auto Information Service.

Contractor, F. J. (1990) 'Ownership Patterns of US Joint Ventures Abroad and the Liberalisation of Foreign Government Regulation in the 1980s: Evidence from the Benchmark Surveys'. Journal of International Business Studies, 21: 55–73.

Corstjens, M. (1991) Marketing Strategy in the Pharmaceutical Industry. London: Chapman & Hall.

Cronk, J. and J. Sharp (1995) 'A Framework for Deciding what to Outsource in Information Technology'. Journal of Information Technology, 10(4): 259–267.

De Bruijn, E. J. and X. Jia (1993) 'Managing Sino-Western Joint Ventures: Product Selection Strategy'. Management International Review, 33(4): 335–360.

De Bruijn, E. J. and X. Jia (1994) 'Managing Sino-Western Joint Ventures: Localisation of Content', in: Stewart, S. (ed.), Joint Ventures in the PRC, Advances in Chinese Industrial Studies, Volume 4. JAI Press, pp. 233–254.

De Wolf, P. (1994) 'The Pharmaceutical Industry', in: Sachwald, F. (ed.), European Integration and Competitiveness: Acquisition and Alliance in Industry. Edward Elgar, pp. 277–317.

Dunning, J. H. (1979) 'Explaining Changing Patterns of International Production: In Defence of The Eclectic Theory'. Oxford Bulletin of Economics and Statistics, November: 269–296.

Dunning, J. H. (1981) 'Explaining the International Direct Investment Position of Countries: Towards a Dynamic or Development Approach'. Weltwirtschaftliches Archiv, 119: 30–64.

Dunning, J. H. (1986) 'The Investment Development Cycle and Third World Multinationals', in: Khan, K. M. (ed.), Multinational of the South: New Actors in the International Economy. London: Frances Printer, pp. 15–47.

Dunning, J. H. (1988) Explaining International Production. London: Unwin Hyman.

Dunning, J. H. (1992a) *Multinational Enterprises and the Global Economy*. Wokingham: Addison-Wesley.

Dunning, J. H. (1992b) 'The Global Economy, Domestic Governance, Strategies and Transnational Corporations: Interactions and Policy Implications'. *Transnational Corporations*, 3: 7–44.

Dunning, J. H. (1997) 'Reconciling Some Paradoxes of Global Economy'. *Paper Presented at Round-Table and Workshop on Globalisation and the Small Open Economy*, May 29, University of Antwerp, Antwerp.

Dunning, J. H. and R. Narula (1994) 'Transpacific Foreign Direct Investment and the Investment Development Path: The Record Assessed'. *Essays in International Business*, No. 10, May, University of South Carolina.

Earl, M. (1996) 'The Risks of Outsourcing IT'. *Sloan Management Review*, Spring: 26–32.

Economist (The) (1998) 'Daimler-Benz: Stalling in China'. *The Economist*, April 18: 74.

European Commission (2001) *European Union Foreign Direct Investment Yearbook 2000*. Luxembourg: EC.

EIU (1992–1996) *Business China*. The Economist Intelligence Unit, Various issues.

EU (1997) *Market Access Sectoral and Trade Barriers Database: China*. http://mkaccdb.eu.int

EU/UNCTAD (1996) *Investing in Asia's Dynamism – European Union Direct Investment in Asia*. Brussels and Geneva.

European Parliament (1996) 'The Dynamics of Economic Change in Asia – Implications for Trade and European Union Presence'. *Working Paper W-12*, Luxembourg.

Eurostat (2001) *Eurostat Yearbook, 2001: The Statistical Guide to Europe*. Luxembourg: Eurostat.

Financial Times (1994) 'China'. *Financial Times Survey*, November 7.

Fortune (1989) *One Company's China Debacle*. November 6: 91–93.

Geringer, M. (1988) *Joint Venture Partner Selection*. Westport, Connecticut: Greenwood Press.

Geringer, M. (1991) 'Strategic Determinants of Partner Selection in International Joint Ventures'. *Journal of International Business Studies*, 22(2): 235–254.

Halbach, A. J. (1989) 'Multinational Enterprises and Subcontracting in the Third World: A Study of Inter-Industrial Linkages'. *ILO Working Paper*, No. 58, Geneva: ILO.

Harrold, P. and R. Lall (1993) 'China: Reform and Development in 1992–93'. *World Bank Discussion Papers*, No. 215, Washington: World Bank.

Harwit, E. (1997) 'Guangzhou Peugeot: Portrait of a Commercial Divorce'. *China Business Review*, November–December: 10–11.

Hauwaert, L. (1997) 'Outsourcing, The European Way'. *Amcham Magazine*, Fourth Quarter: 23–25.

Hedlund, G. (1986) 'The Hypermodern MNC-A Heterarchy'? *Human Resource Management*, 1: 9–35.

Hedlund, G. (1992) 'A Model of Knowledge Management and the Global N-Form Corporation'. *Paper Presented at the EIBA Annual Meeting*, Reading, December.

Henley, J., C. Kirkpatrick and G. Wilde (1999) 'Foreign Direct Investment in China: Recent Trends and Current Policy Issues'. *The World Economy*, 22(2): 223–243.

Hickman, M. and J. B. Mendelsohn (1998) 'China's Law Now Give Investors More Options'. *The National Law Journal*, March.

Hoechst (1997) *A Seminar on the Restructuring*. Presentation by Horst Waesche, Member Board of Management, Beijing, December 16.

Huang, G. Y. (1995) *The Universal Dictionary of Foreign Business in Modern China*. Chengdu: Sichuan People's Publishing House (in Chinese).

International Economic Review (1994) *Foreign Investment in China*. July: 12–17.

Kotabe, [...] Multinational Companies', in: Boyd, G. (ed.), *Structural Competitiveness in the Pacific: Corporate and State Rivalries*. Edward Elgar: Cheltenham.

Kotabe, M. and G. Omura (1989) 'Sourcing Strategies of European and Japanese Multinationals: A Comparison'. *Journal of International Business Studies*, 20(1): 26–43.

Kotabe, M. and K. S. Swan (1994) 'Offshore Sourcing: Reaction, Maturation, and Consolidation of U.S. Multinationals'. *Journal of International Business Studies*, First Quarter: 115–140.

Lall, S. (1980) 'Vertical Interfirm Linkages: An Empirical Study'. *Oxford Bulletin of Economics and Statistics*, 42: 203–206.

Lall, S. (1985) 'Multinationals and Technology Development in Host Countries', in: Lall, S. (ed.), *Multinationals, Technology and Exports*. London: Macmillan.

Lardy, N. R. (1994) *China in The World Economy*. Washington, DC: Institute for International Economics.

Lasserre, P. and H. Schütte (1995) *Strategy for Asia-Pacific*. Basingstoke: Macmillan.

Lee, C. H. (1983) 'International Production of the United States and Japan in Korean Manufacturing Industries: A Comparative Study'. *Weltwirtshaftliches Archiv*, 119(4): 745–753.

Lin, Danming (1996) 'Hong Kong's China Invested Companies and their Reverse Investment in China', in: John Child and Yuan Lu (eds), *Management Issues in China: Volume II, International Enterprises*. London: Routledge.

Marukawa, T. (1995) 'Industrial Groups and Division of Labour in China's Automobile Industry'. *The Development Economies*, 33(3): 300–355.

Mcmillan, C. H. (1993) 'The Role of Foreign Direct Investment in the Transition from Planned to Market Economies'. *Transnational Corporations*, 3: 97–119.

Ministry of Machinery (1996) *Third National Industrial Census of the People's Republic of China, 1995*. Beijing (in Chinese).

MOFTEC (1983–1998) *Almanac of China's Foreign Economic Relations and Trade*. Hong Kong.

MOFTEC (2000) *Statistics on FDI in China*. Beijing.

MOFTEC (2001) *Recent Statistics on FDI in China* (www.moftec.gov.cn).

Moxon, R. W. (1982) 'Offshore Sourcing, Subcontracting, and Manufacturing', in: Walter, I. (ed.), *Handbook of International Business*. New York: John Wiley and Sons.

Murray, G. (1995) 'China further Restricts Foreign Investment Incentives'. *Japan Economic Newswire*, March 24.

NERI (2001) 'Foreign Investment Inflows During the First Three Quarters'. National Economic Research Institute, China (*China Online Marketplace*).

Nishiguchi, T. (1994) *Strategic Industrial Sourcing: The Japanese Advantage*. New York: Oxford University Press.

Nohria, N. and S. Ghoshal (1994) 'Differentiated Fit and Shared Values Alternatives for Managing Headquarters–Subsidiary Relations'. *Strategic Management Journal*, 15(6): 491–502.

OECD (1992) *Globalisation of Industrial Activities, Four Case Studies: Auto Parts, Chemicals, Construction and Semiconductors*. Paris: OECD.

OECD (1995) *Foreign Direct Investment, OECD Countries and Dynamic Economics of Asia and Latin America*. Paris: OECD.

Ostry, S. (1992) 'The Domestic Domain: The New International Policy Arena'. *Transnational Corporations*, 1: 7–26.

Plasschaert, S. (1989) 'The Foreign Exchange Adequacy Requirement for Equity Joint Ventures in the People's Republic of China, in Dynamics of International Business'. *15th Annual Conference of EIBA*, Helsinki, pp. 1156–1173.

Plasschaert, S. and D. Van Den Bulcke (1992) 'Changing Dynamics of International Production: Globalisation and Collaborative Schemes in Multinational Enterprises', in: van den Broeck, J. and D. Van Den Bulcke (eds), *Changing Economic Order*. Antwerp: Wolters-Noordhof Publishers, pp. 93–116.

Ravenhill, J. (1996) 'Japanese and US Subsidiaries in East Asia: Host Economy Effects'. *MIT JP Working Paper*, 96-07.

Reuber, G. L., H. Crookell, M. Emerson and G. Gallais-Hamonno (1973) *Private Foreign Investment in Development*. Oxford: Clarendon Press.

Rugman, M. and A. Verbeke (1992) 'Multinational Enterprise and National Economy Policy', in: Buckley, P. J. and M. Casson (eds), *Multinational Enterprise in the World Economy*. Aldershot: Edward Elgar.

Schroath, F. W., M. Y. Hu and H. Y. Chen (1993) 'Country-of-Origin Effects of Foreign Investments in the People's Republic of China'. *Journal of International Business Studies*, 4: 278–290.

Schütte, H. (1997) 'Strategy and Organisation: Challenges for European MNCs in Asia'. *European Management Journal*, 4(15): 436–445.

Shaw, S. M. and J. Meier (1994) 'Second-Generation MNCs in China'. *The China Business Review*, September–October: 10–15.

Shen, Y. H. (1994) *Foreign Direct Investment from Western Europe*. Beijing: Shishi Publishing House (in Chinese).

Simon, J. D. (1982) 'Political Risk Assessment: Past Trends and Future Prospects'. *Columbia Journal of World Business*, Fall: 62–71.

Singh, I. (1992) 'China: Industrial Policies for an Economy in Transition'. *World Bank Discussion Papers*, No. 143, Washington: World Bank.

Sohn, J. H. D. (1993) 'Social Knowledge as a Control System: A Proposition and Evidence from the Japanese FDI Behaviour'. *Journal of International Business Studies*, Quarter: 296–324.

Swamidass, P. M. (1993) 'Import Sourcing Dynamics: An Integrative Perspective'. *Journal of International Business Studies*, Fourth Quarter: 671–691.

Swamidass, P. M. and M. Kotabe (1992) 'Component Sourcing Strategies of Multinationals: An Empirical Study of European and Japanese Multinationals'. *Journal of International Business Studies*, First Quarter: 81–99.

SYP (2001) *SYP Purchases of Guangdong Float Glass Co.*, http://www.sypglass.com

Thomas, H., W. Bogner and J. Mcgee (1994) 'A Longitudinal Study of the Competitive Positions and Entry Paths of European Firms in the US Pharmaceutical Market', in: Obloj, K. (ed.), *High Speed Competition in a New Europe, Proceedings of the 20th Annual Conference of EIBA*. Warsaw: International Postgraduate Management Centre, University of Warsaw, pp. 77–99.

Tolentino, E. E. (1993) *Technological Innovation and Third World Multinationals*. London and New York: Routledge.

UNCTC (1992) *The Determinants of Foreign Direct Investment, A Survey of the Evidence, Division of Transnational Corporations and Investment.* New York: UN.

Unilever (1999) 'China in Transition'. *Unilever Magazine,* June: 7-9.

UN/UNCTAD (1992) *The Determinants of Foreign Direct Investment: A Survey of the Literature.* New York: UN.

UN/UNCTAD (1997) *World Investment Report 1997: Transnational Corporations, Market Structure and Competition Policy.* New York and Geneva: UN.

UN/UNCTAD (1999) *World Investment Report 1999: Foreign Direct Investment and the Challenge of Development.* New York and Geneva: UN.

UN/UNCTAD (2000) *World Investment Report 2000: Cross-Border Mergers and Acquisitions and Development.* New York and Geneva: UN.

UN/UNCTAD (2001) *World Investment Report 2001: Promoting Linkages.* New York and Geneva: UN.

Urata, S. (1995) *Emerging Patterns of Production and Foreign Trade in Electronics Products in East Asia: An Examination of a Role Played by Foreign Direct Investment.* San Francisco: Asia Foundation.

Van Den Bulcke, D. (1988) 'Deregulation of Foreign Direct Investment in Developing Countries', in: Van Den Bulcke, D. (ed.), *Recent Trends in International Development: Direct Investment, Services, Aid and Human Rights.* Antwerp: University of Antwerp, pp. 29–63.

Van Den Bulcke, D. and H. Zhang (1994a) 'Belgian Equity Joint Ventures in China, Some Considerations and Evidence', in: Stewart, S. (ed.), *Joint Ventures in the People's Republic of China, Advances in Chinese Industrial Studies,* Volume 4. JAI Press, pp. 165–183.

Van Den Bulcke, D. and H. Zhang (1994b) 'The Development of Local Marketing Knowledge Within Joint Ventures: An Analysis of the Performance of Belgian Multinationals in China', in: Obloj, K. (ed.), *High Speed Competition in a New Europe, Proceedings of The 20th Annual Conference of EIBA,* Volume 2. Warsaw: International Postgraduate Management Centre, University of Warsaw, pp. 129–162.

Van Den Bulcke, D. and H. Zhang (1997) 'Significance of Central and Eastern Europe in the Strategic Restructuring of Belgian Transnational Corporations: Four Case Studies'. Proceedings, *The 5th Annual Conference of Marketing Strategies for Central and Eastern Europe,* Vienna, 10–12 December 1997.

Van Den Bulcke, D. and H. Zhang (1998) 'Foreign Direct Investment in China: Interactions between Government Policies and Multinational Investment Strategies', in: Tharakan, P. K. M. and D. Van Den Bulcke (eds), *International Trade, Foreign Direct Investment and Economic Environment.* Macmillan: London.

Van Den Bulcke, D., H. Zhang and X. Li (1999) 'Interaction between the Business Environment and the Corporate Strategic Positioning of Firms in the Pharmaceutical Industry: A Study of the Entry and Expansion Path of MNEs into China'. *Management International Review,* 4: 353–377.

Wang, Z. (1996) *Investment of Transnational Corporations.* Beijing: Chinese Economy Edition (in Chinese).

Wong, L. (1997) 'Honda Wins Guangzhou Base'. *South China Morning Post,* November 14.

Woodcock, C. P., P. W. Beamish and S. Makino (1994) 'Ownership-Based Entry Mode Strategies and International Performance'. *Journal of International Business Studies,* Second Quarter: 253–273.

World Bank (1993) *China Industrial Organisation and Efficiently Case Study: The Automotive Sector.* Report No. 12134-CHA.

The World Bank (1999) *World Development Report 1999/2000: Entering the 21st Century*. Washington, D.C.: The World Bank.

Xing, W. J. (1997) 'Shifting Gears'. *The China Business Review*, November–December: 8–18.

Yip, G. S. (1989) 'Global Strategy in a World of Nations'? *Sloan Management Review*, Fall: 9–41.

Young, S., N. Hood and J. Hamill (1985) *Decision-making in Foreign Owned Multinational Subsidiaries in the United Kingdom*. Geneva: International Labour Office.

Zaloom, E. A. and H. Liu (1999) 'Old Methods, New Terrain'. *The China Business Review*, March–April: 34–37.

Zander, I. and O. Sölvell (1992) 'Transfer and Creation of Knowledge in Local Firm and Industry Clusters – Implications for Innovation in the Global Firm'. *Paper Presented at the Annual Meeting of AIB*, Brussels, November, pp. 21–22.

Zhan, J. (1993) 'Role of Foreign Direct Investment in Market-Oreinted Reforms and Economic Development: The Case of China'. *Transnational Corporations*, 2: 121–148.

Zhang, H. (2000) *The Restructuring of China's Industrial Landscape: Understanding the Challenges of the New Chinese Market Place: A Sampling of the Literature*. Research Report, Antwerp: CIMDA.

Zhang, H. and D. Van Den Bulcke (1996) 'Rapid Changes in The Investment Development Path of China', in: Dunning, J. H. and R. Narula (eds), *Foreign Direct Investment and Governments: Catalysts For Economic Restructuring*. London: Macmillan.

Zhang, H. and D. Van Den Bulcke (2000) 'The Restructuring of The Chinese Automotive Industry: The Role of FDI and Impact of European Multinational Enterprises', in: Millar, C. and C. J. Choi (eds), *International Business: Emerging Issues and Emerging Markets*. London: MacMillan.

Zysman, J. and M. Borrus (1994) 'From Failure to Fortune? European Electronics in the Changing World Economy'. *BRIE Working Paper*: 10.

Index